Chant My Mantra & Color My Mala

108 Days of Meditation, Manifestation & Mindfulness

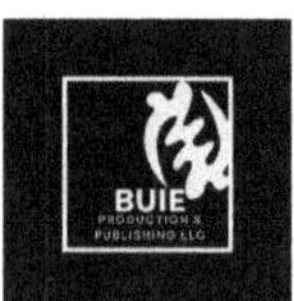

The Owner of This Book:

____

Dear journeyer,

I hope this letter finds you in a moment of calm and tranquility. I wanted to take a moment to express my heartfelt gratitude for choosing "Chant My Mantra & Color My Mala" as a companion on your path to peace and mindfulness. In a world that often feels hurried and chaotic, it's easy to forget the importance of slowing down, taking a breath, and grounding ourselves in the present moment. This coloring book was created with the intention of providing you with a haven of serenity, a space where you can escape the noise of the outside world and rediscover the beauty of the here and now. A space to focus the mind, cultivate positivity, and deepen one's connection to their intentions and inner peace.

As you embark on this coloring journey, I invite you to approach each page with an open heart and a mindful spirit. Mindfulness is not about achieving perfection but about embracing the process. It's about savoring every stroke of your coloring pencil, feeling the textures of the paper, immersing yourself in the colors you choose, and the intention you set.

Here are some tips to guide you along the way:

__1. Breathe__: Before you start coloring, take a moment to center yourself. Inhale deeply, exhale slowly and release any tension you may carry.
__2. Be Present__: As you apply color to the page, let your mind fully engage with the task at hand. Notice the sensations, the colors, and the shapes as they emerge.

3. Let Go: *Release the need for perfection. Remember there are no mistakes when making you or in this creative process. Each stroke is a unique expression of your inner self.*
4. Find Joy: *Embrace the joy that coloring brings. It's a simple pleasure that can profoundly impact your well-being.*
5. Reflect: *How do you feel as you color? What thoughts come and go? This self-awareness is an integral part of mindfulness.*

Remember that mindfulness is not a destination but a lifelong journey. "Chant My Mantra & Color My Mala" is here to support you on that journey, page by page. Whether you are seeking a moment of solitude, an affirming activity, or a tool to manage stress, I hope you find what you seek within these pages.

Thank you for embarking on this coloring journey with me. May it bring you the peace, serenity, and mindfulness you deserve.

Peace and Blessings,

B.A.Buie

The Origins and Meaning of Mala Beads

Mala beads, also known as prayer beads or meditation beads, are ancient and meaningful tools used in various spiritual and religious traditions across the world. Originating from India thousands of years ago, these beads hold deep significance and serve as a tangible connection to one's spiritual practice.

Historical Origins: The word "mala" is derived from the Sanskrit word for "garland" or "meditative string." Mala beads have their roots in India, where they are primarily associated with Hinduism and Buddhism. The use of beads for meditation and prayer can be traced back to the 8th century BCE, and their form and purpose have evolved over time.

Materials and Construction: Traditional mala beads are typically made from natural materials like wood, seeds, or gemstones. Each material carries its own symbolism. For example, Rudraksha seeds are believed to have a strong connection to Lord Shiva in Hinduism, while different gemstones are associated with specific healing properties in various cultures.

A mala necklace typically consists of 108 beads, although variations with 27 or 54 beads also exist. The number 108 holds spiritual significance in Hinduism, Buddhism, and other spiritual traditions. The necklace is often completed with a larger, more decorative bead known as the "guru bead" and a tassel, which symbolizes the connection of all beings.

Meaning and Purpose: Mala beads are primarily used as a meditation aid and a tool for prayer. Here's how they are typically used:

1. **Meditation**: Practitioners use mala beads to count breaths or mantras during meditation. As one repeats a chosen mantra or affirmation, they move their fingers along the beads, allowing them to focus their mind and create a meditative rhythm.
2. **Prayer**: In various religious traditions, mala beads are used to count prayers, chants, or affirmations. The process of moving from one bead to the next is a tactile and meditative way to deepen one's connection to their faith.
3. **Mindfulness**: Mala beads serve as a reminder of one's intentions and spiritual goals throughout the day. Wearing them can encourage mindfulness and a sense of presence in daily life.
4. **Healing and Energy**: In some cultures, the choice of gemstone in a mala is believed to have healing properties. Different stones enhance specific qualities such as love, protection, or clarity.

Cultural Significance: The use of mala beads extends beyond India. They have been adopted by various cultures and religions, including Buddhism, Hinduism, Jainism, and, more recently, the mindfulness and wellness movements in the West. Mala beads symbolize the universal desire for inner peace, spiritual growth, and connection to the divine.

In conclusion, mala beads are more than just beautiful pieces of jewelry; they are potent tools for meditation, prayer, and mindfulness, with a rich history and profound meaning. These sacred garlands bridge cultures and faiths, reminding us of our shared human quest for spiritual awakening and inner harmony.

African Spirituality and Mala Beads: African spirituality is a diverse and intricate system of belief that varies across the continent's many regions and communities. It is deeply connected to nature, ancestors, and the divine. While mala beads are not indigenous to Africa, they have been incorporated into African spiritual practices, especially in areas where syncretism, the blending of different belief systems, has occurred.

1. **Syncretism and Cultural Exchange**: In many parts of Africa, the arrival of various religious traditions, such as Christianity and Islam, led to the fusion of indigenous spiritual practices with these imported faiths. Mala beads, with their universal meditative and prayerful qualities, have been embraced as a tool for devotion and connection to the divine in this syncretic context. They have been integrated into rituals and ceremonies, often taking on meanings specific to the local culture.

2. **Ancestral Connection:** African spirituality strongly emphasizes connecting with ancestors and seeking their guidance and protection. With their repetitive counting and tactile nature, Mala beads can be used in prayers or meditations dedicated to ancestors. Each bead becomes a symbolic step towards connecting with the ancestral realm, bridging the gap between the living and the deceased.

3. **Protection and Healing:** As in other spiritual traditions, specific materials used to create mala beads can have a unique significance in African spirituality. For example, certain African communities may use beads from locally sourced materials, such as seeds, shells, or stones, believed to possess protective or healing properties. These beads are worn or used in rituals to ward off negative energies or promote well-being.

4. **Rituals and Ceremonies:** Mala beads are incorporated into various African rituals and ceremonies, such as initiations, rites of passage, or healing ceremonies. They are a tangible tool to facilitate focused meditation or prayer during these sacred events.

In the context of African spirituality, mala beads showcase their adaptability and universality. They become a bridge between the traditional practices of indigenous cultures and the modern world, allowing for the preservation of spiritual heritage while adapting to contemporary needs.

The adoption of mala beads by various cultures and spiritual traditions underscores their versatility as a tool for meditation, prayer, and mindfulness. Their universal appeal lies in their simplicity, functionality, and ability to facilitate focused and repetitive practices that promote inner peace and spiritual growth.

To that end, I offer this adaptation of a long tradition in hopes that it promotes wellness, healing, and mindfulness that transcend religious practices and culture.

The Origins and Meaning of Mantras

Mantras, ancient and potent tools for spiritual growth and self-discovery, have traversed centuries and cultures, transcending geographical boundaries to become a universal practice. Rooted in the profound wisdom of ancient civilizations, mantras have found their place in contemporary society as powerful instruments for mental and emotional well-being. This page explores the origins, uses, and benefits of mantras, shedding light on their enduring relevance in our fast-paced world.

Historical Origins: The word "mantra" has its roots in Sanskrit, where 'man' translates to 'mind' and 'tra' means 'tool' or 'instrument.' Originating from ancient Vedic traditions in India, mantras were initially recited as hymns during rituals and ceremonies. Over time, the practice evolved, encompassing various spiritual traditions, including Hinduism, Buddhism, and Jainism.

1. **Spiritual Practice:** Mantras are often integral to spiritual practices, acting as a bridge between the practitioner and the divine. In Hinduism and Buddhism, specific mantras are associated with deities or enlightened beings, serving as a means of invoking their presence and guidance.
2. **Meditation and Mindfulness:** Mantras serve as focal points during meditation, aiding in concentration and mindfulness. Repeating a mantra helps silence the chatter of the mind, fostering a sense of inner peace and clarity. The rhythmic chanting of mantras can lead to a deep meditative state, promoting relaxation and stress reduction.

3. Self-Reflection and Affirmation: Beyond spiritual contexts, mantras are embraced for personal development. Individuals use affirmational mantras to shift their mindset, overcome challenges, and manifest positive change in their lives. These self-empowering mantras serve as reminders of one's strength and resilience.

Benefits:

1. Stress Reduction and Relaxation: The rhythmic repetition of mantras induces a relaxation response, reducing stress and promoting a sense of calm. This can have positive effects on overall mental and physical well-being, contributing to lower blood pressure and improved sleep.
2. Enhanced Concentration: The focused repetition of a mantra during meditation enhances concentration and mindfulness. Regular practice can lead to improved cognitive functions, heightened awareness, and better mental clarity.
3. Emotional Healing: Mantras are often employed as tools for emotional healing. Whether dealing with grief, anxiety, or negative emotions, the soothing vibrations of mantra chanting can bring emotional release and balance, fostering a greater sense of well-being.

Mantras, with their deep historical roots and versatile applications, continue to be a source of strength and inspiration for individuals seeking spiritual growth and personal development. As we navigate the complexities of modern life, the age-old practice of chanting mantras stands as a timeless beacon, guiding us towards inner peace, self-discovery, and a harmonious connection with the universe.

Building Your Mantra

1. Prepare your space and body by finding a quiet area and sitting comfortably.

2. Remove any distractions

3. Take deep breaths while focusing on your intention.

4. Build your mantra by combining two phrases.
This template is a guide, not a rule.
Listen to the voice within.

I AM
I WILL
I HAVE

+

Love Blessed Peace Joy Strong
Beautiful Courage Light Precious
On Purpose Healed Abundant
Kind Gentle Infinite Powerful Full
Protected Calm Present Open
Available To Grace   Vibrant

I AM Infinite
____

Counting & Coloring Malas

Pick a Color and begin

Repeat your mantra aloud as you color a counting bead one at a time.

Proceed counterclockwise, starting to the east of the Guru Bead.

Once complete, say "thank you" and color your Guru and Tassel.

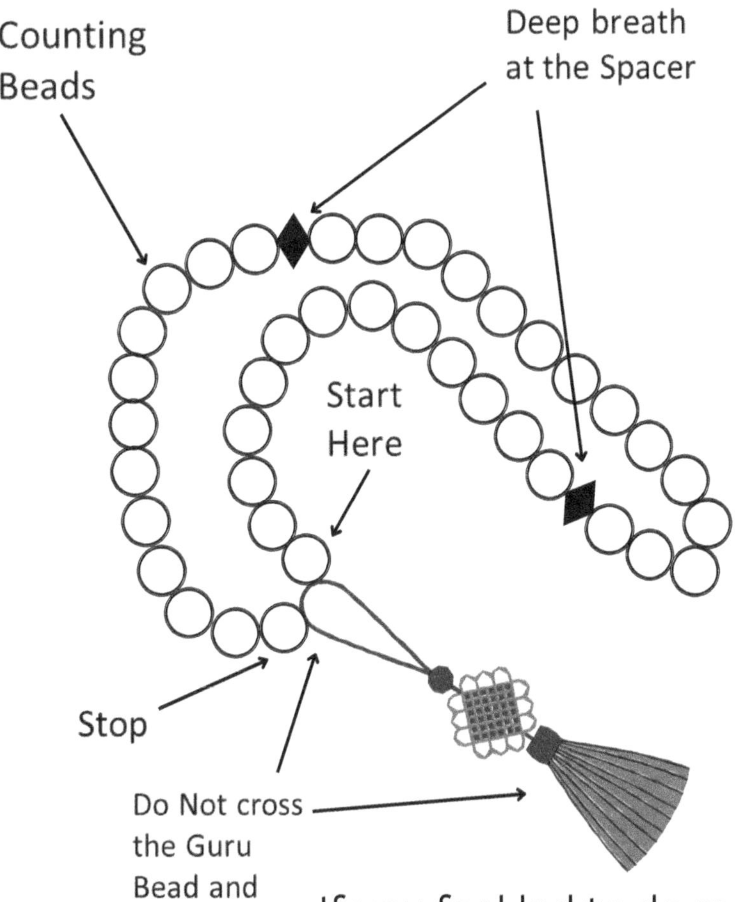

If you feel led to do more, retrace the beads counterclockwise or adorn the background images with color.

Mantra Building Tool

Mantras are personal declarative statements designed to affirm what we desire to manifest. Use this list of words as a guide, not a boundary.

Intent : I know   I See   I Speak   I Love   I Do   I Feel   I Am   I Will   I Have

Courageous	Worthy	Kind	Guided
Passionate	Light	Brave	Unbroken
Successful	Purpose	Smart	Gifted
Powerful	Affirmed	Helpful	Patient With Myself
Honest	Driven	Important	Patient With Others
Healed	Unique	Confident	Necessary
Calm	Wise	Creative	Organized
Prosperous	Thoughtful	Happy	Energized
Protected	Bold	Love	Healthy
Friendly	Open	Free	Thankful
Grounded	Boundless	Abundant	Hopeful
Unstoppable	Forgiving	Full	A Good Listener
Fearless	Safe	Grateful	Creative
Supported	Fun	Life	Disciplined
Treasured	Talented	Beautiful	Open
Whole	Able	Intelligent	Enough
Infinite	Boundless	Resilient	Highly Favored

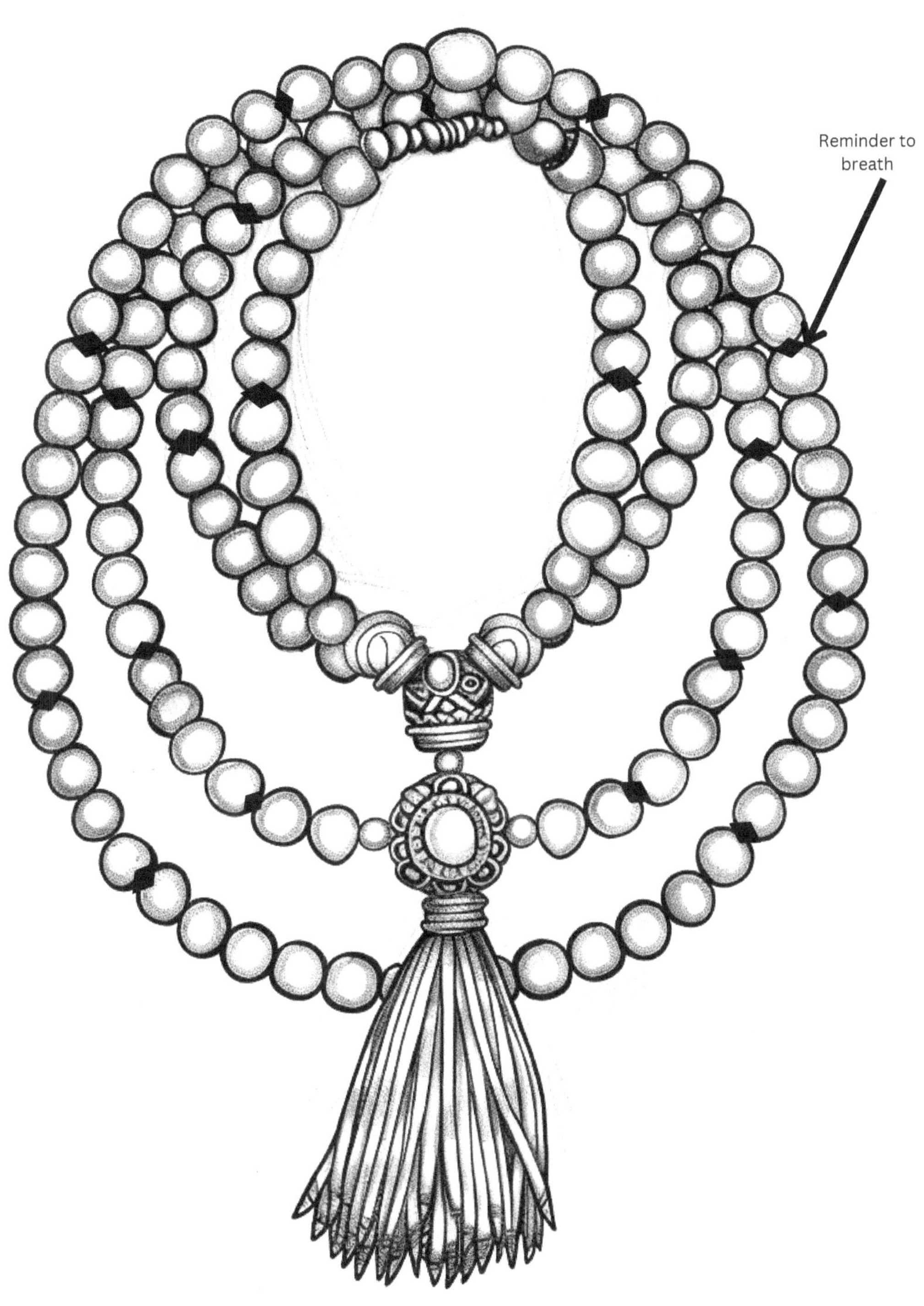
Reminder to
breath

Day 2

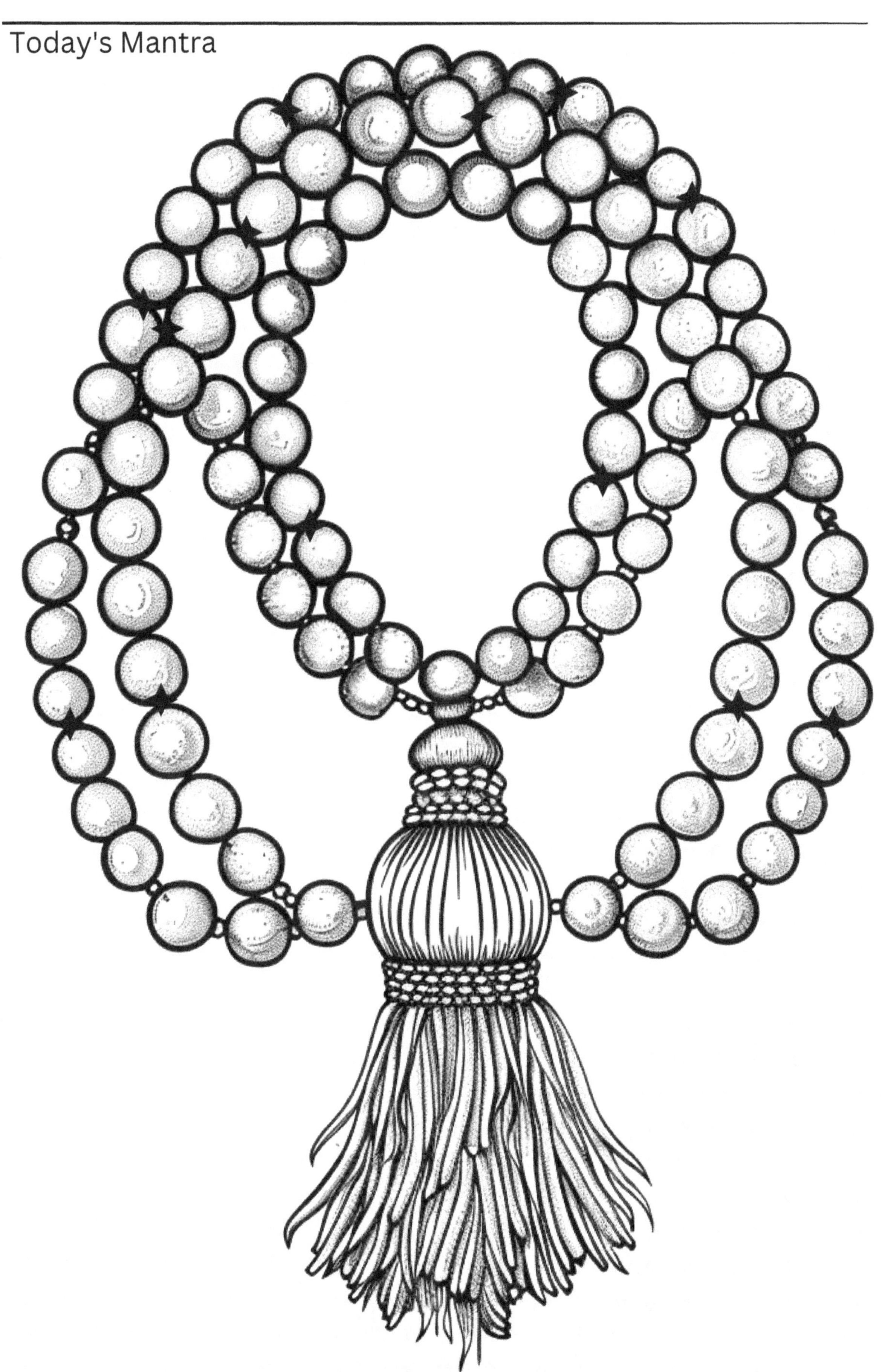

Day 3

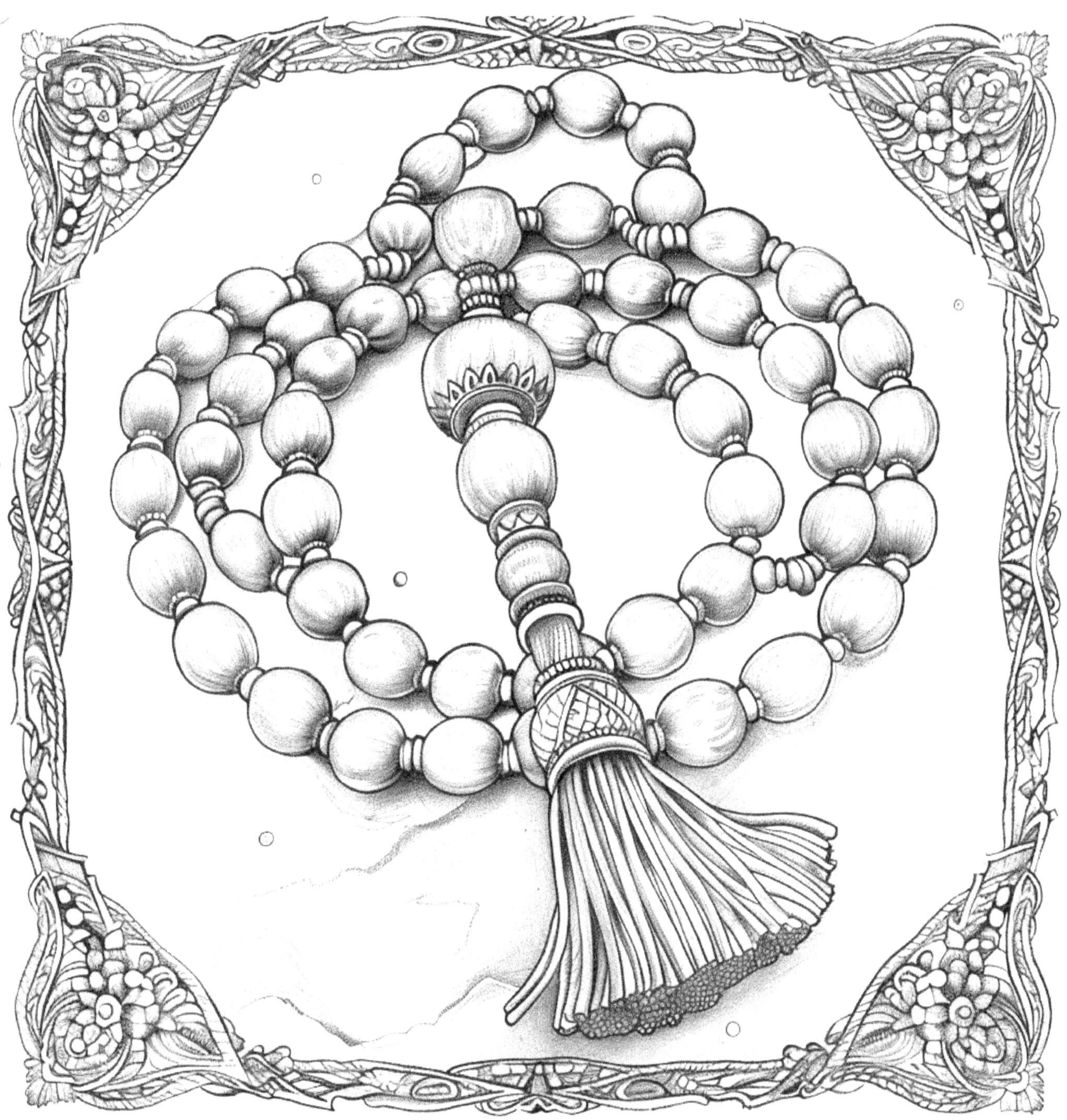

Day 4

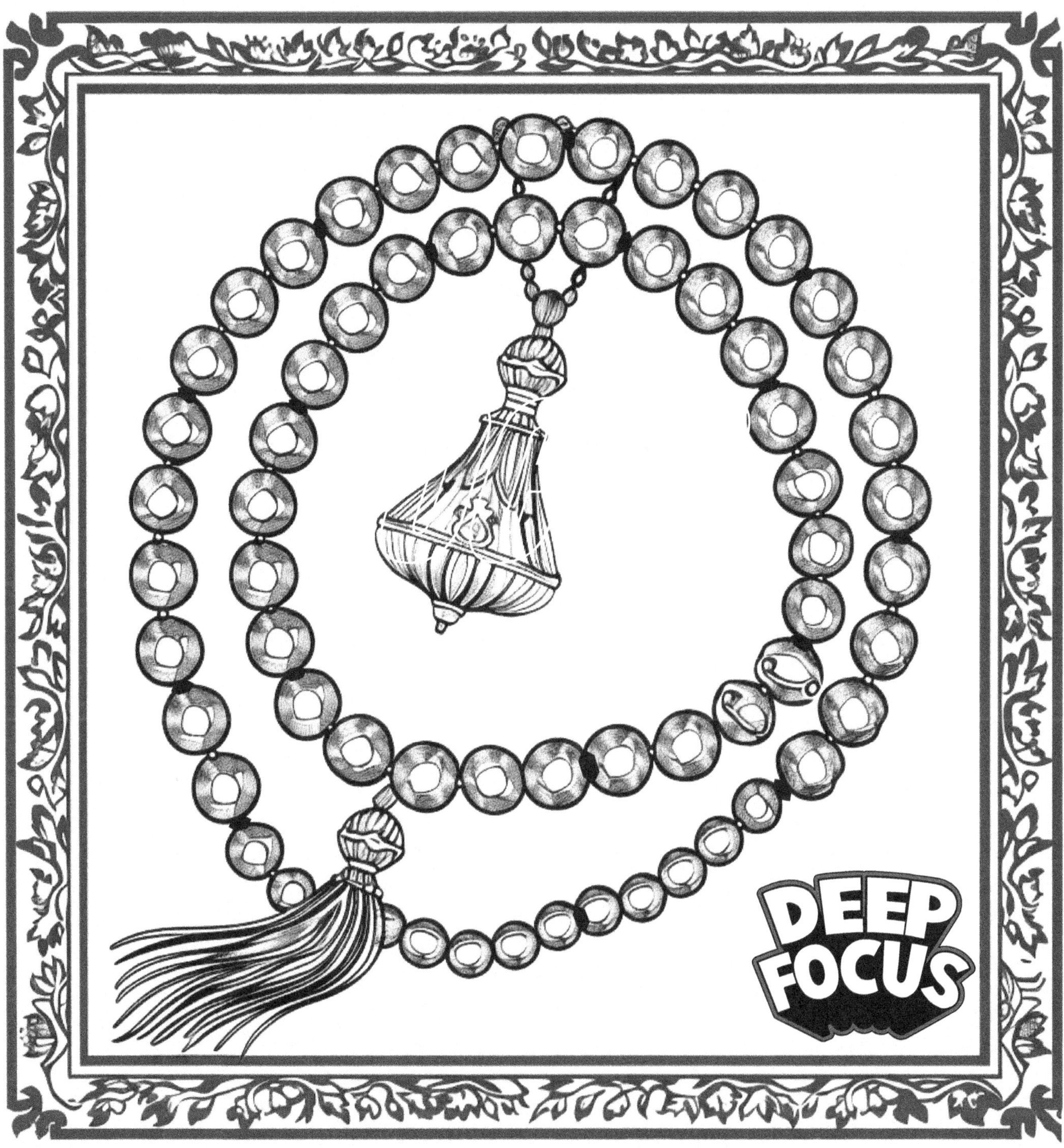
DEEP
FOCUS

Day 5

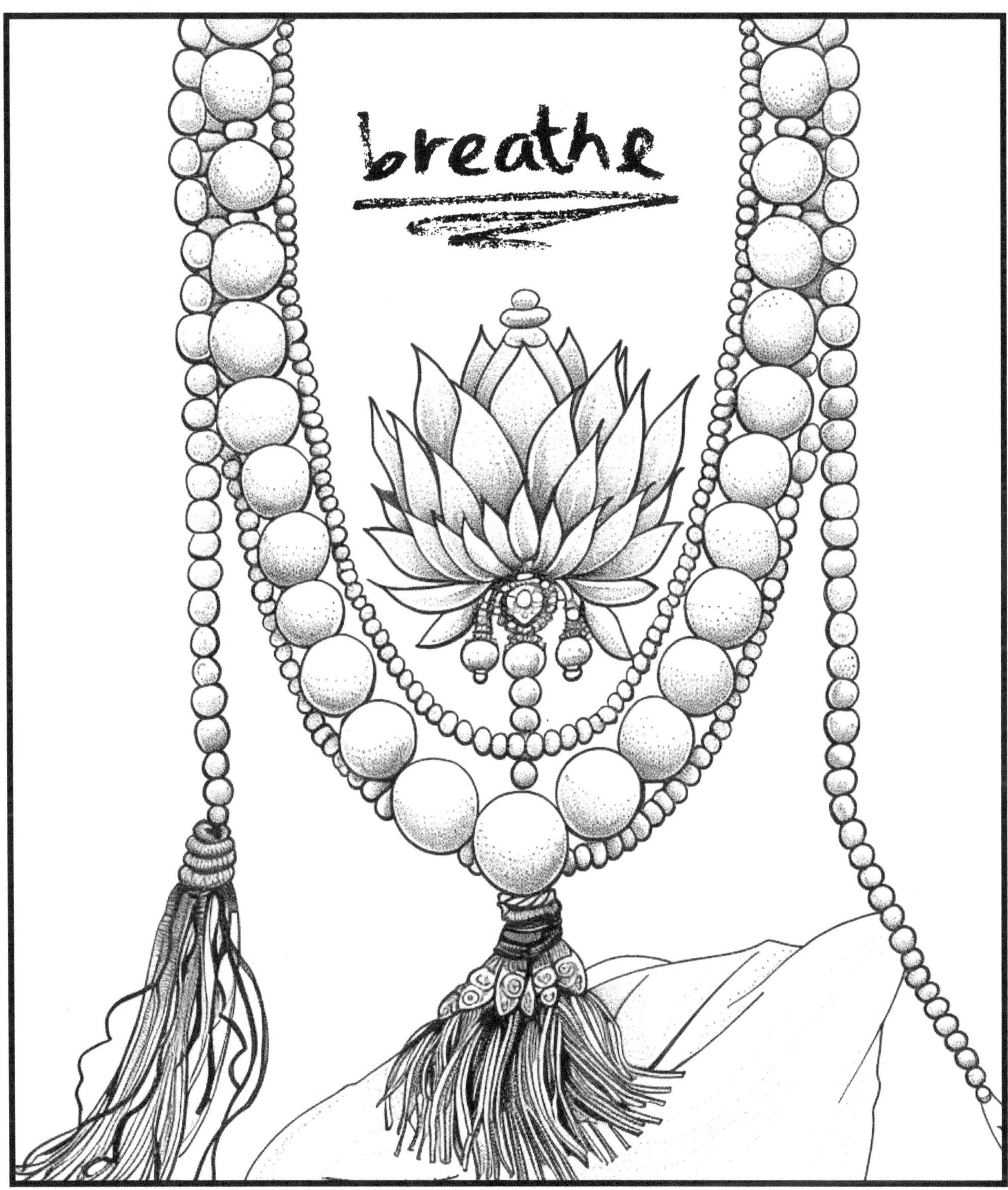
breathe

Day 6

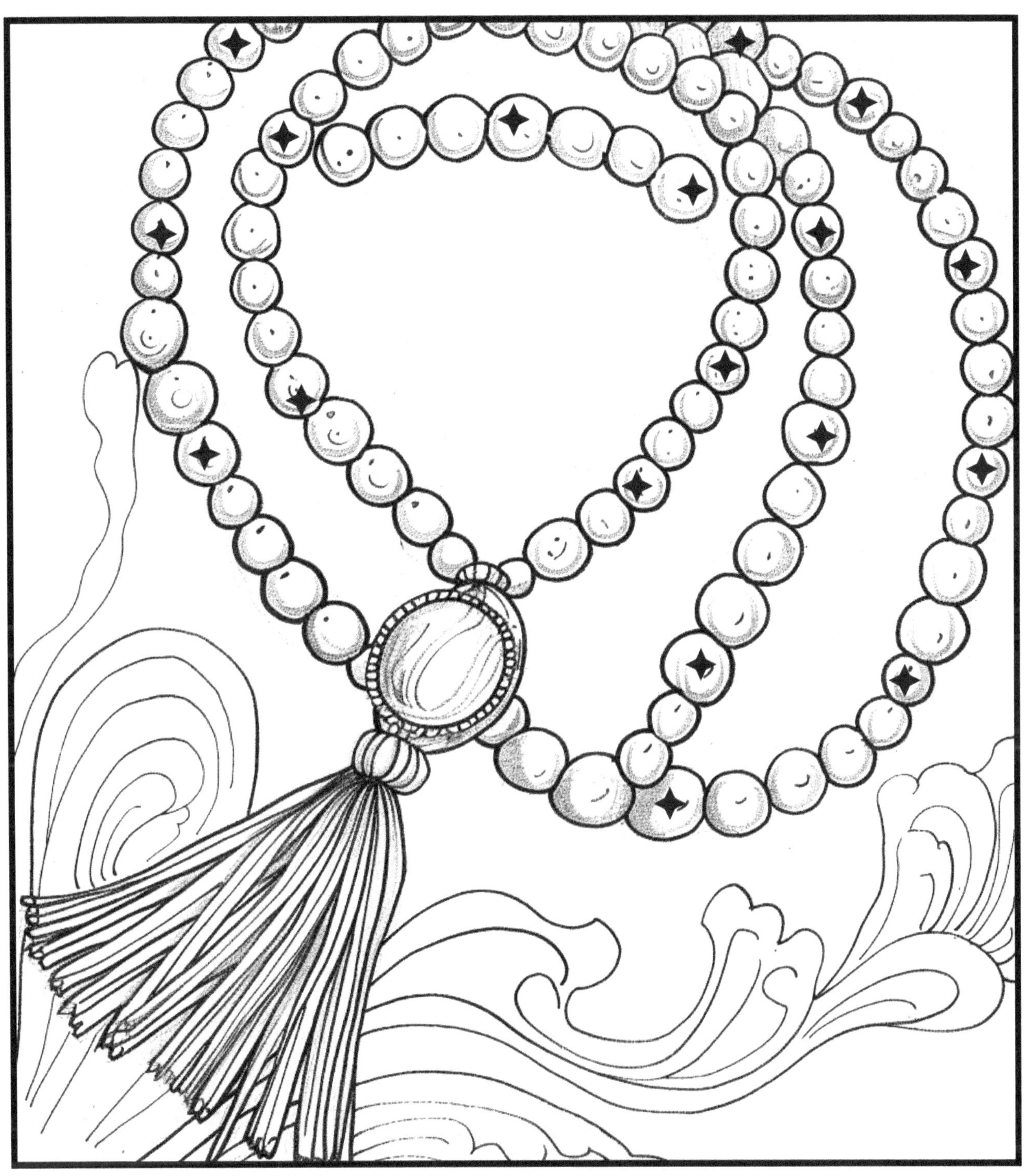

Day 7

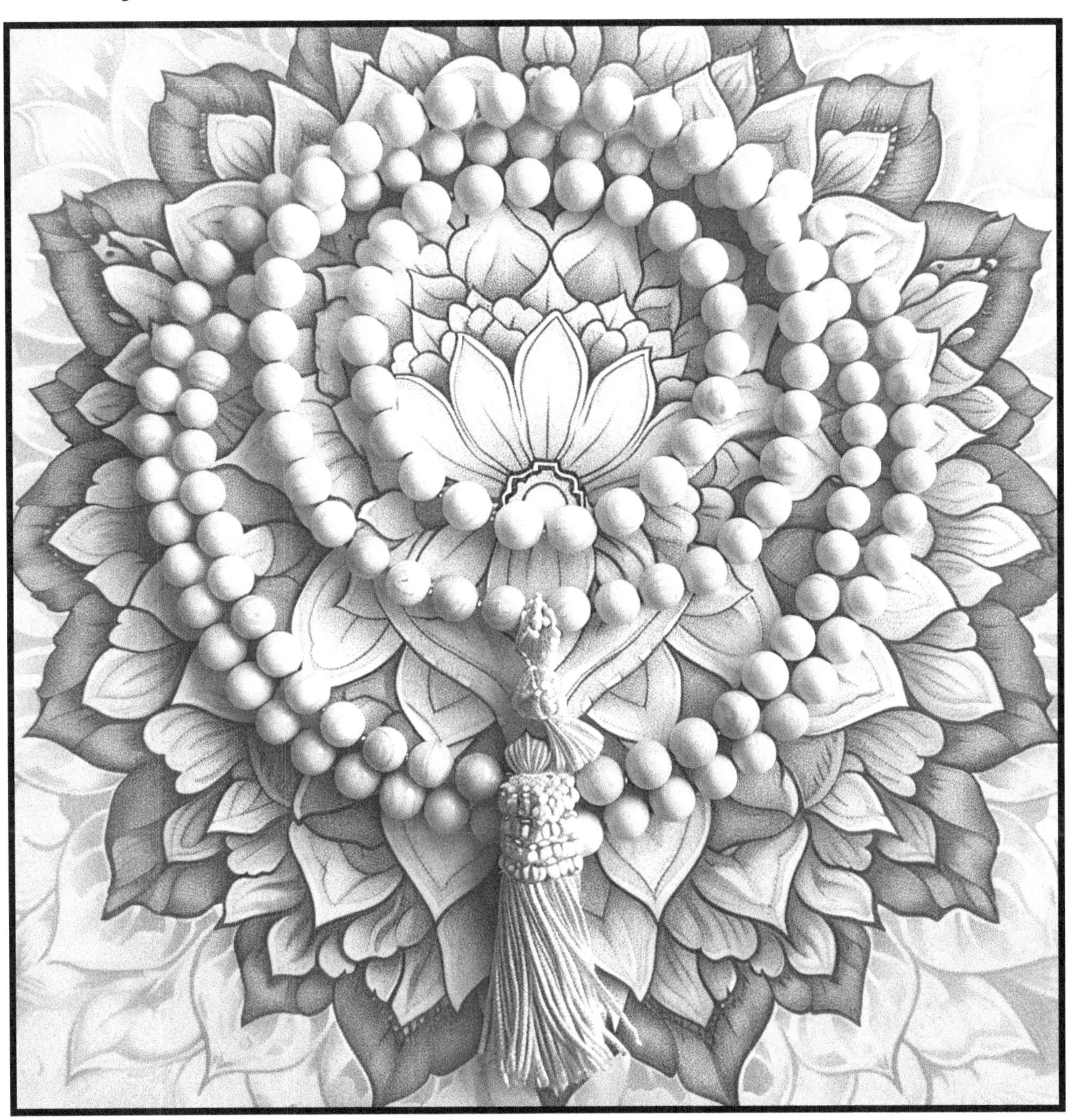

Peace &
BLESSINGS

Day 8

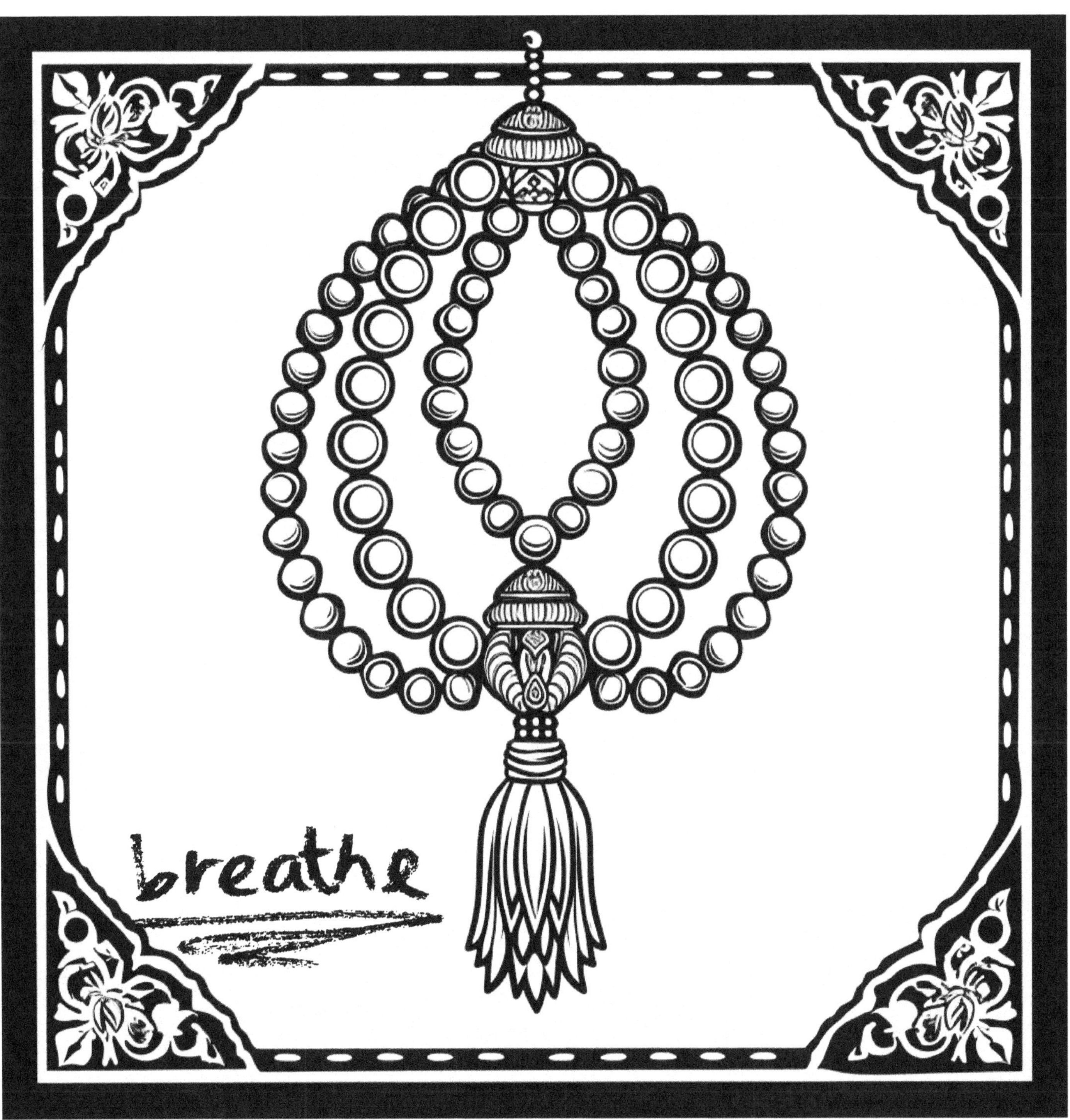
breathe

Day 9

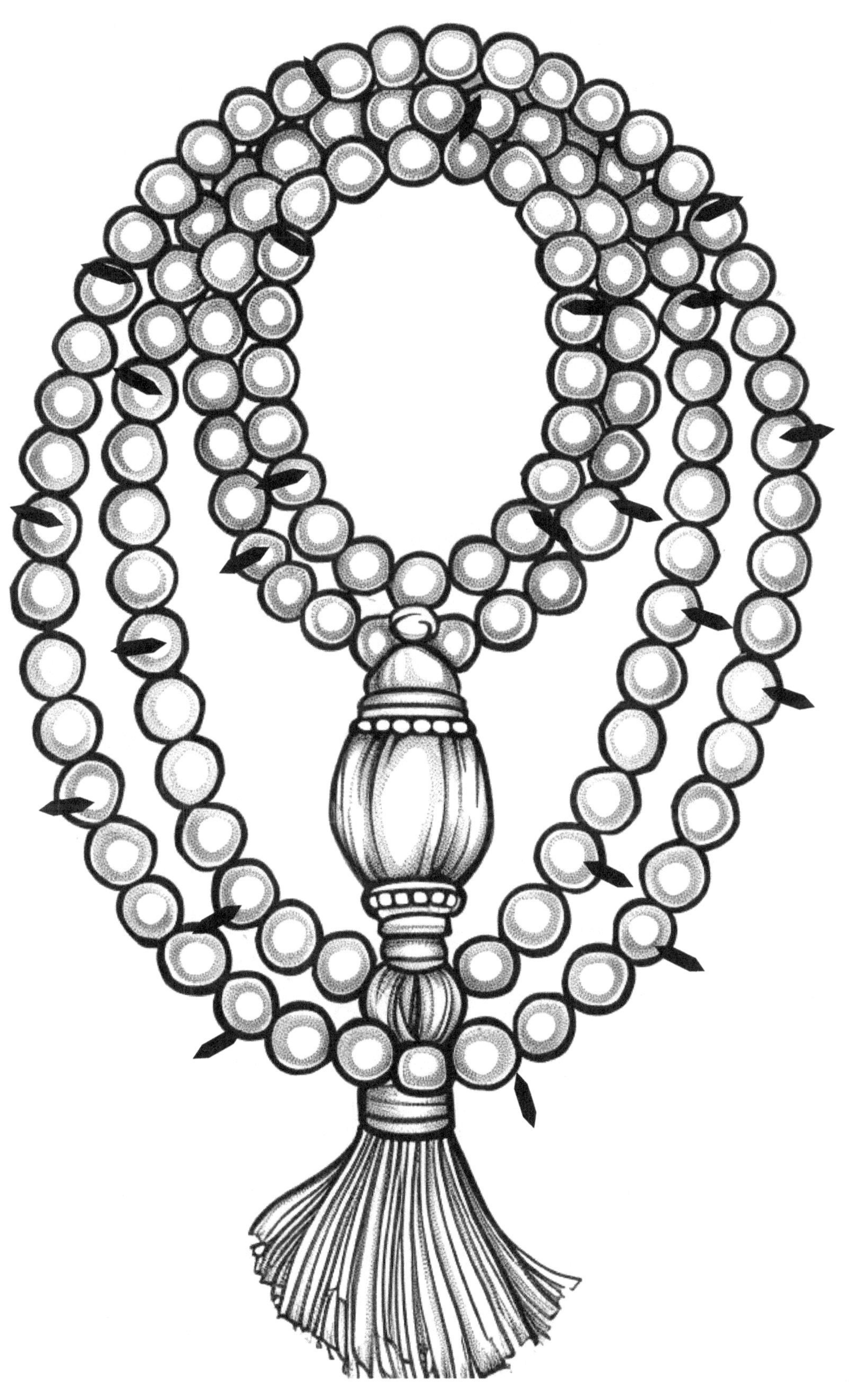

Day 10

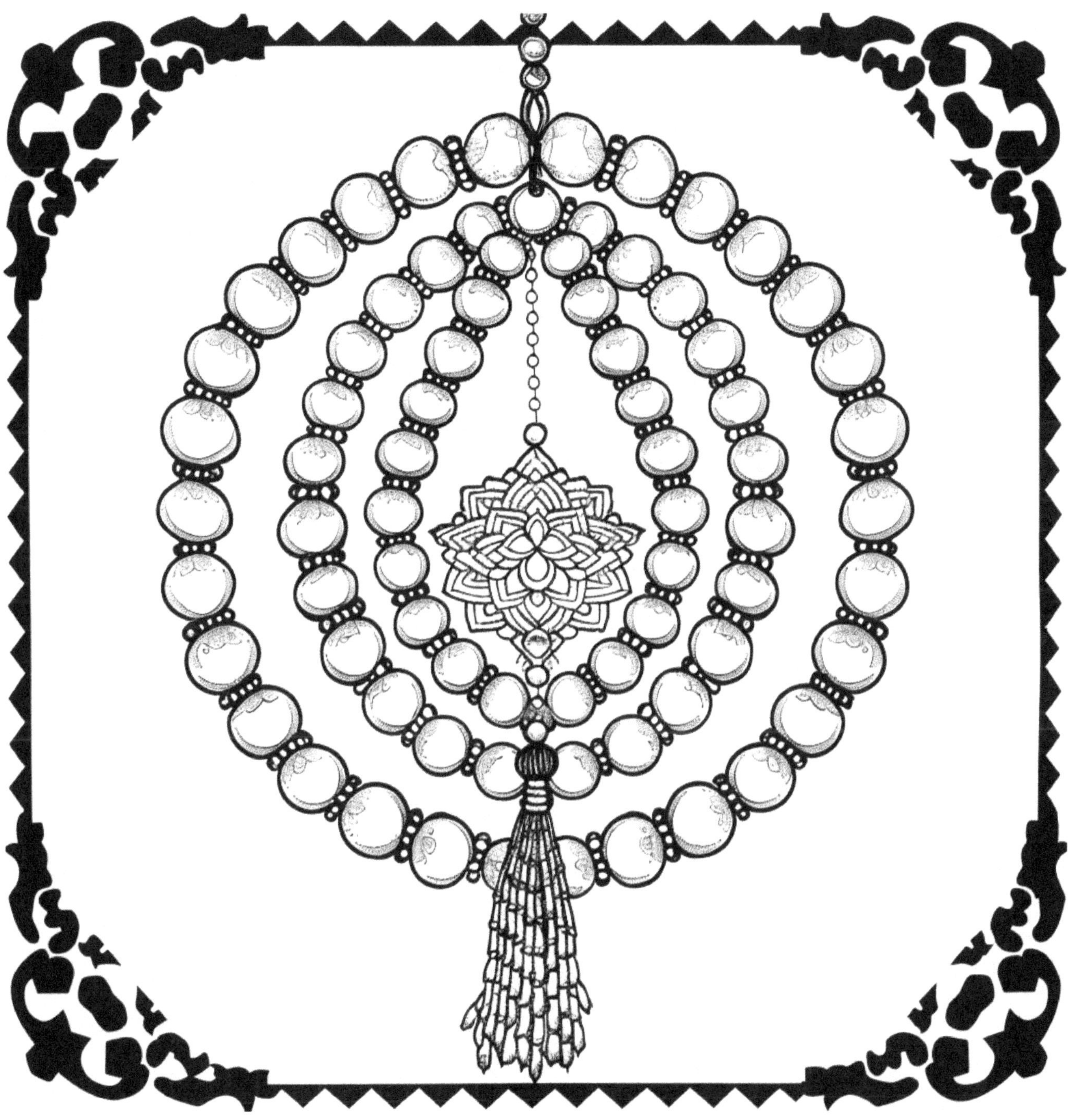

Day 11

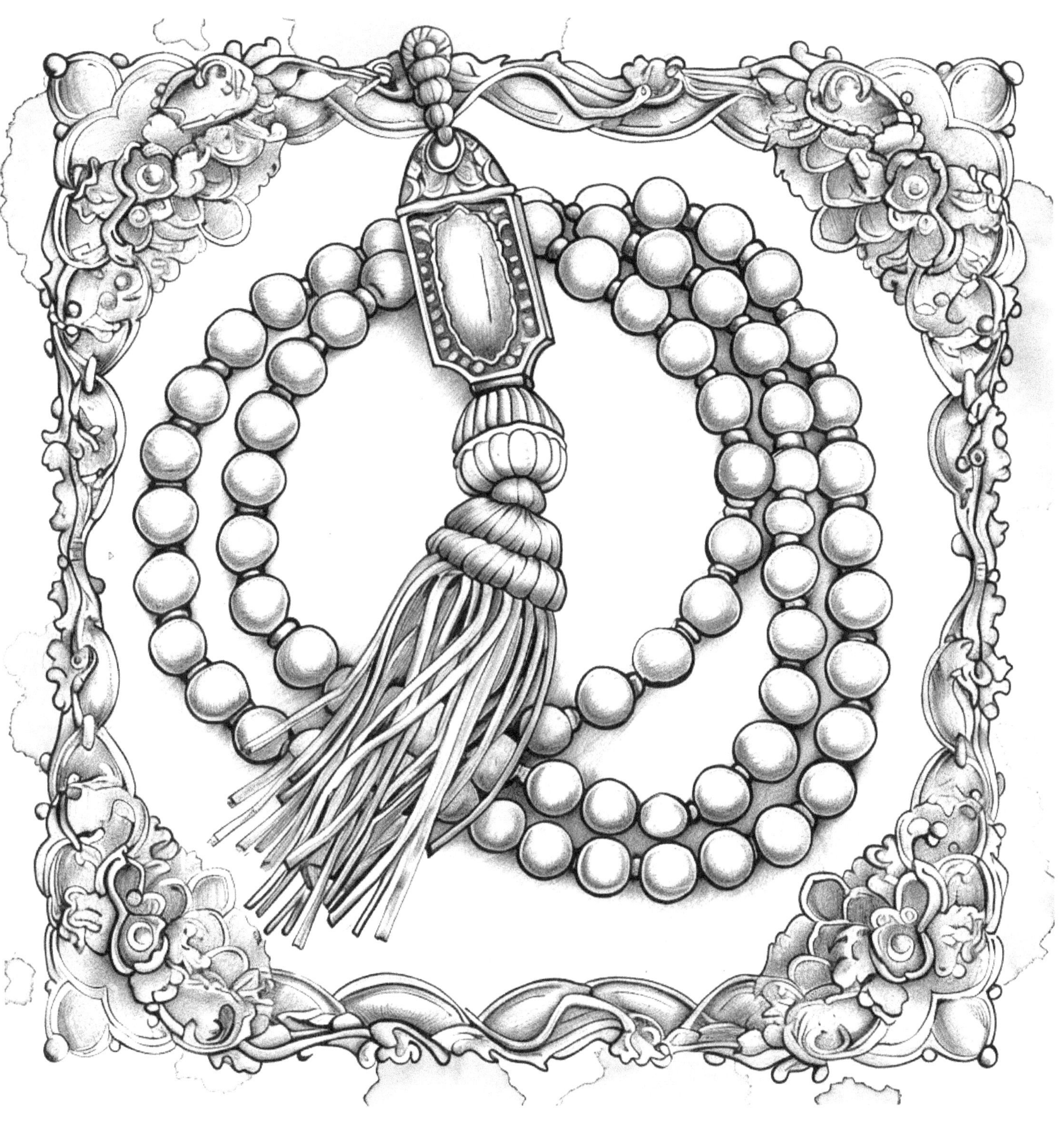

Day 12

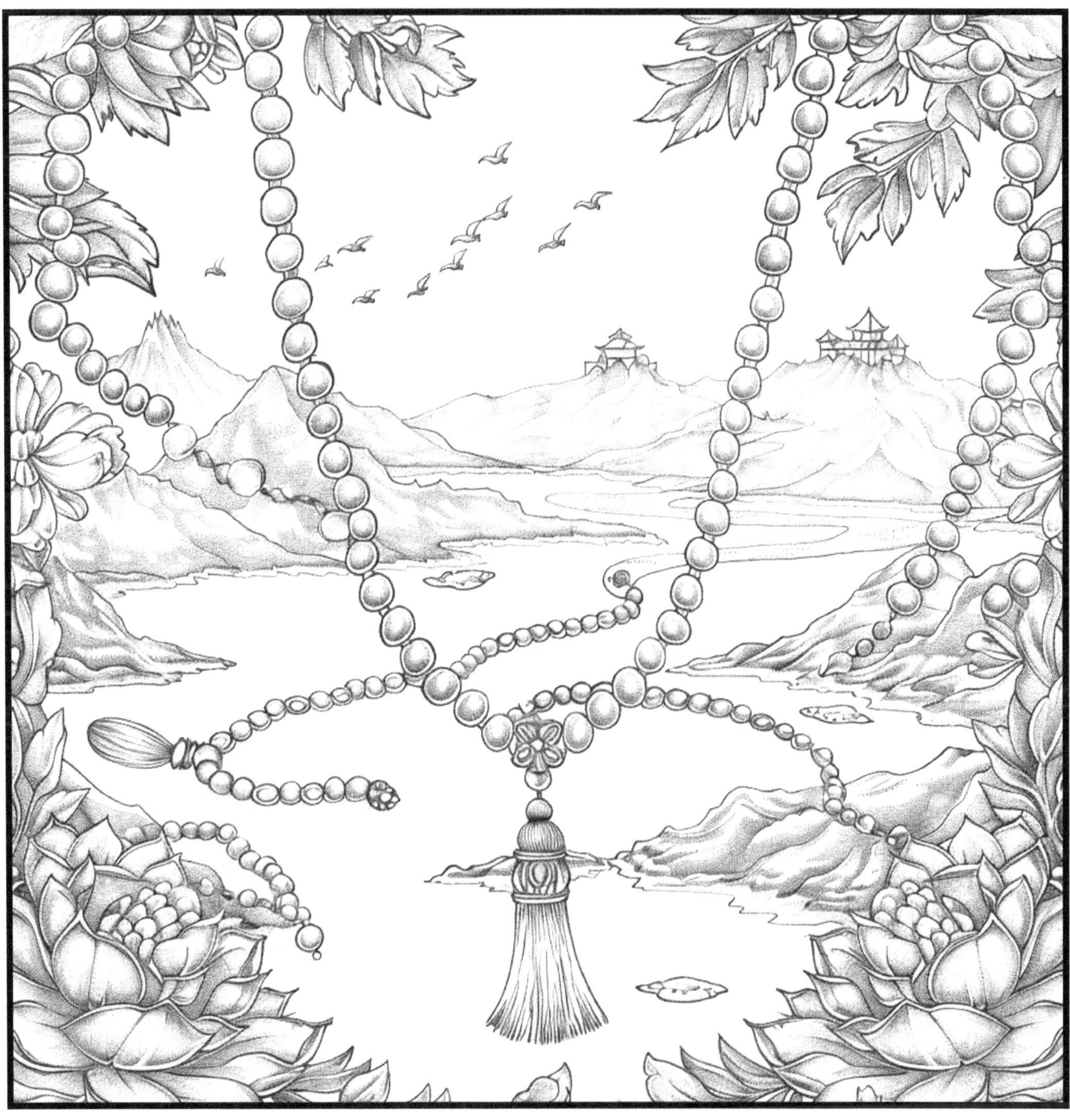

Day 13

Inhale Confidence

Exhale Doubt!

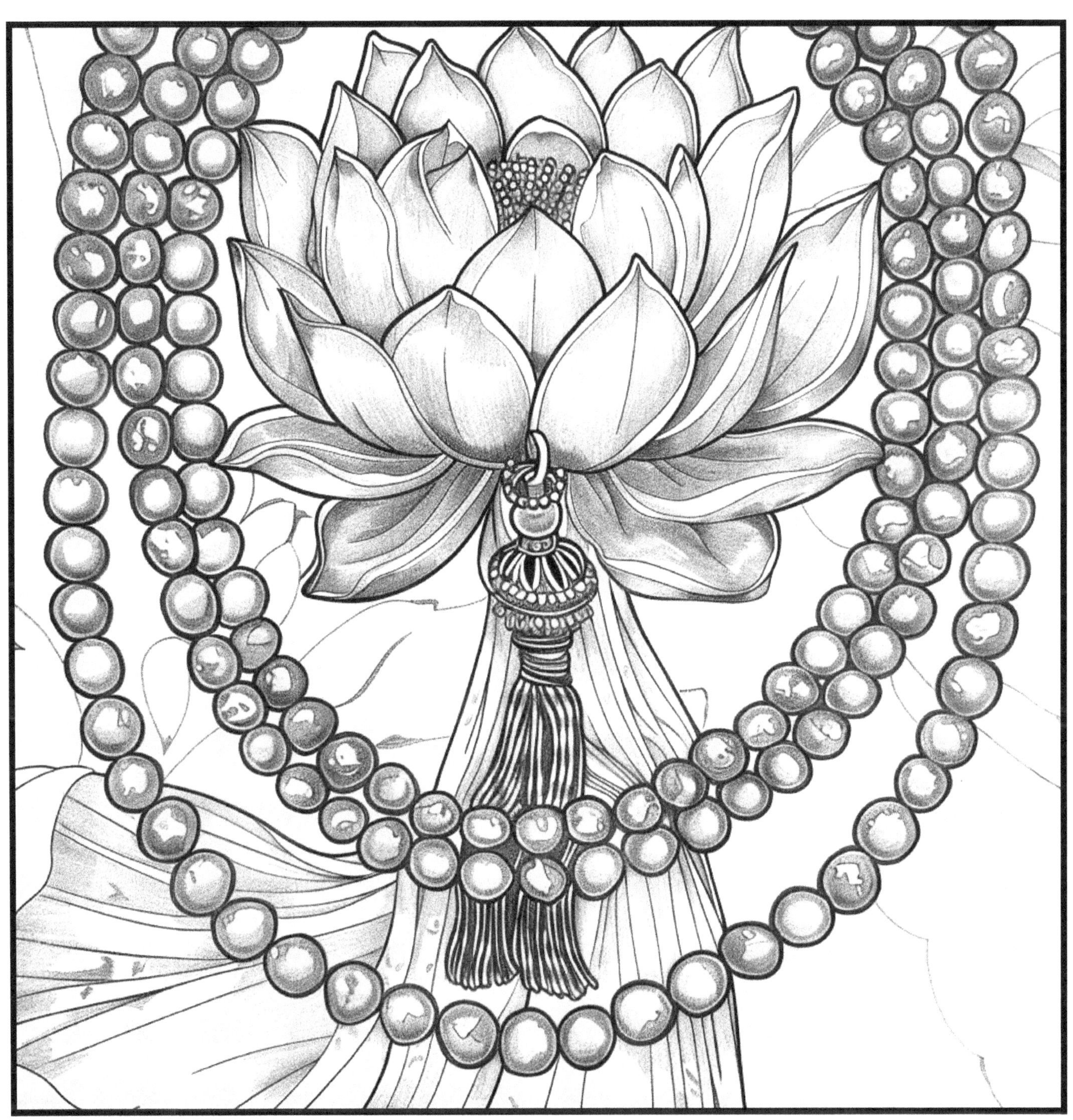

Breath In, Breath Out, Rock On!

Day 14

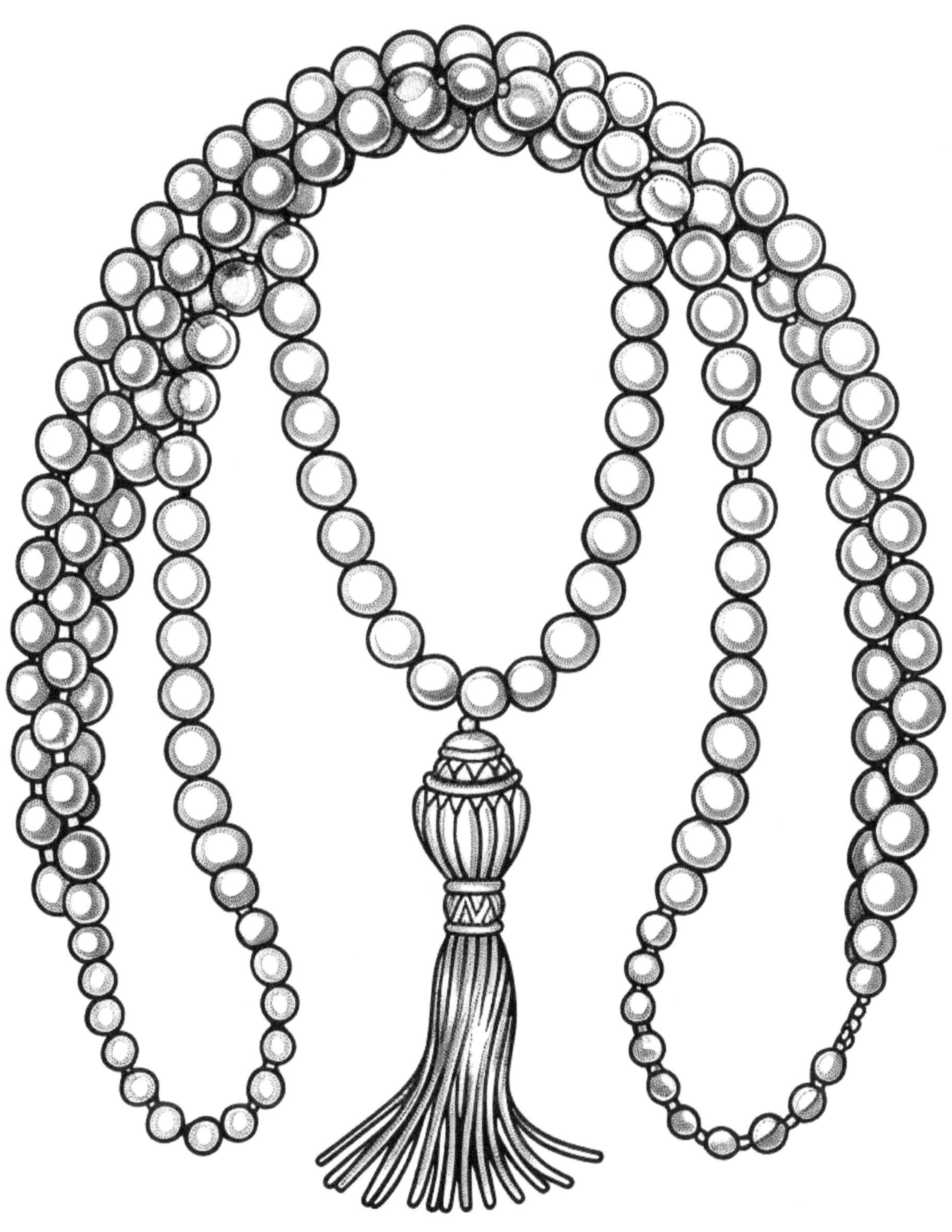

Day 15

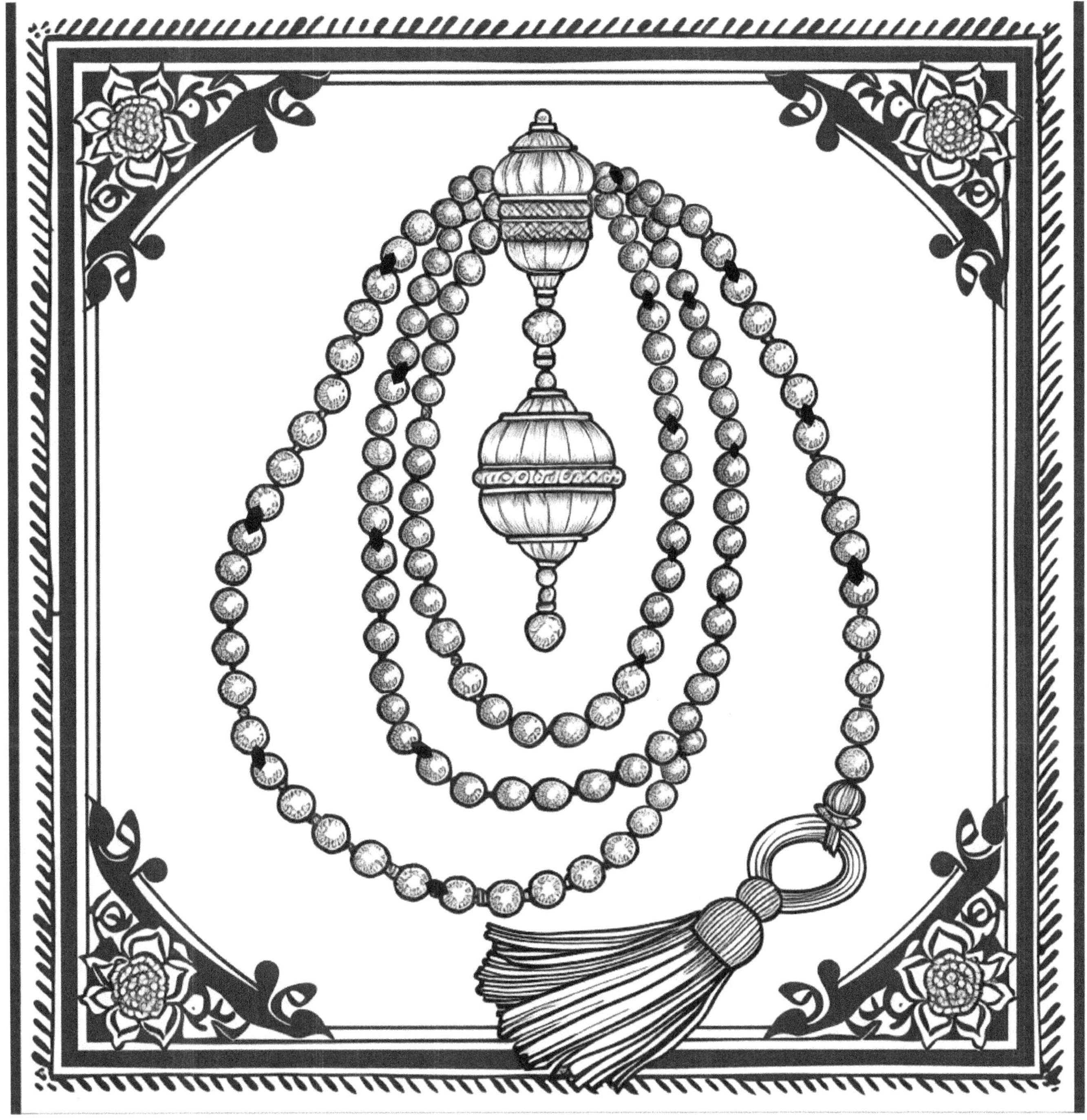

Day 16

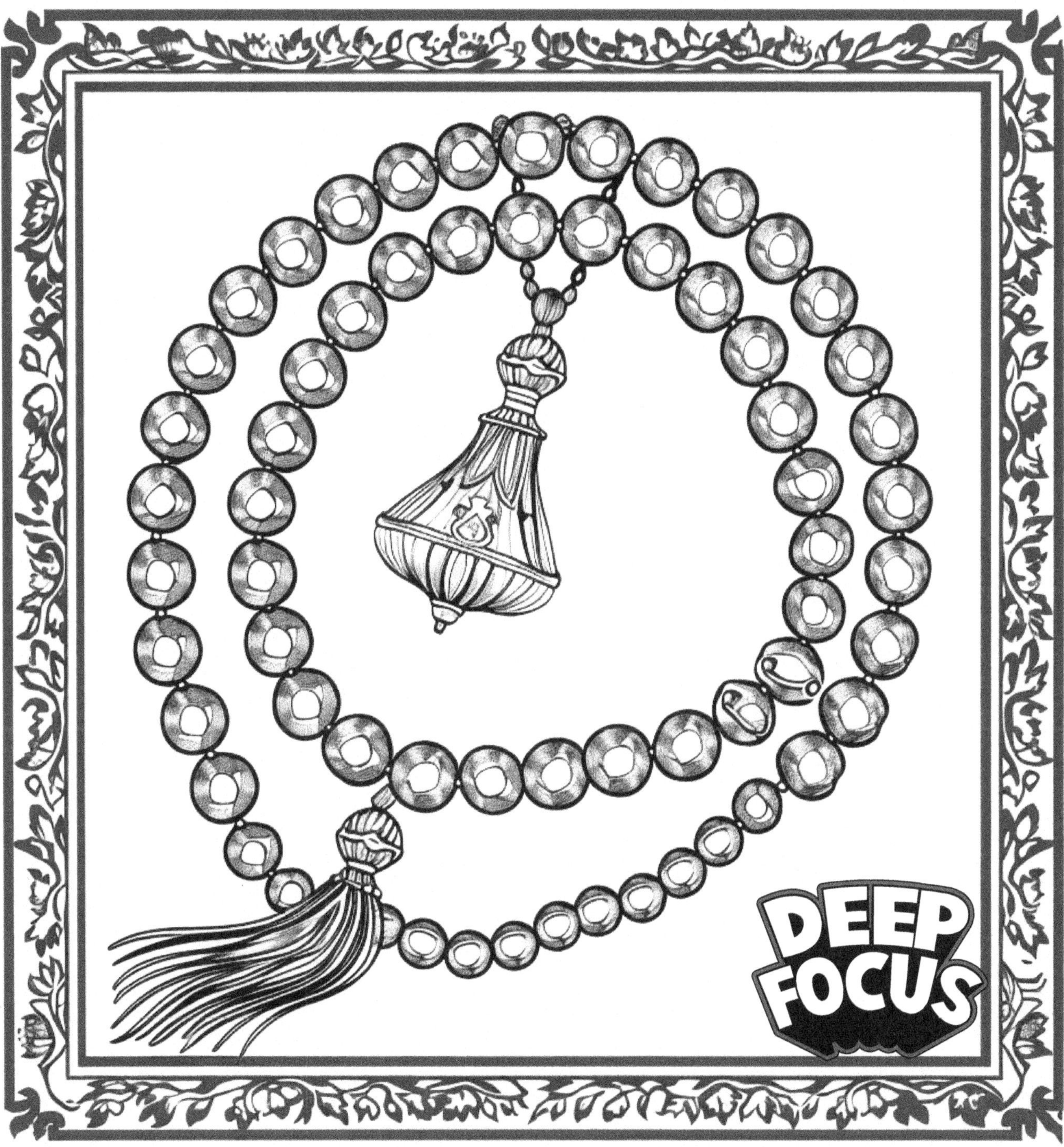

DEEP
FOCUS

Day 17

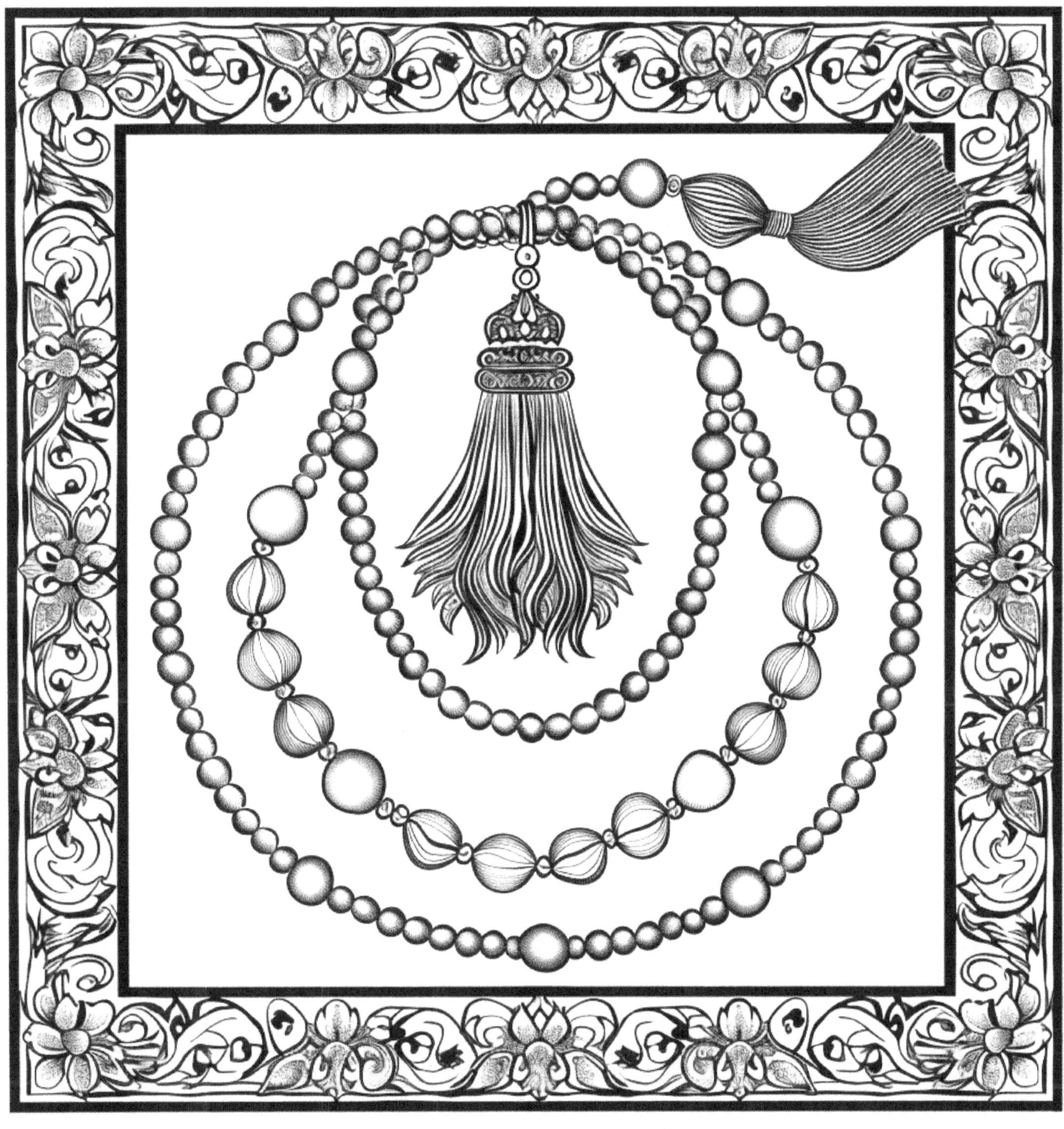

Day 18

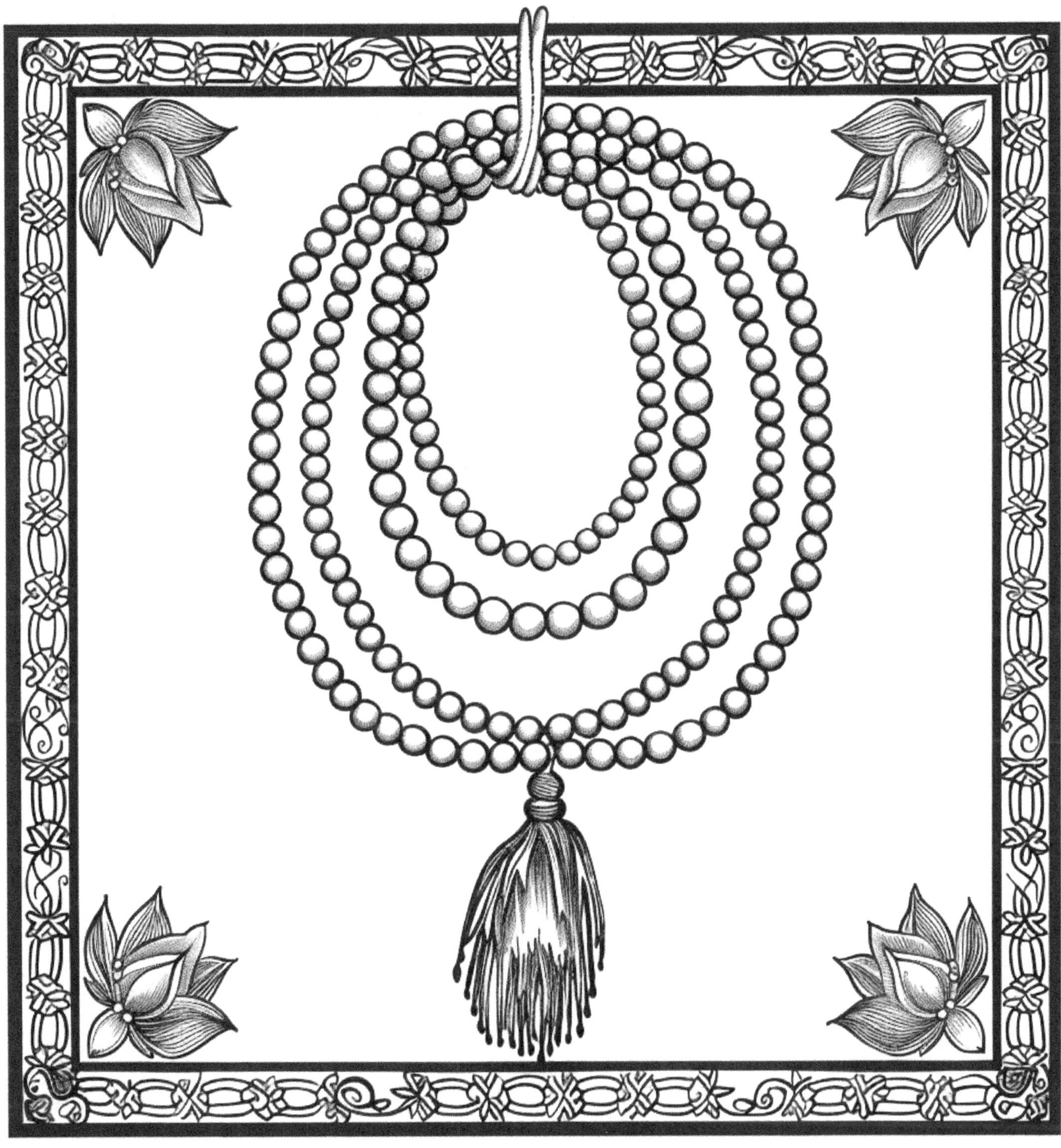

Day 19

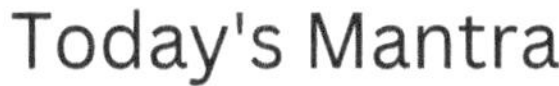

Inhale.
Chant Mantra.
Color Mala.
Exhale.
Repeat.

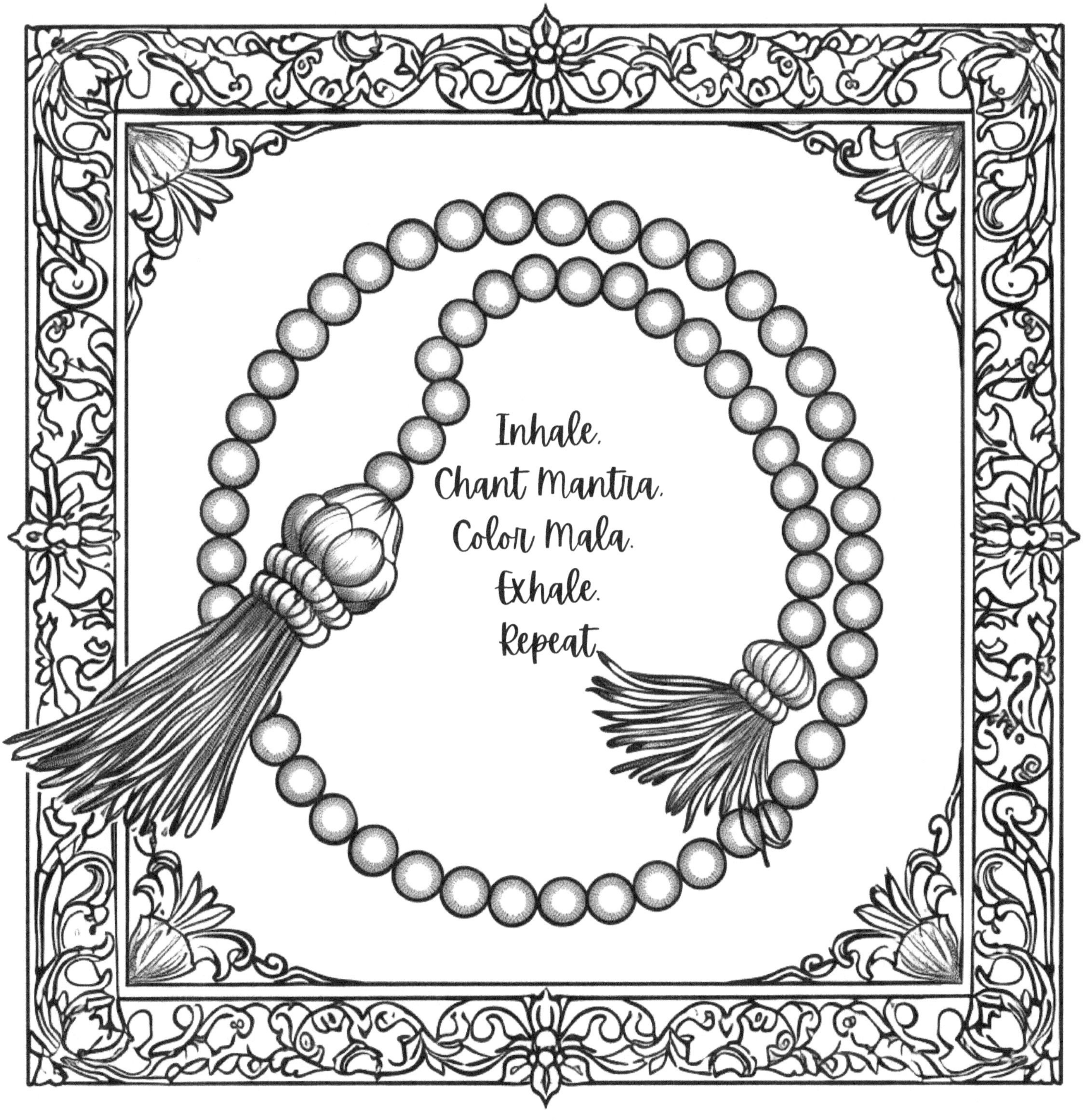

Day 20

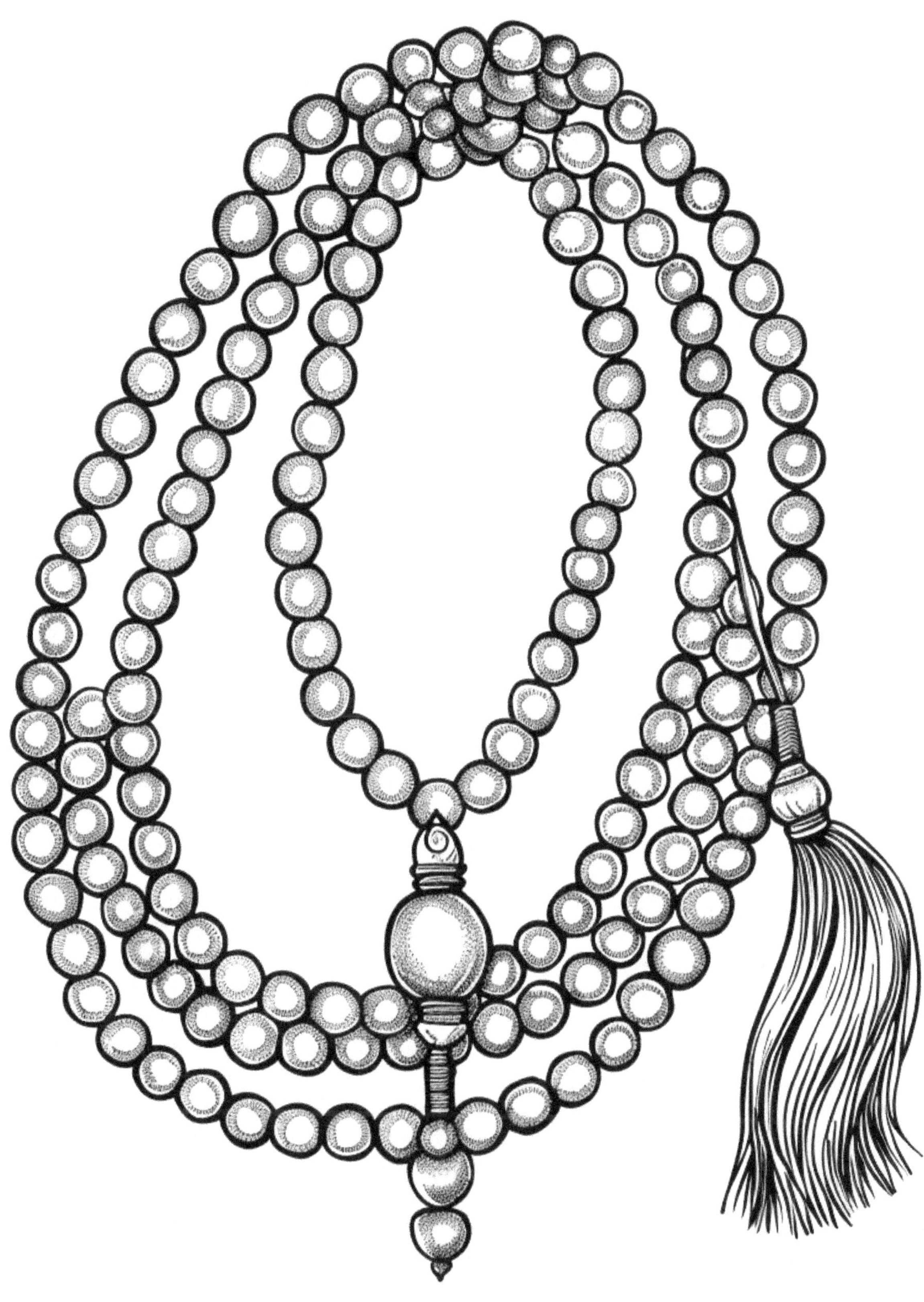

Day 21

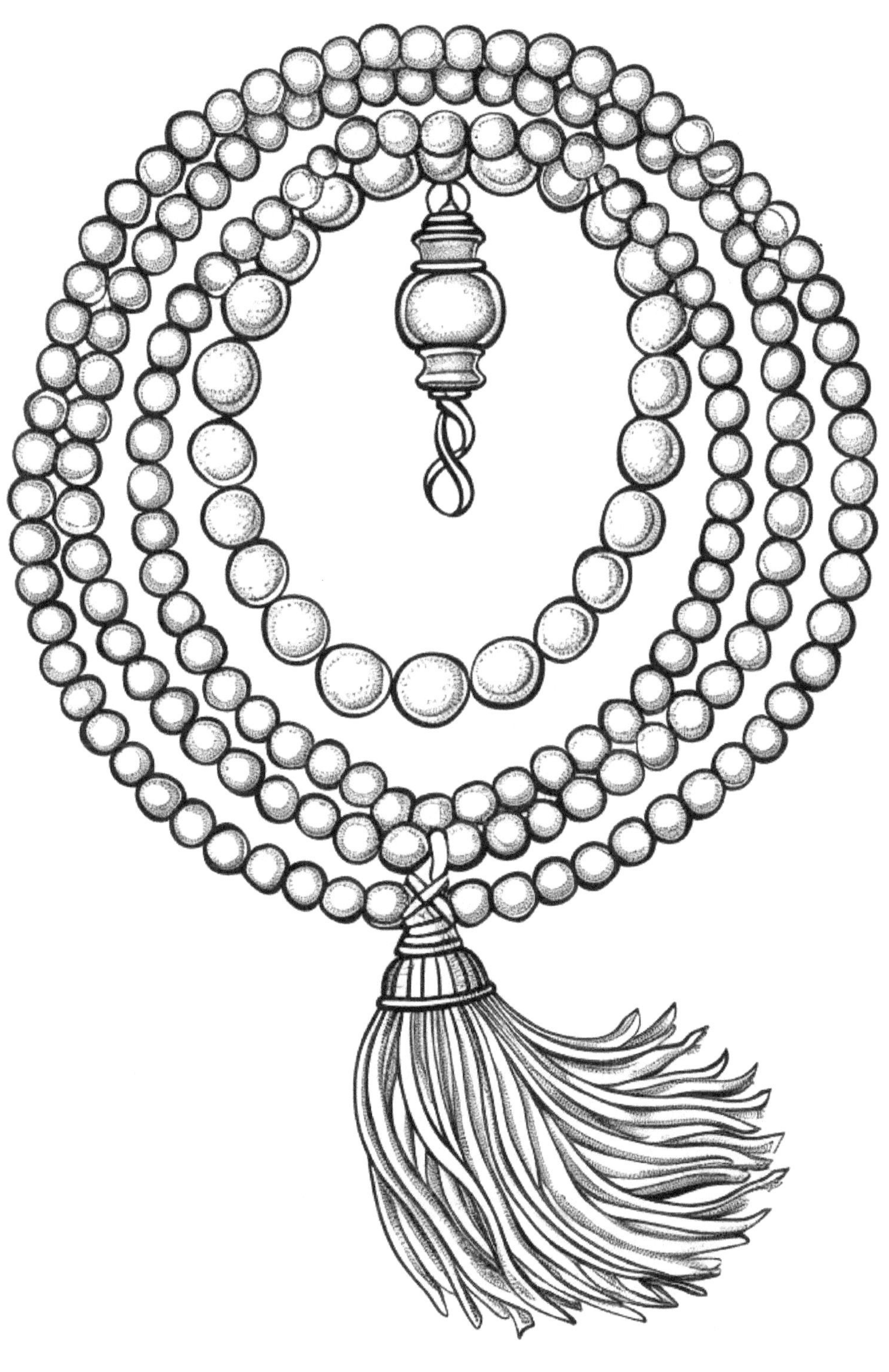

Day 22

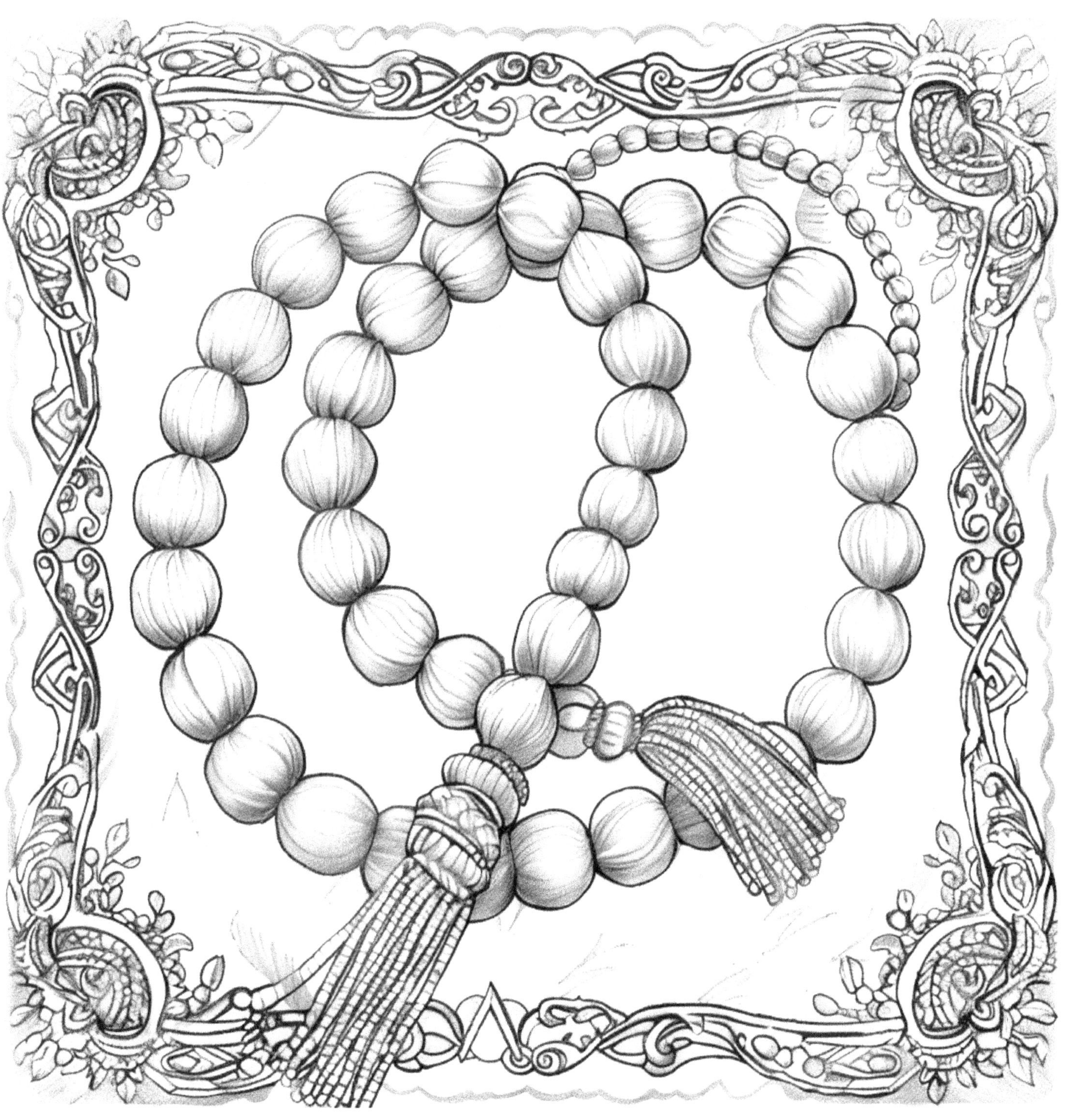

Day 23

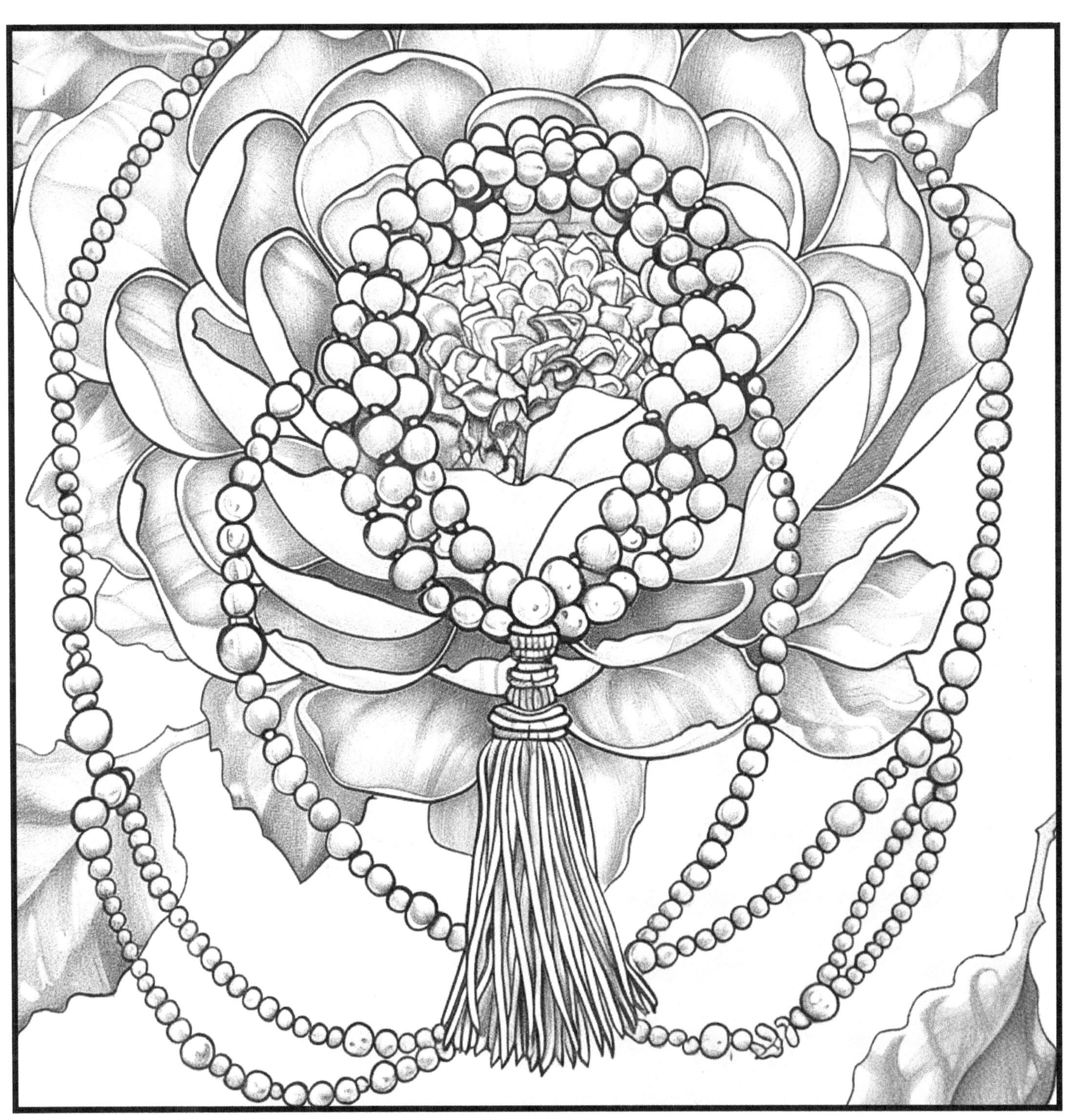

Day 24

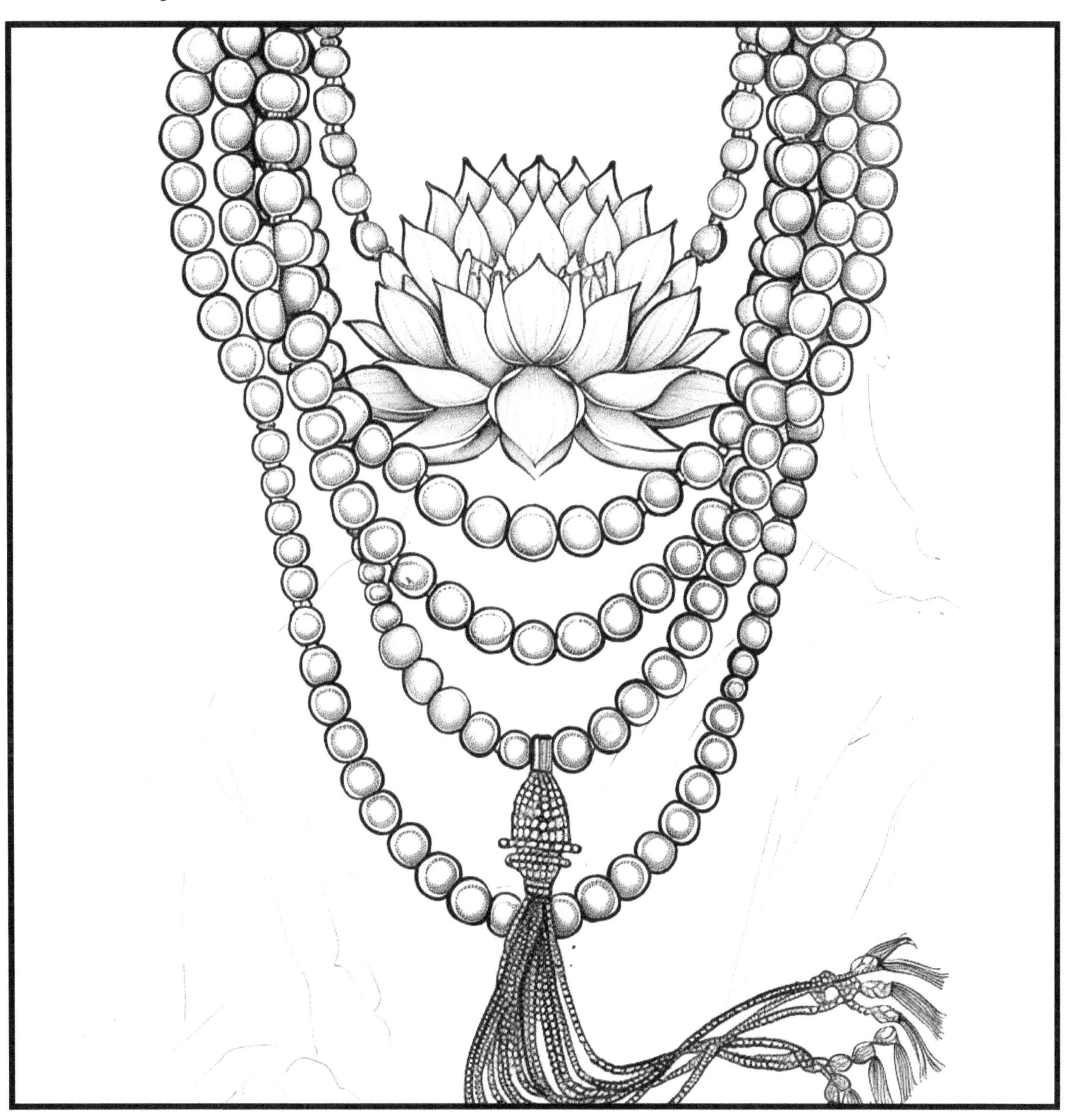

The lotus flower symbolizes purity and spiritual awakening as it emerges pristine from the muddy waters, reflecting resilience and enlightenment.

Day 25

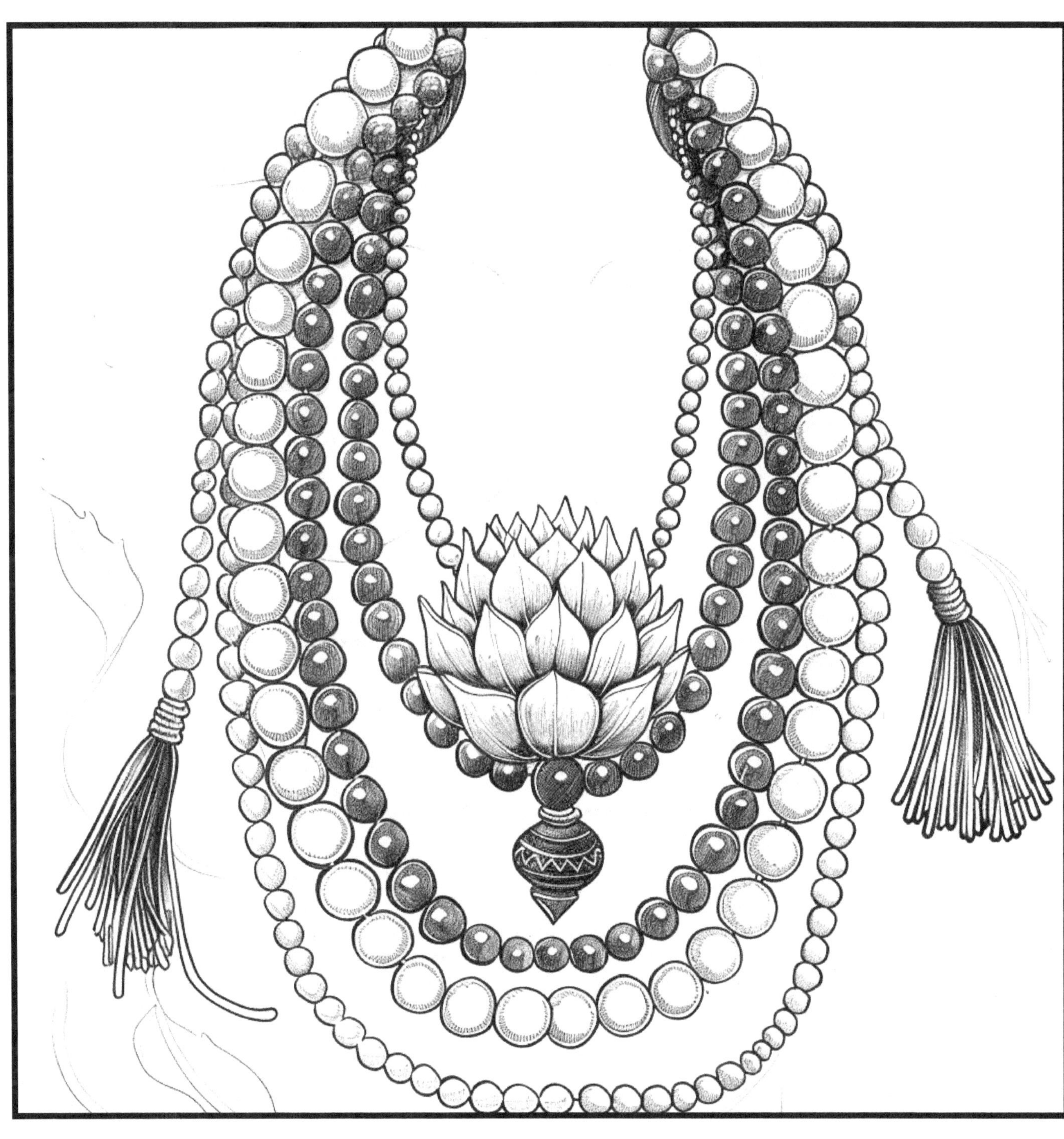

Day 26

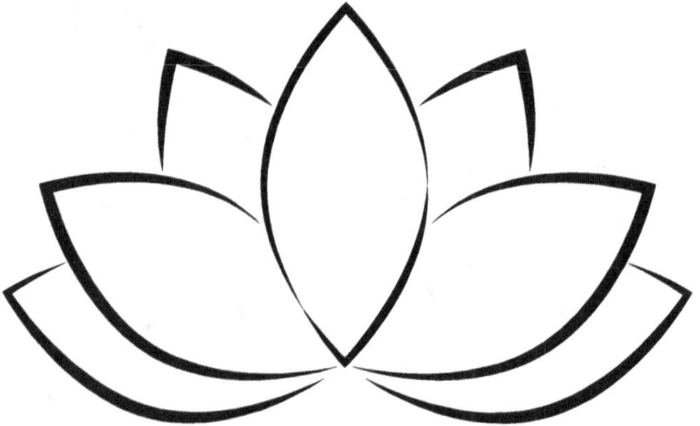

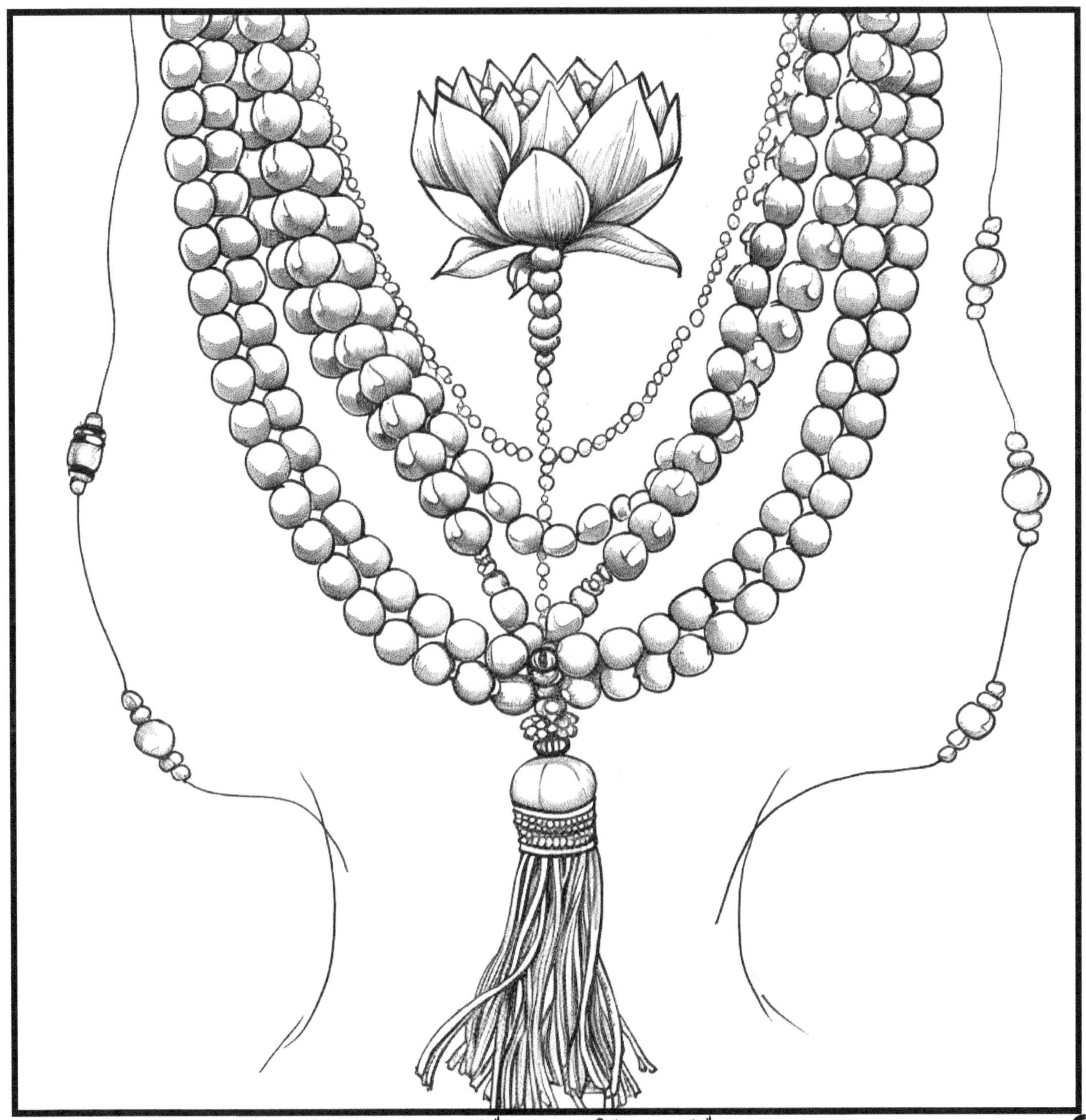

"Remember to breathe - it's the body's way of saying, 'Hey, I'm here. I'm alive! Thank you'"

Day 27

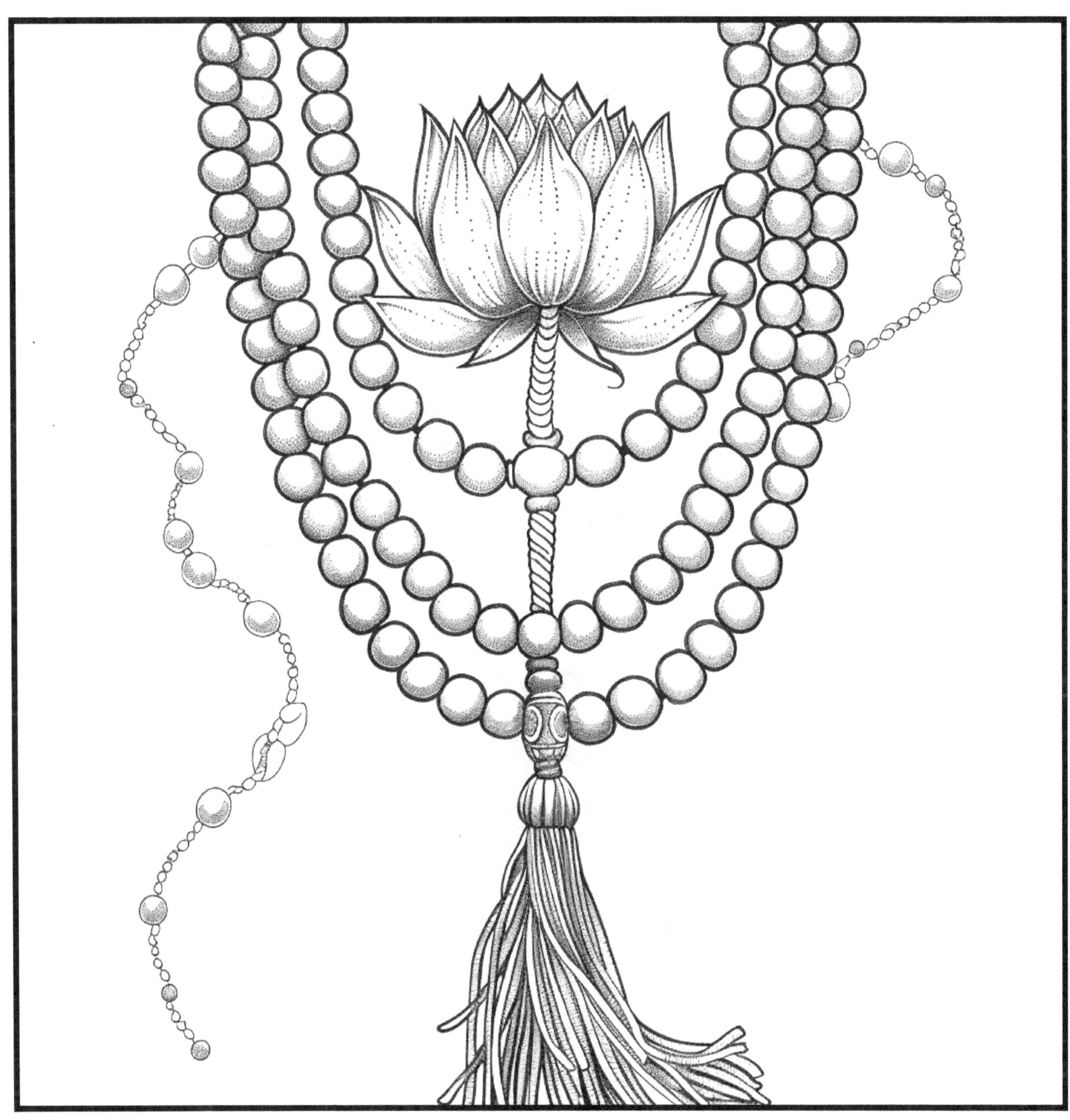

Day 28

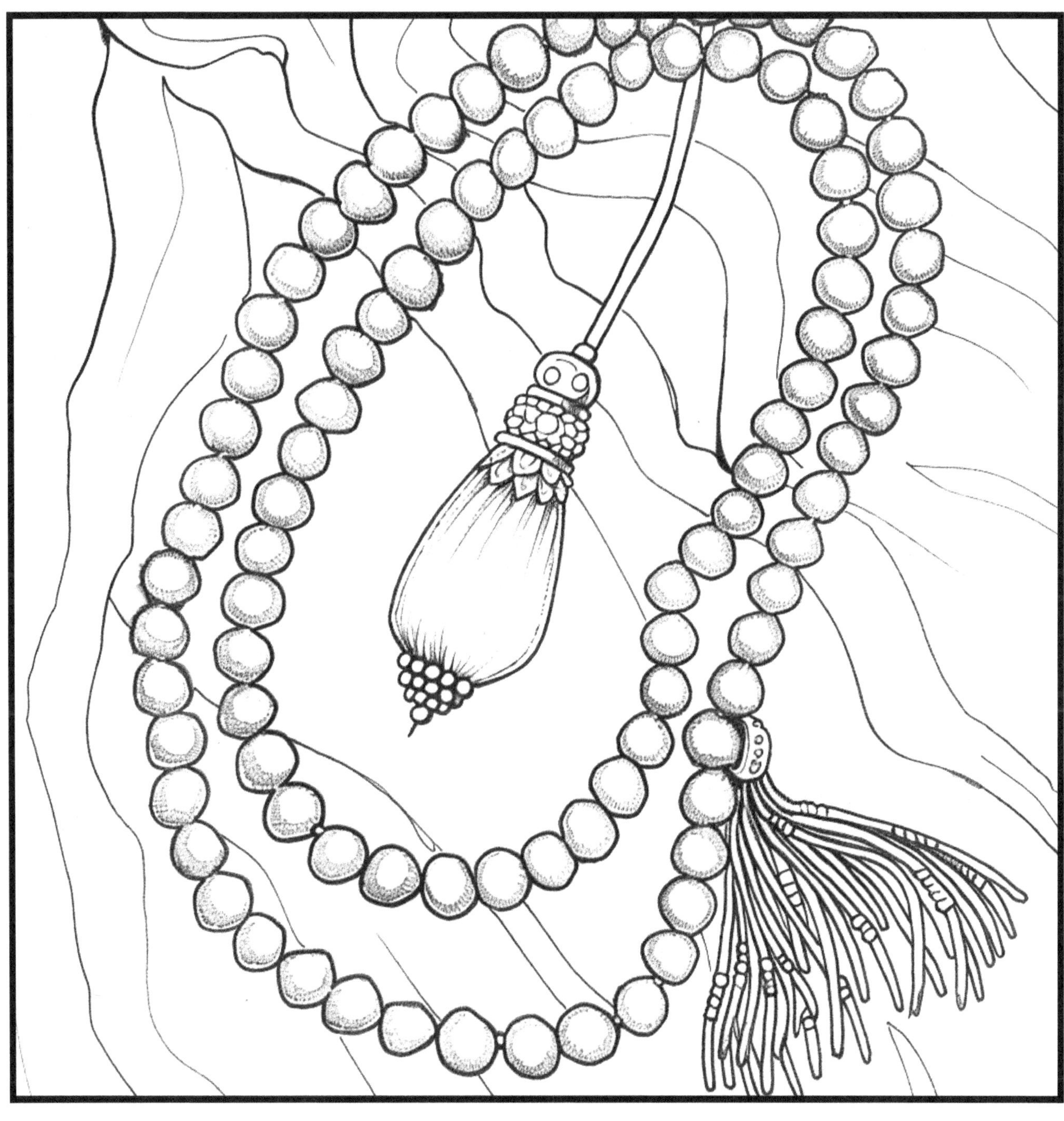

Day 29

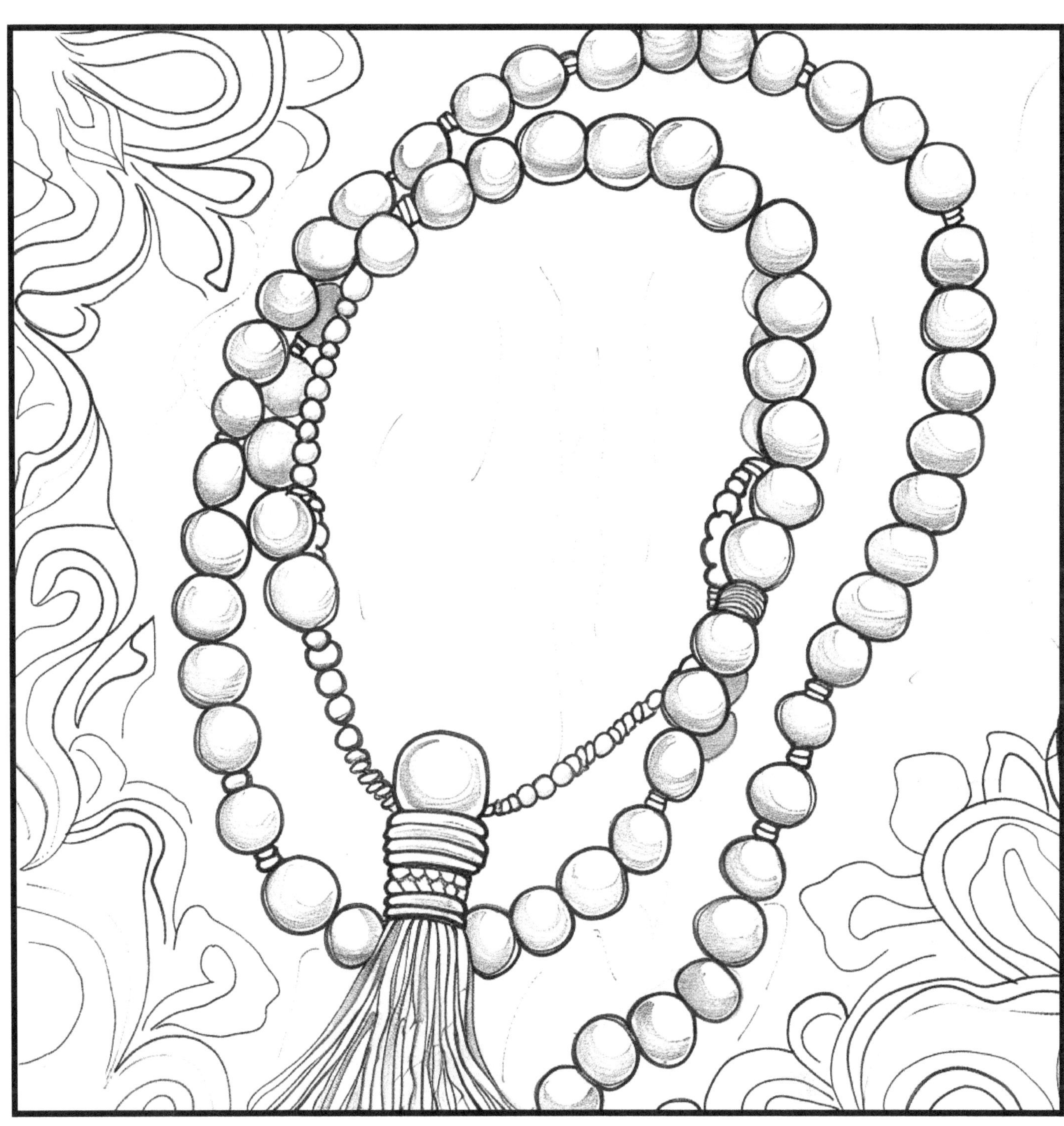

Day 30

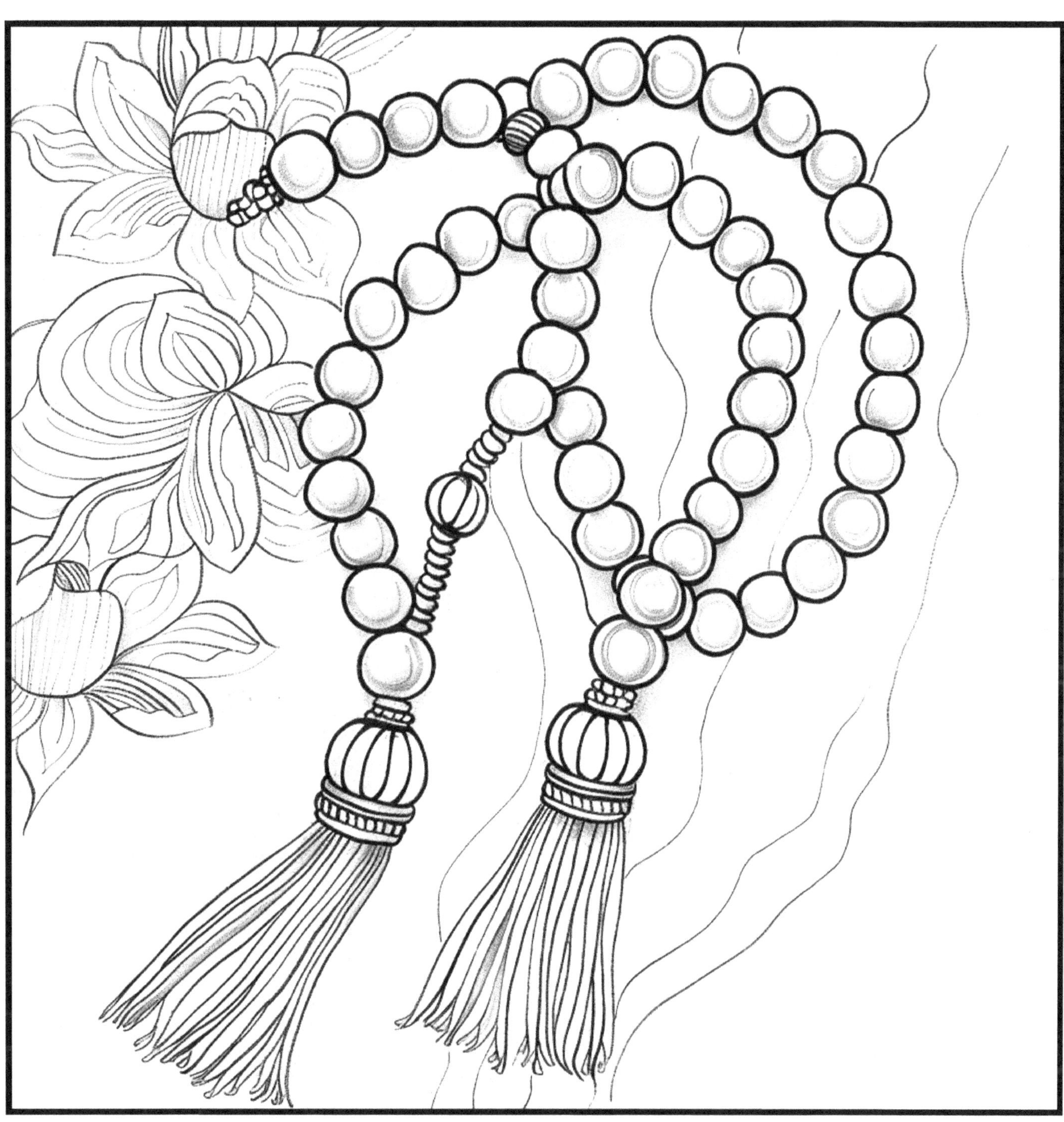

Day 31

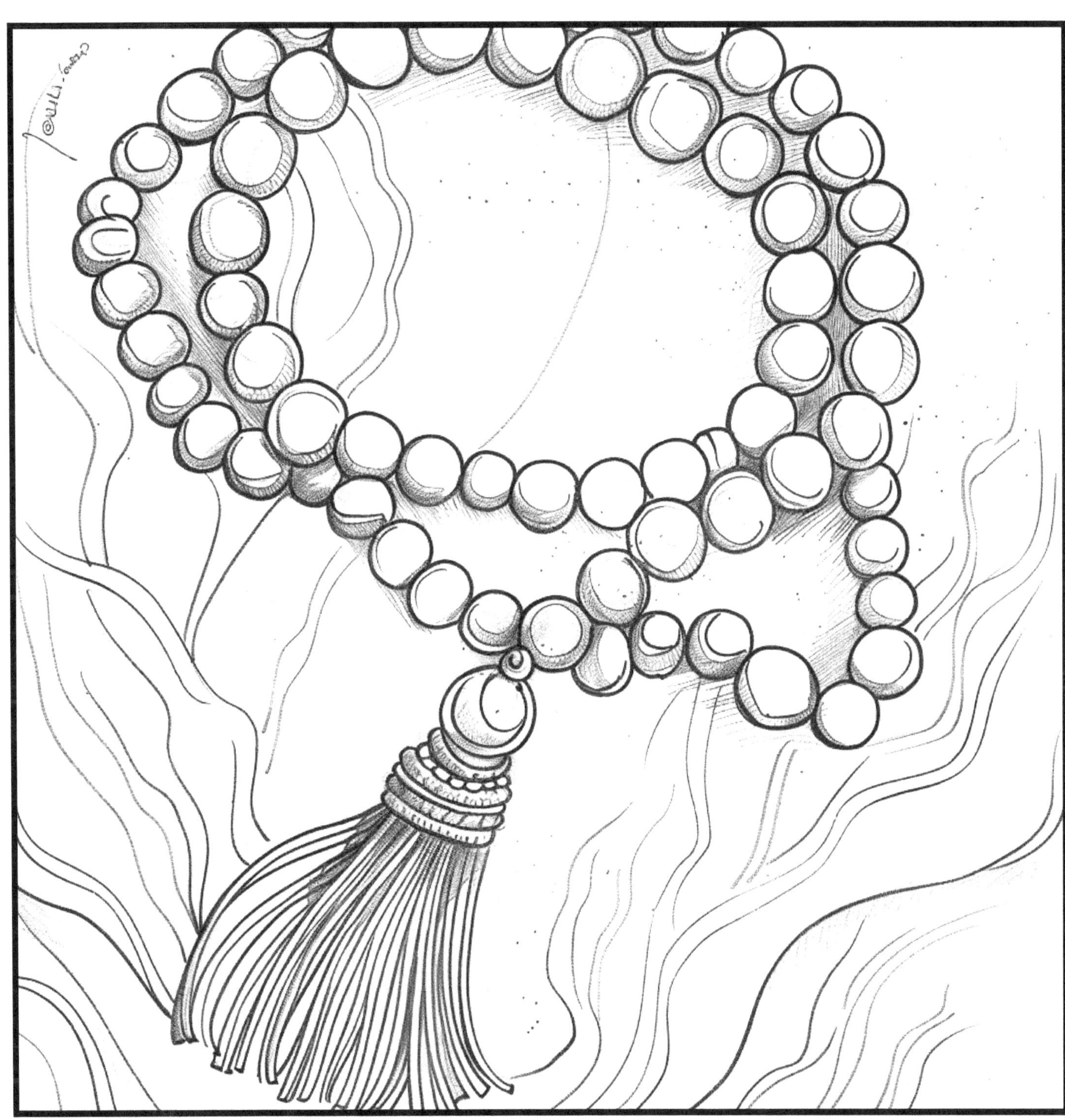

Day 32

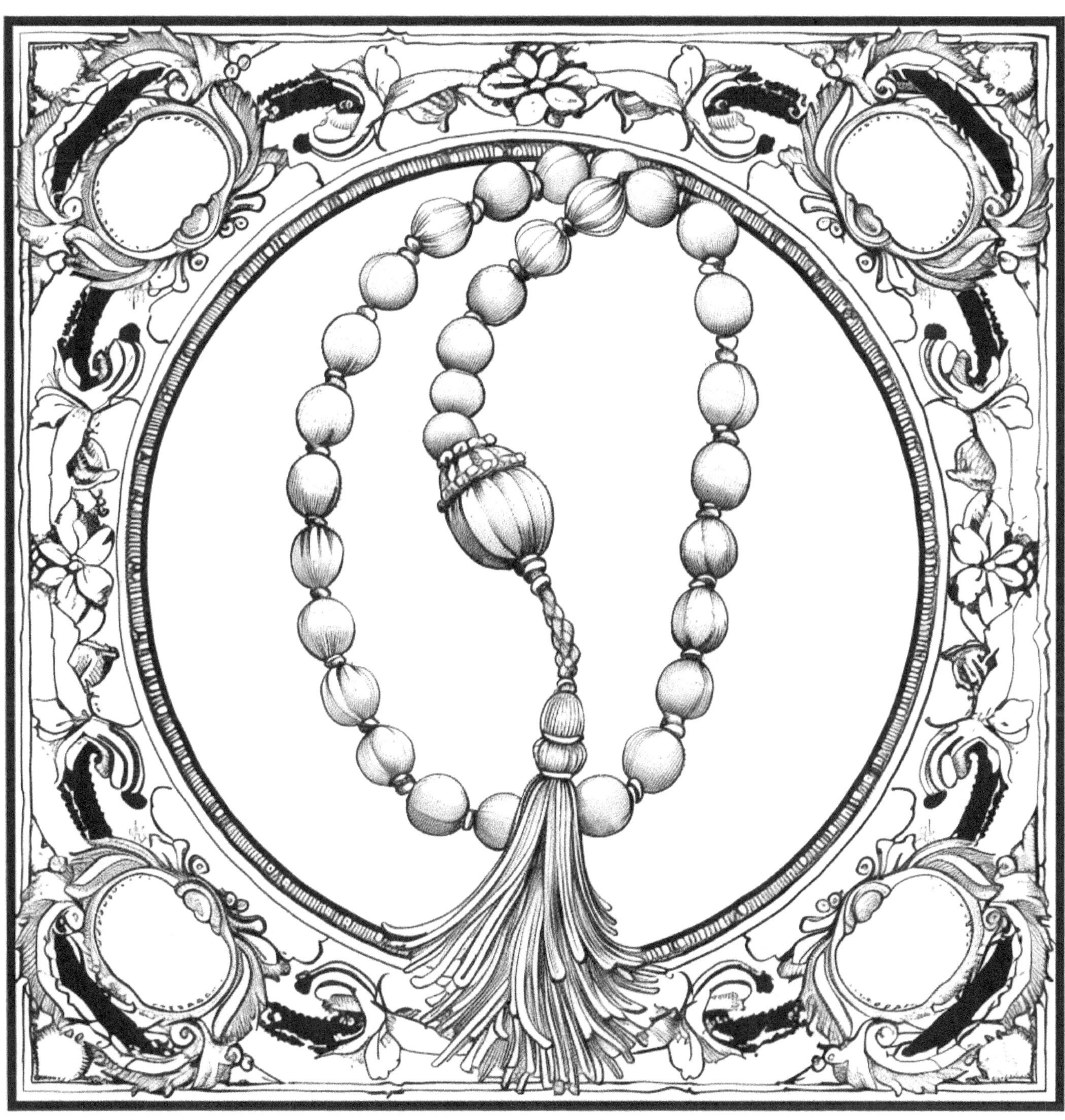

Day 33

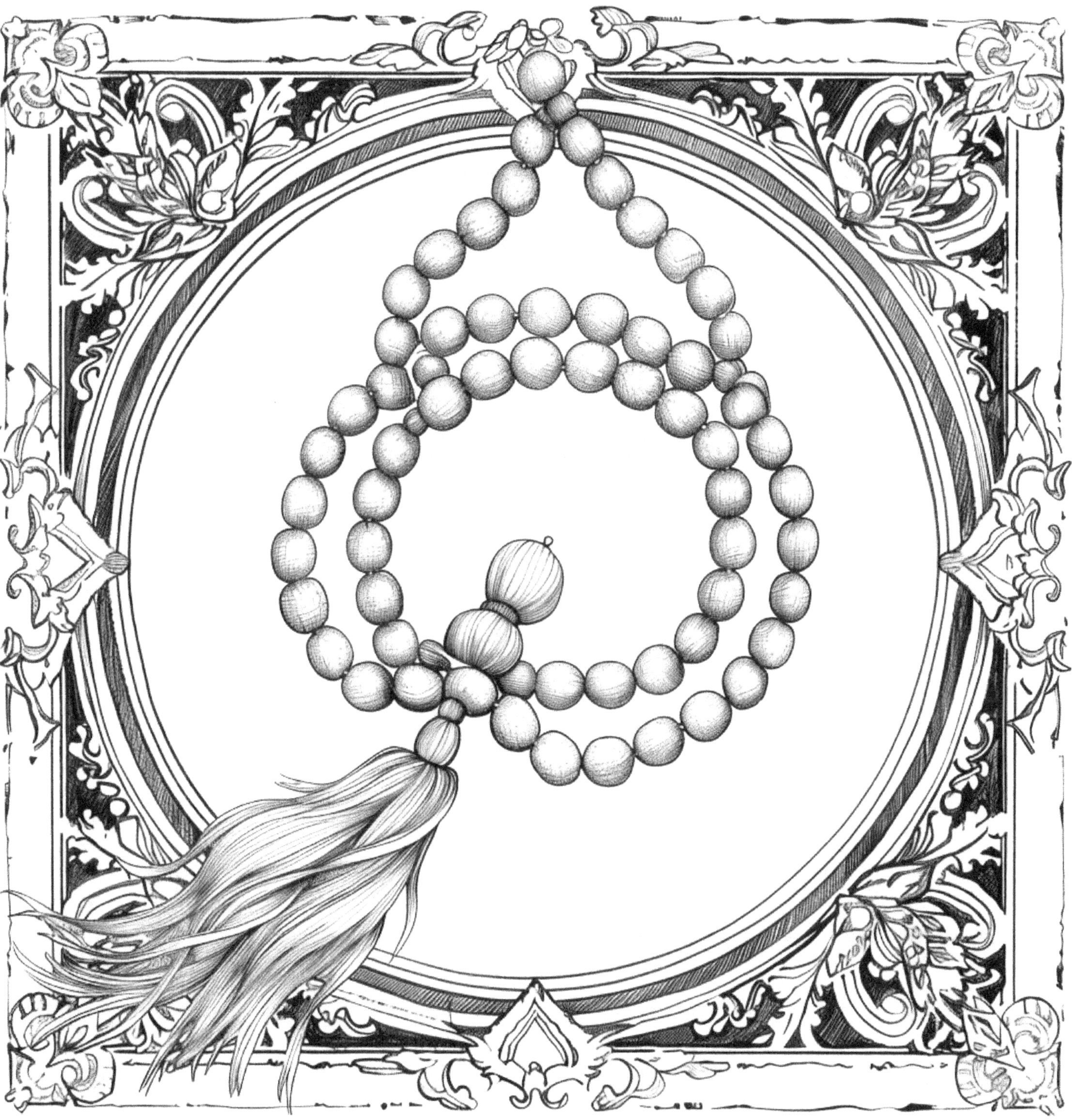

Day 34

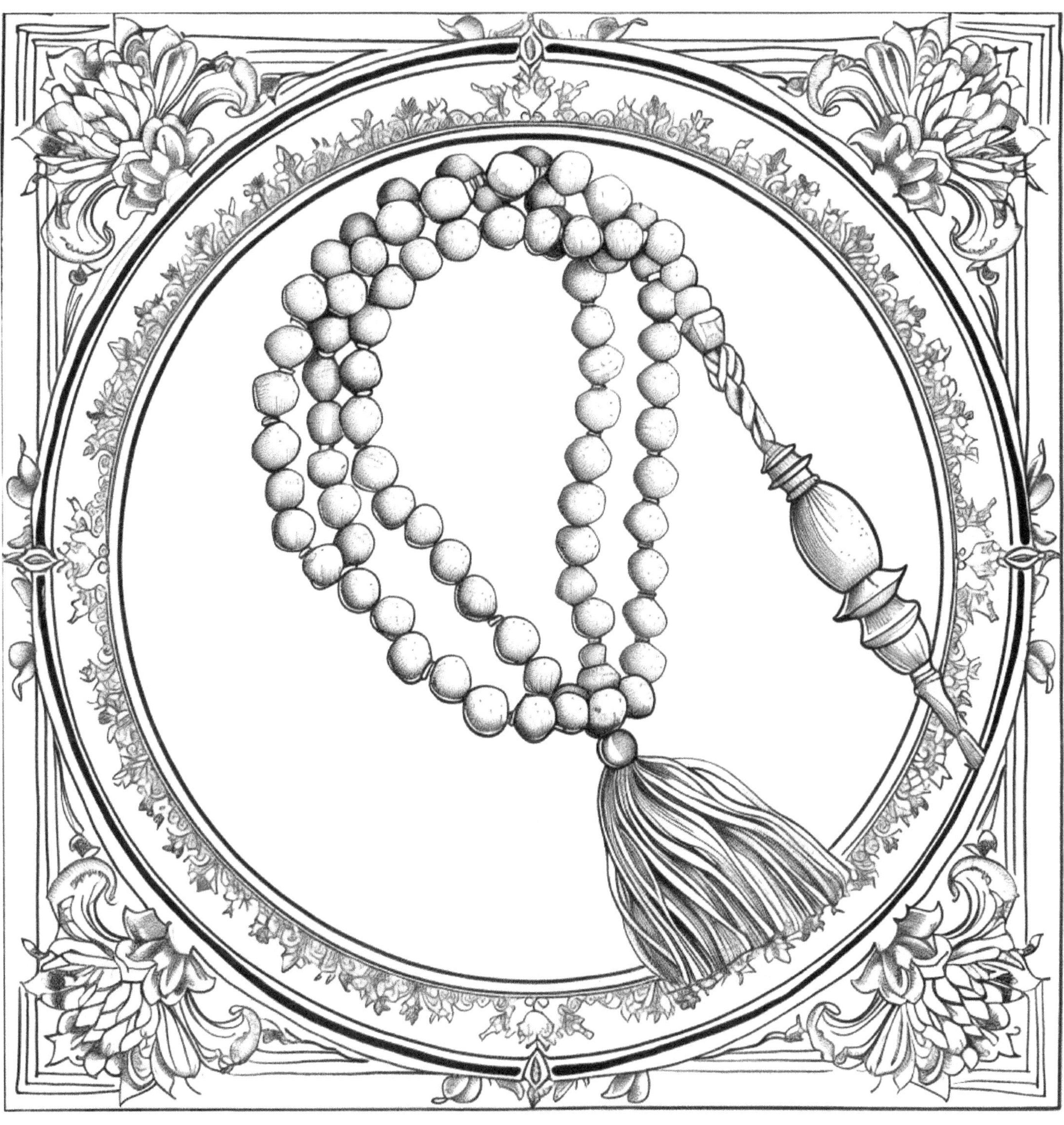

Day 35

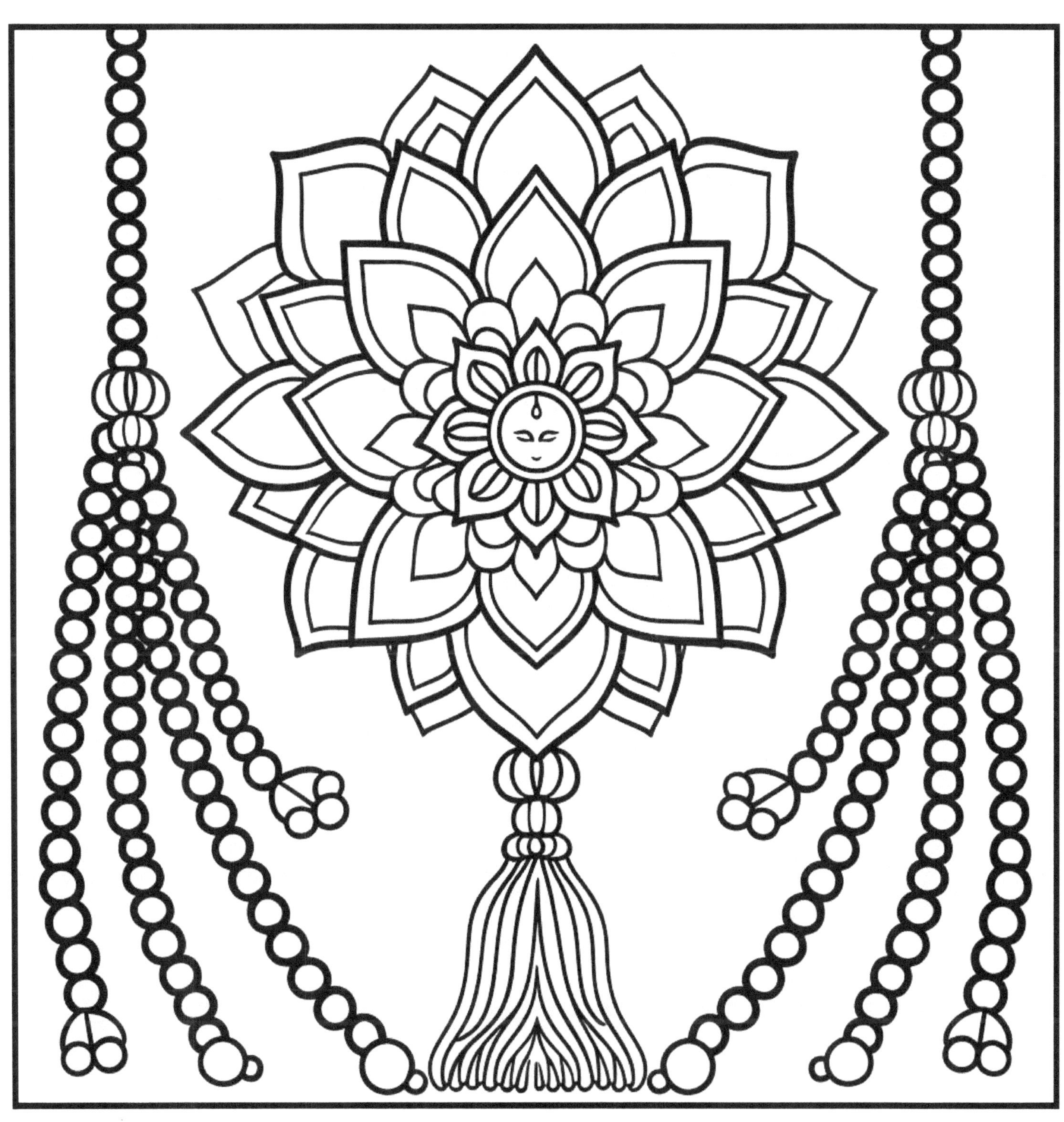

Day 36

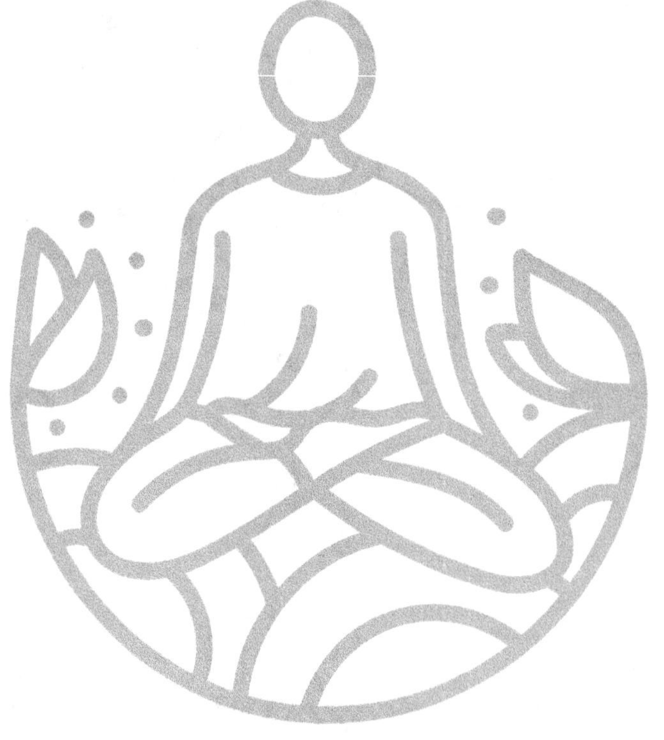

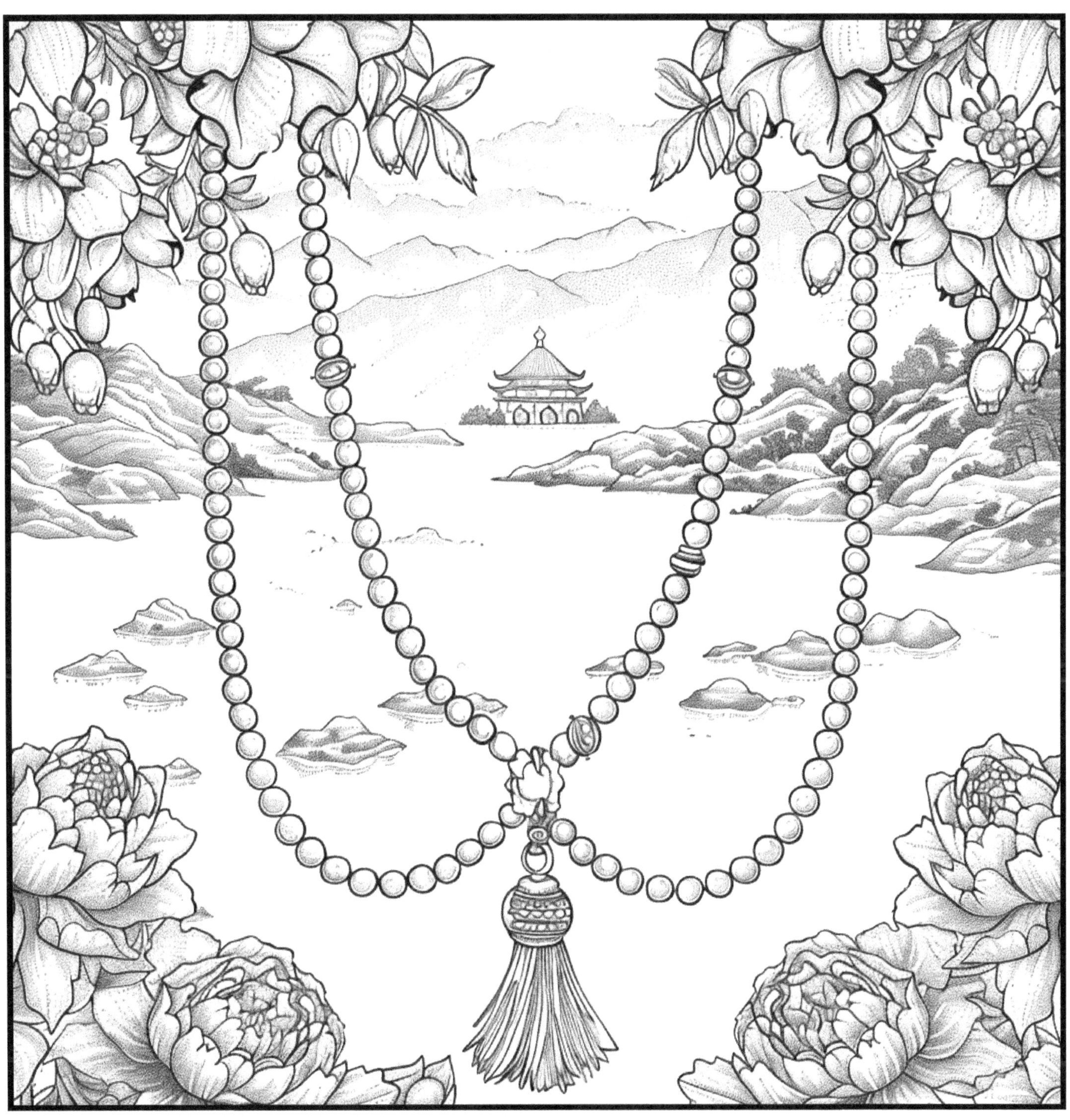

Day 37

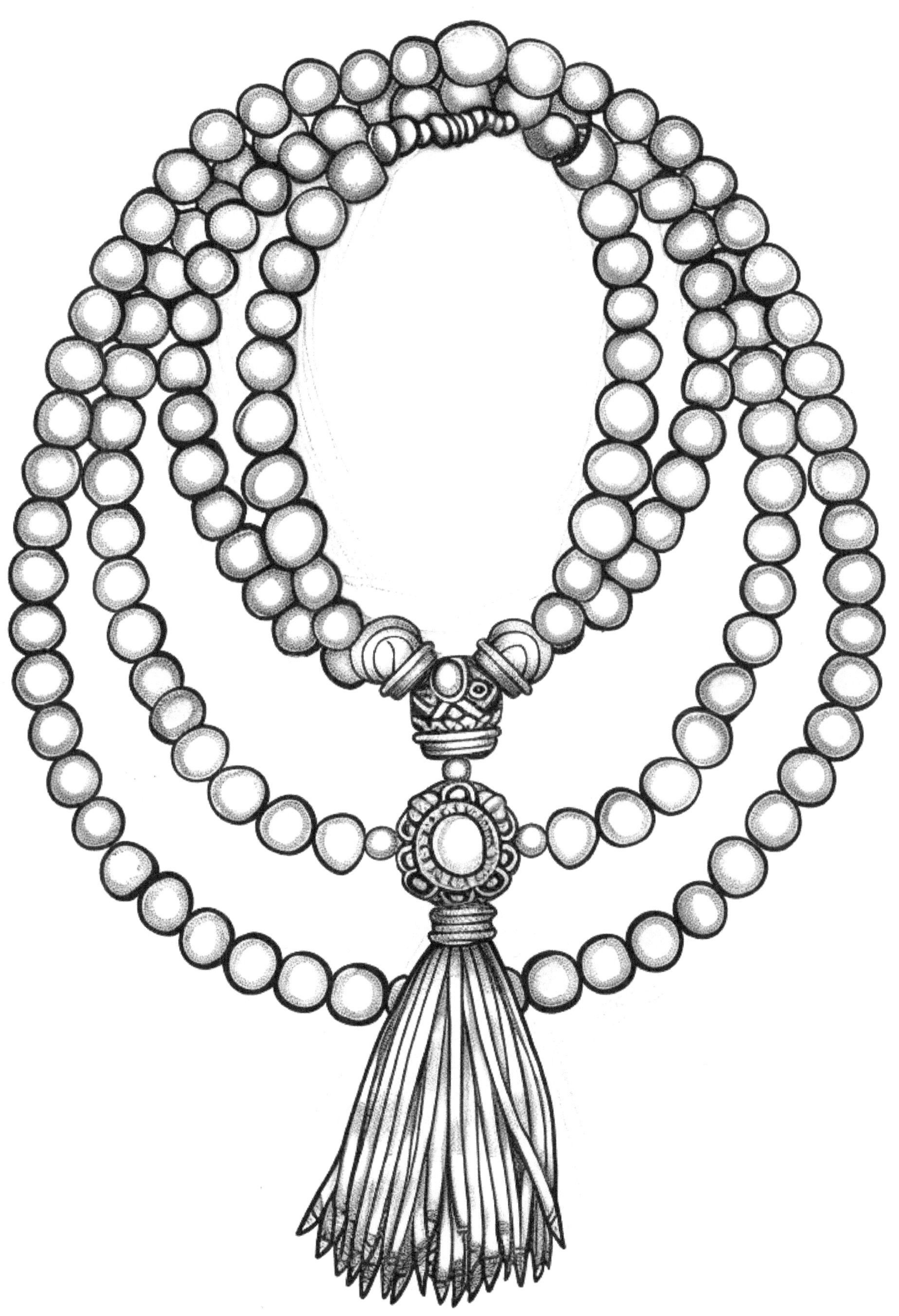

Day 38

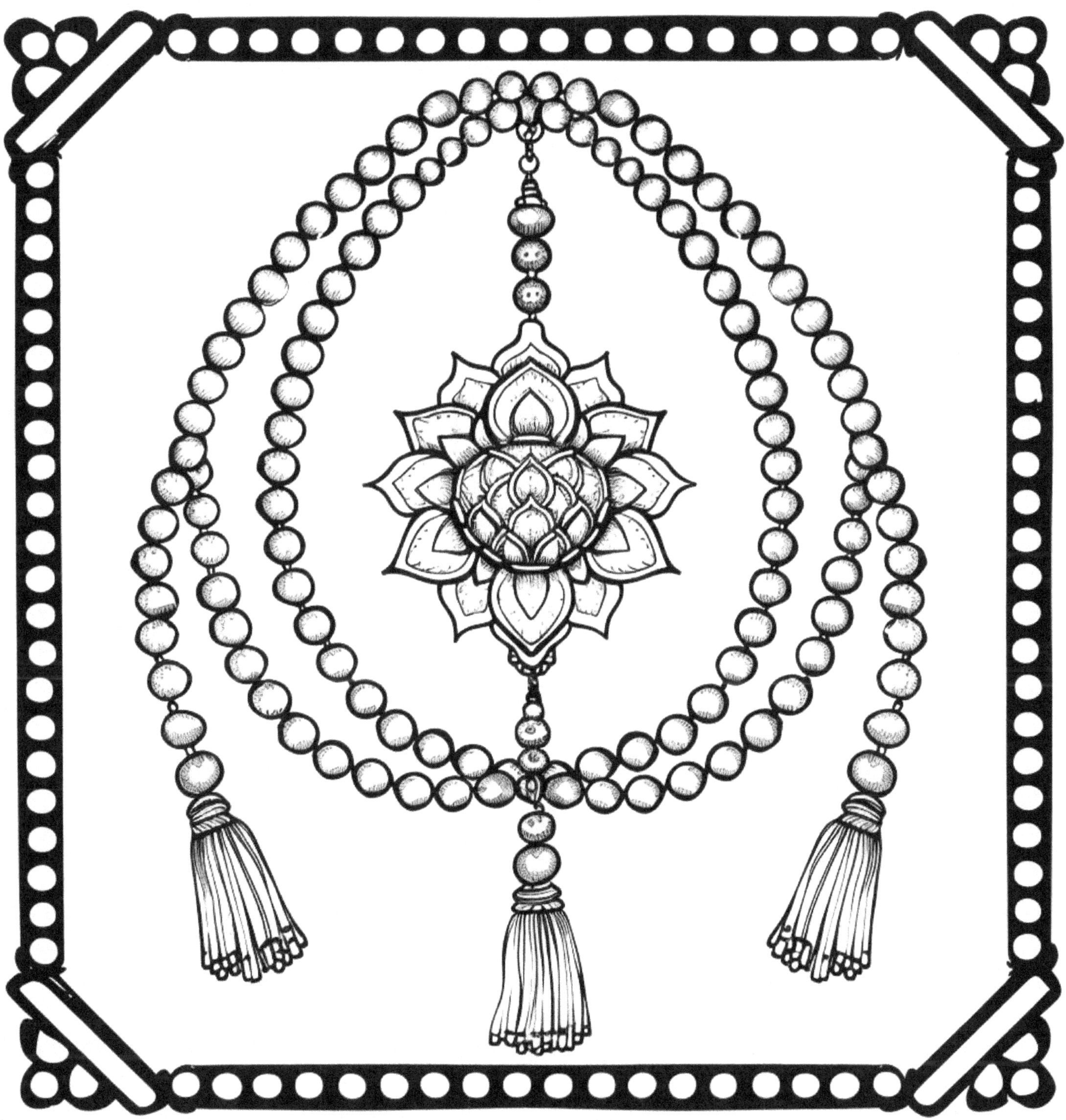

Day 39

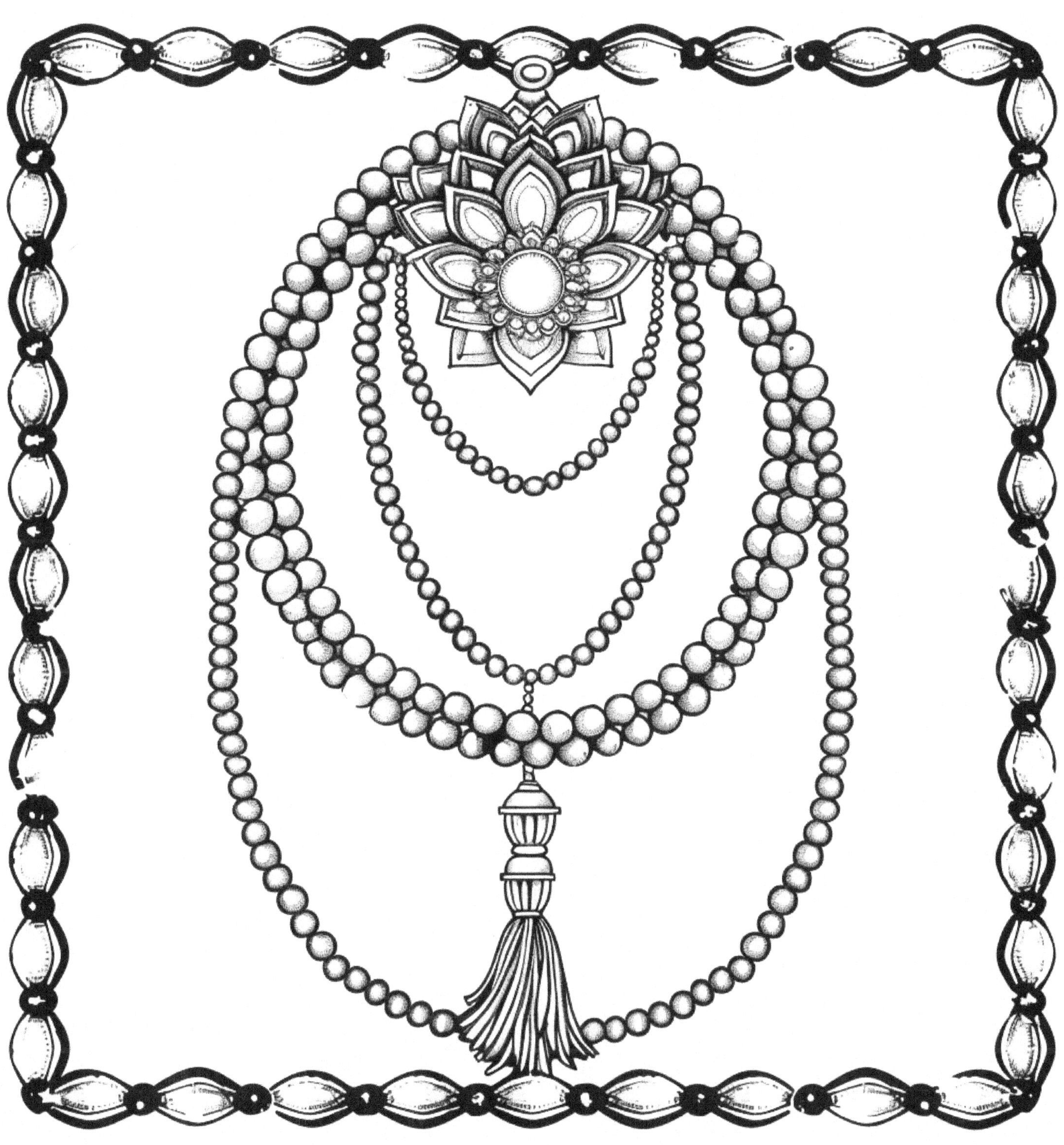

Day 40

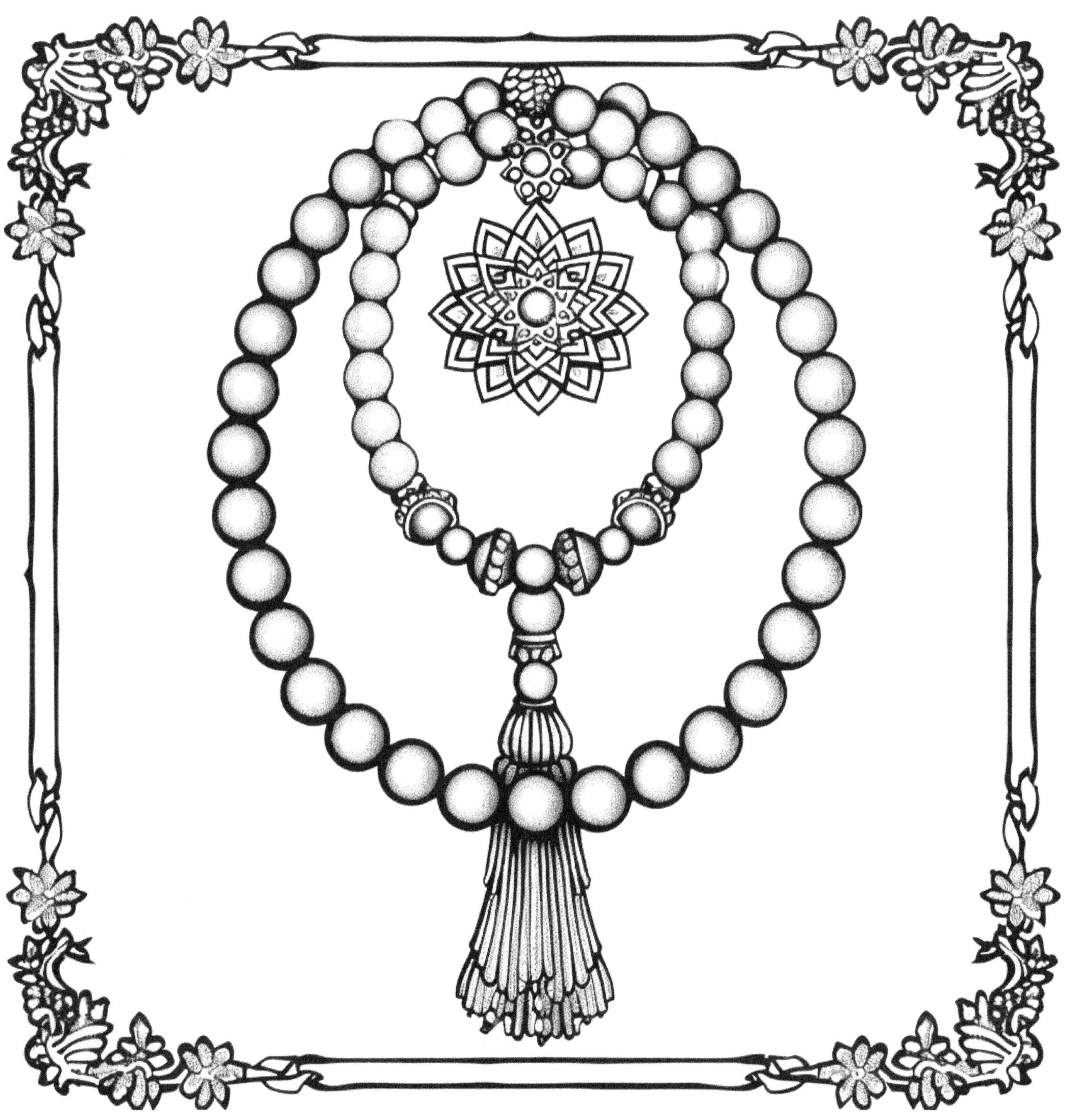

Day 41

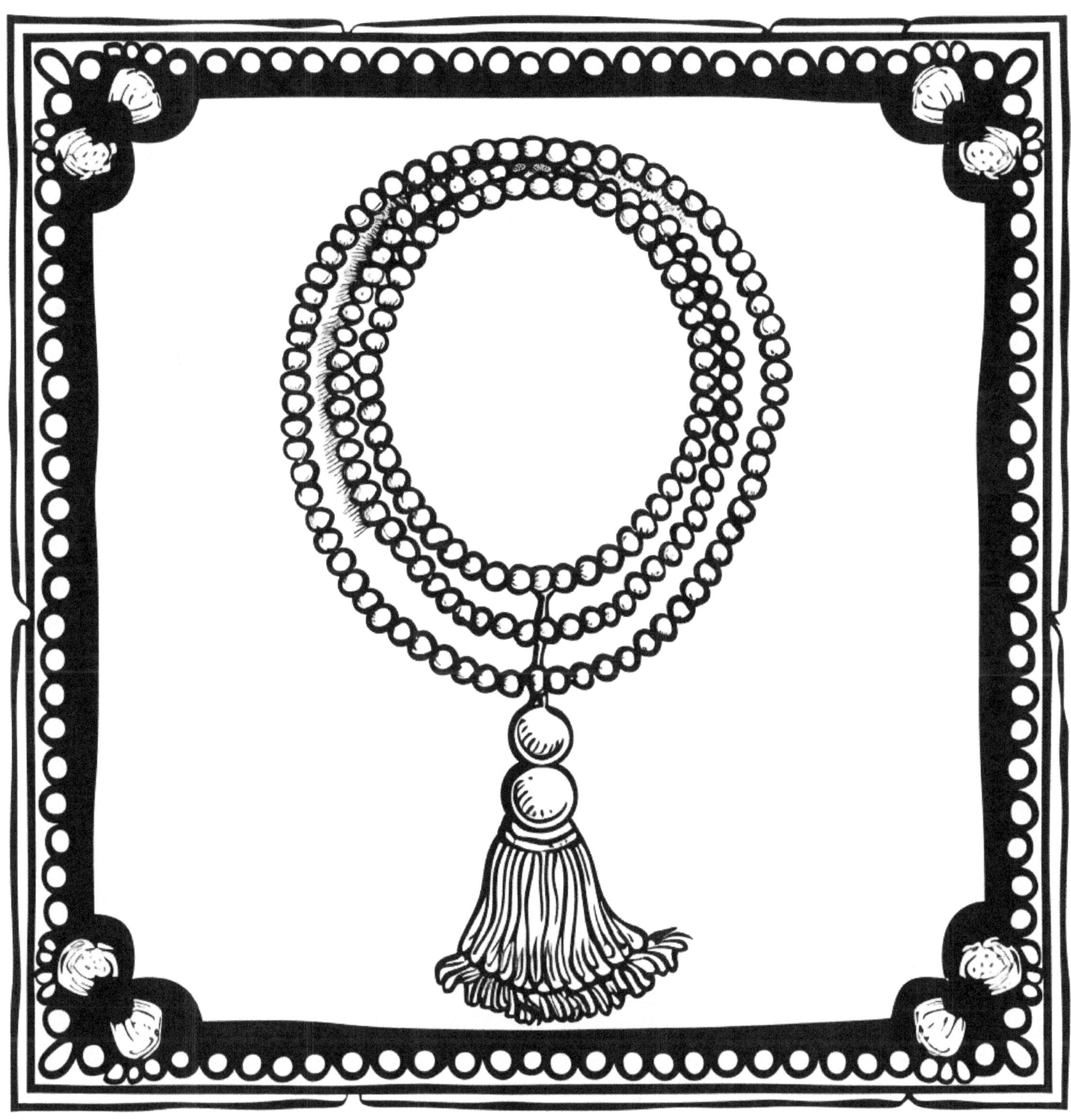

Day 42

Day 43

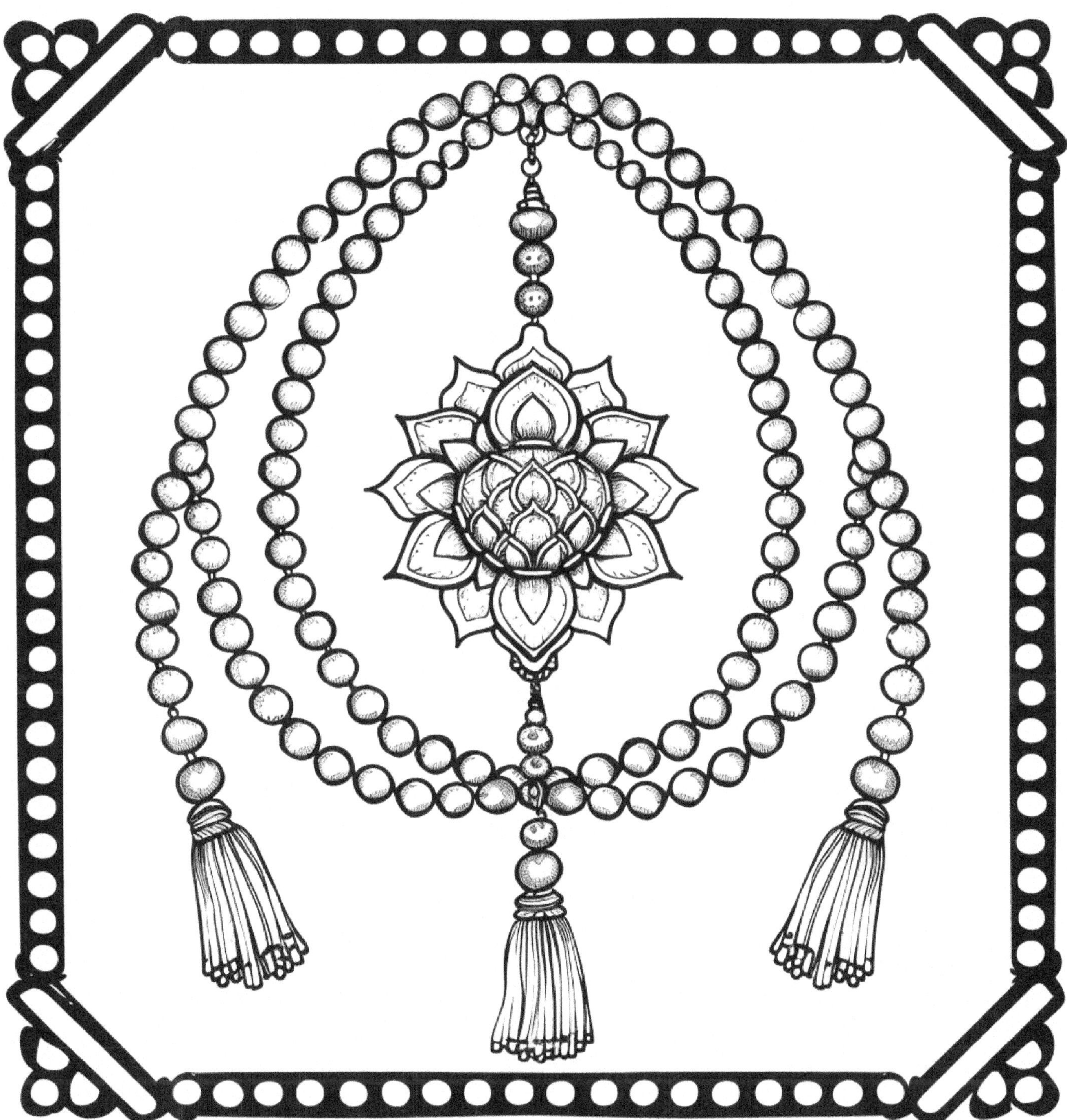

Day 44

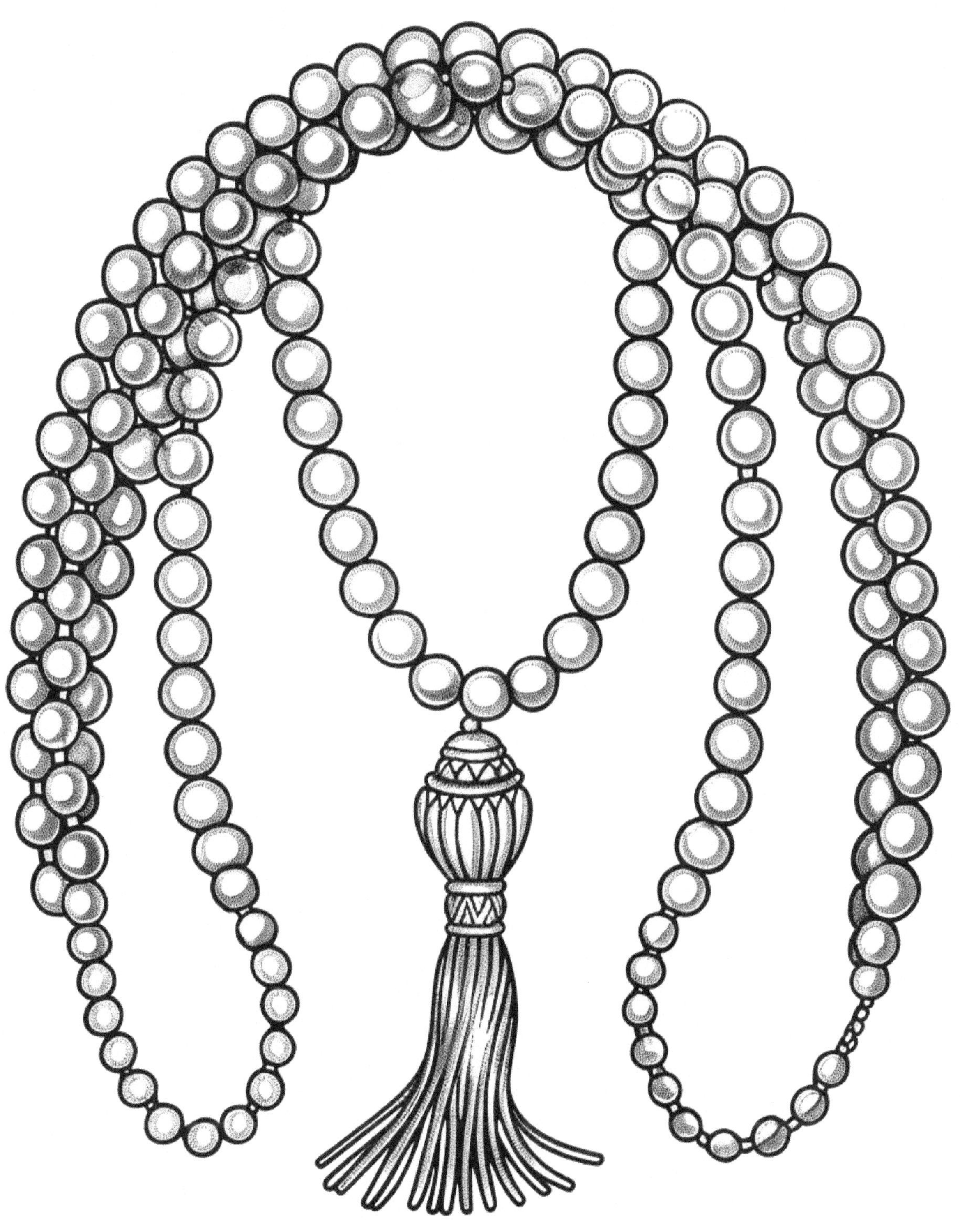

Day 45

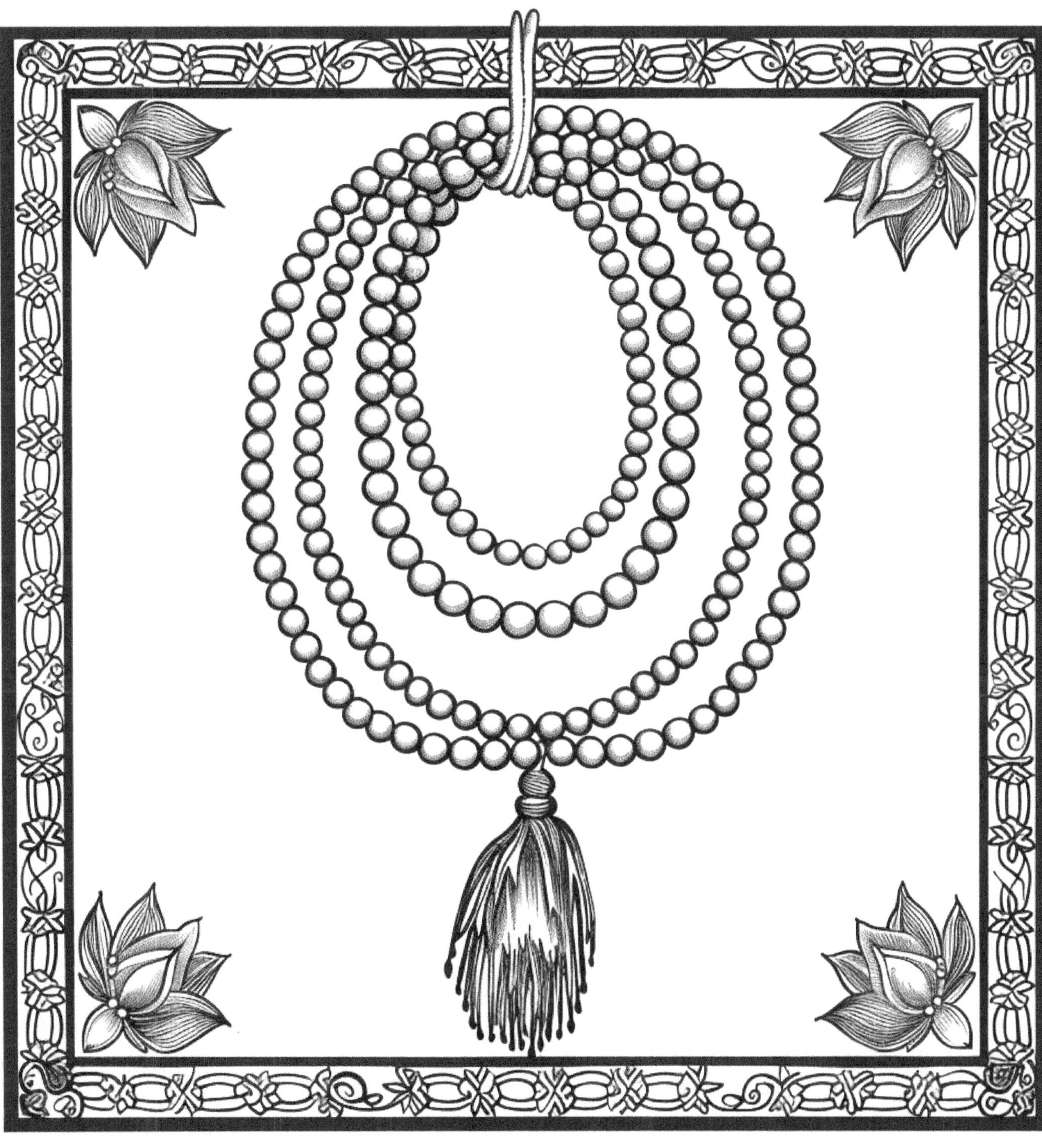

Day 46

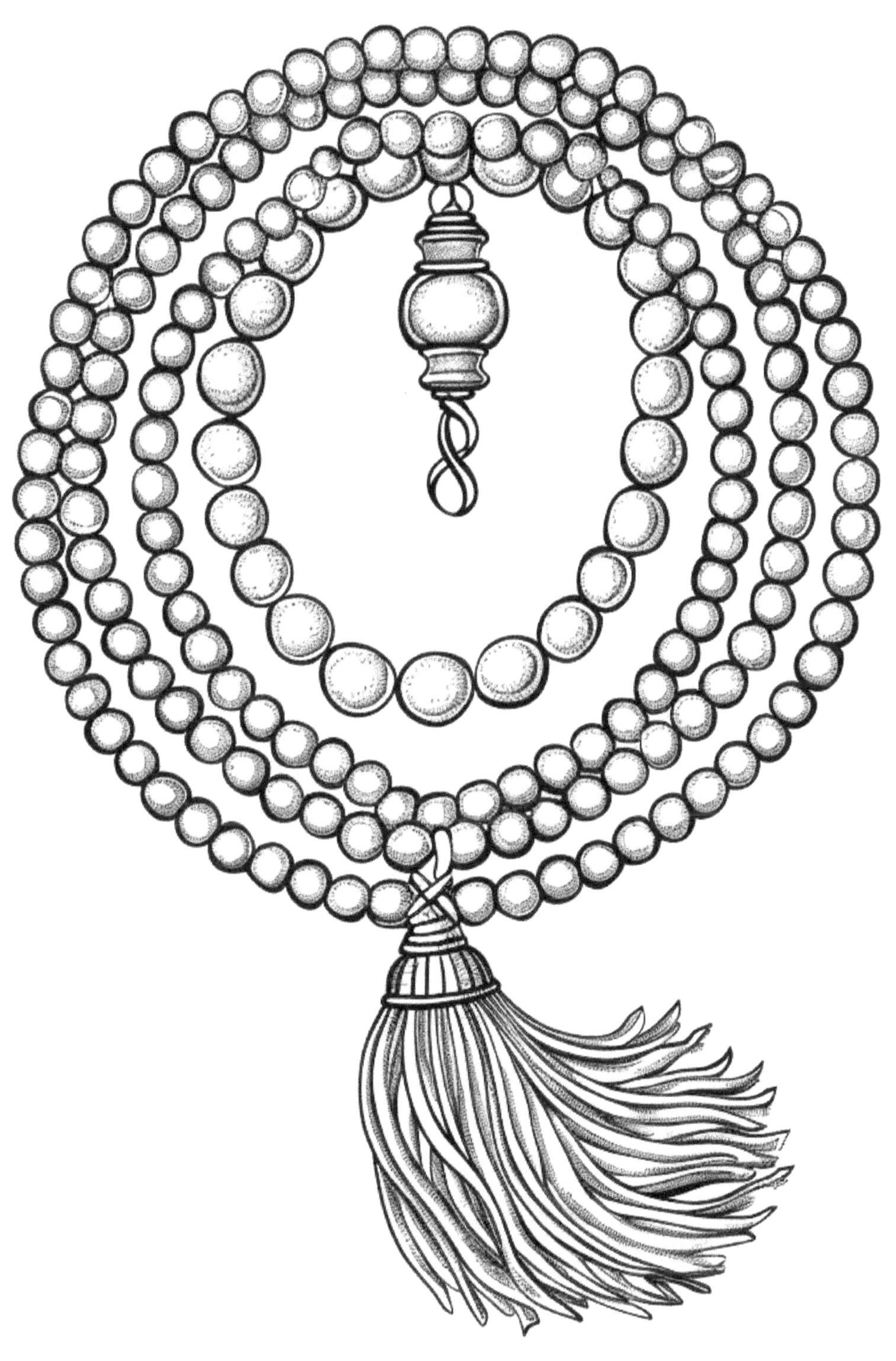

Day 47

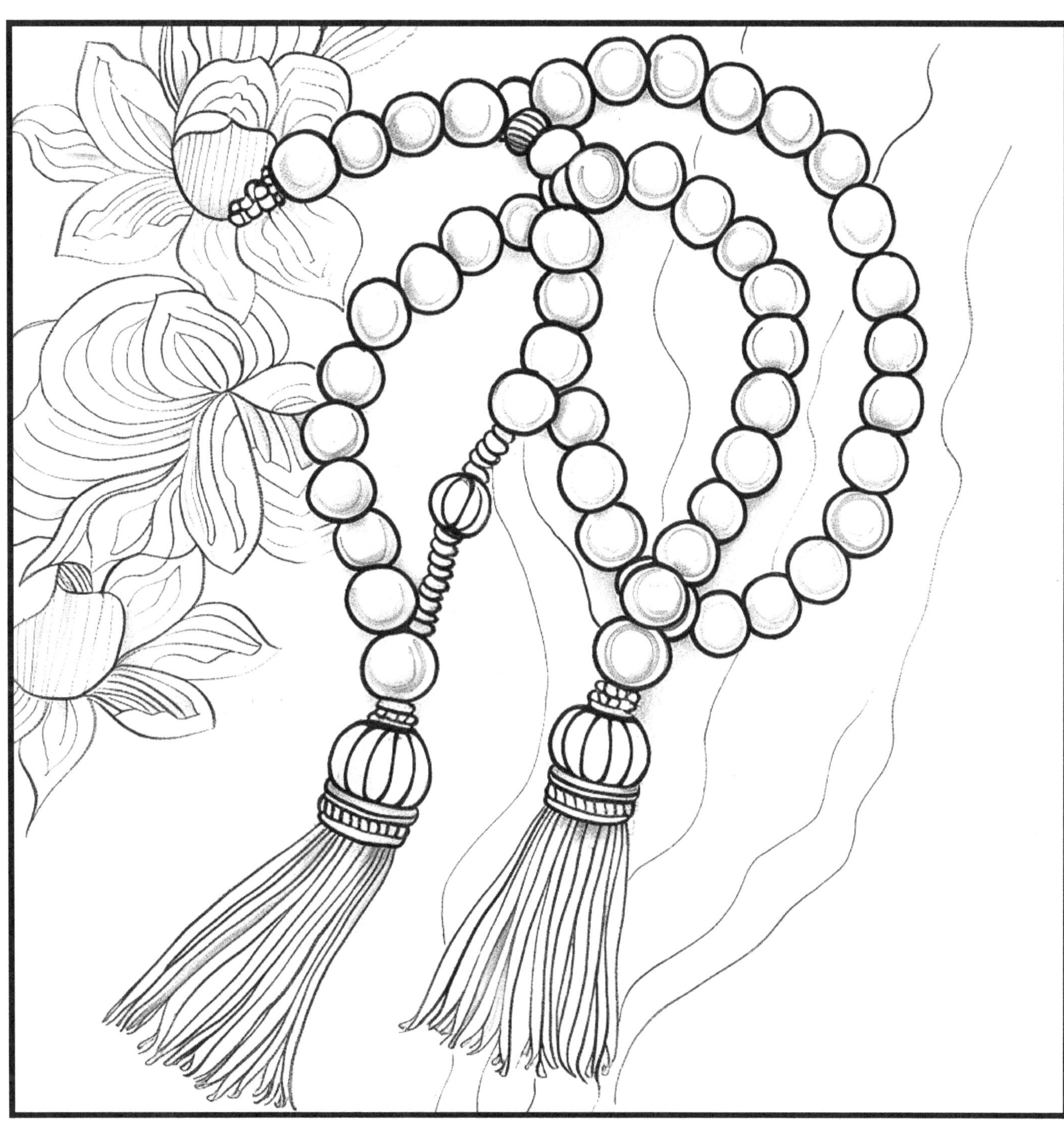

Day 48

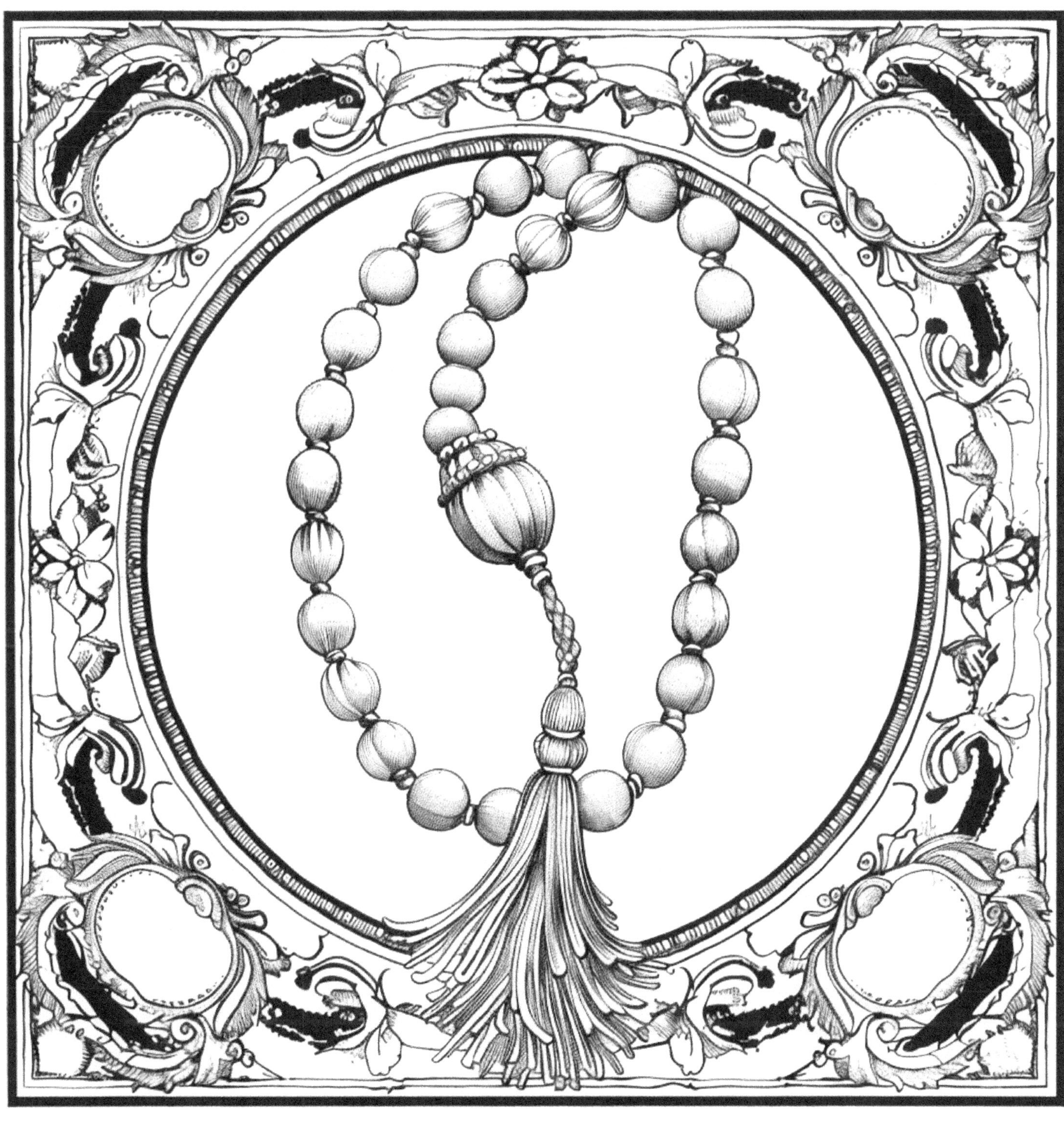

Day 49

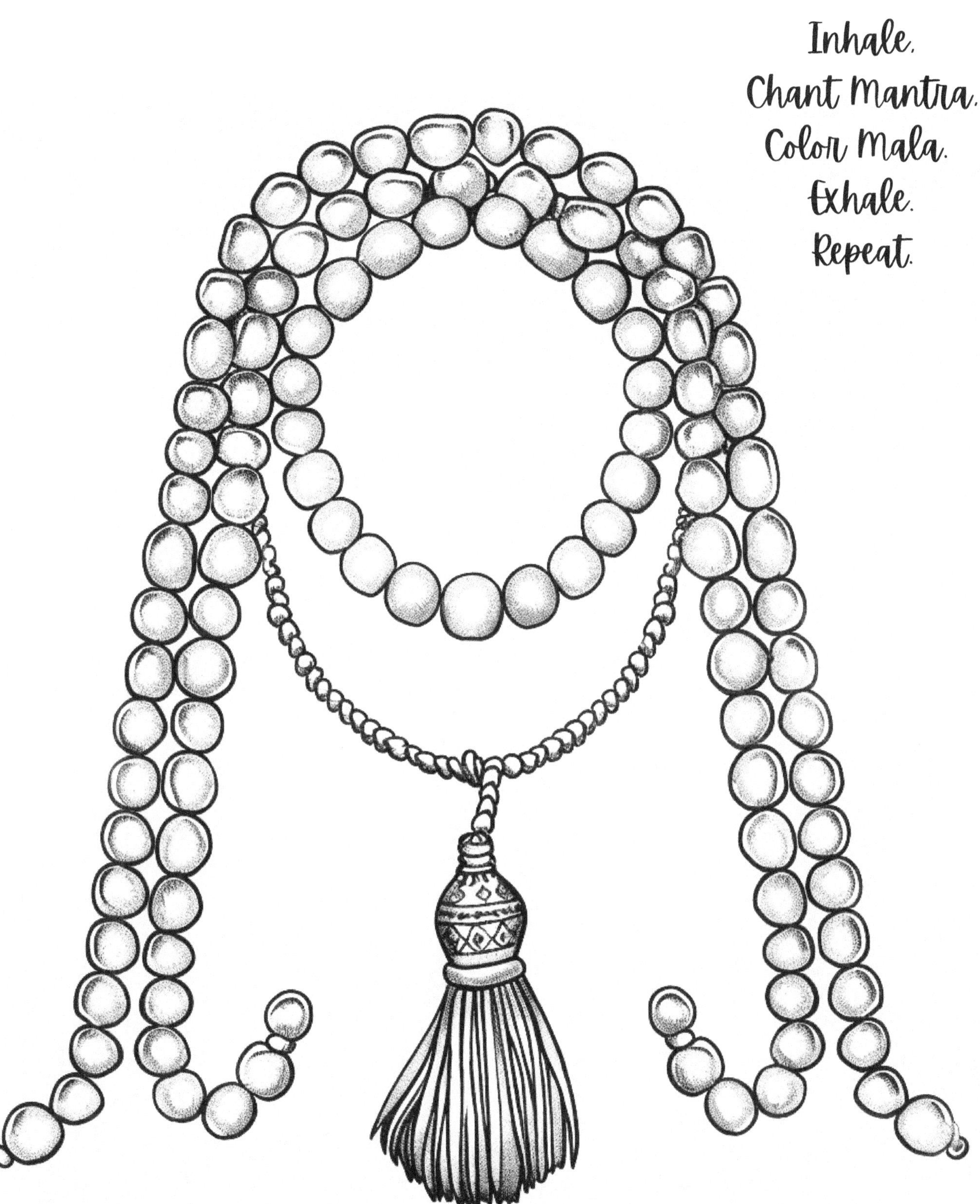
Inhale.
Chant Mantra.
Color Mala.
Exhale.
Repeat.

Day 50

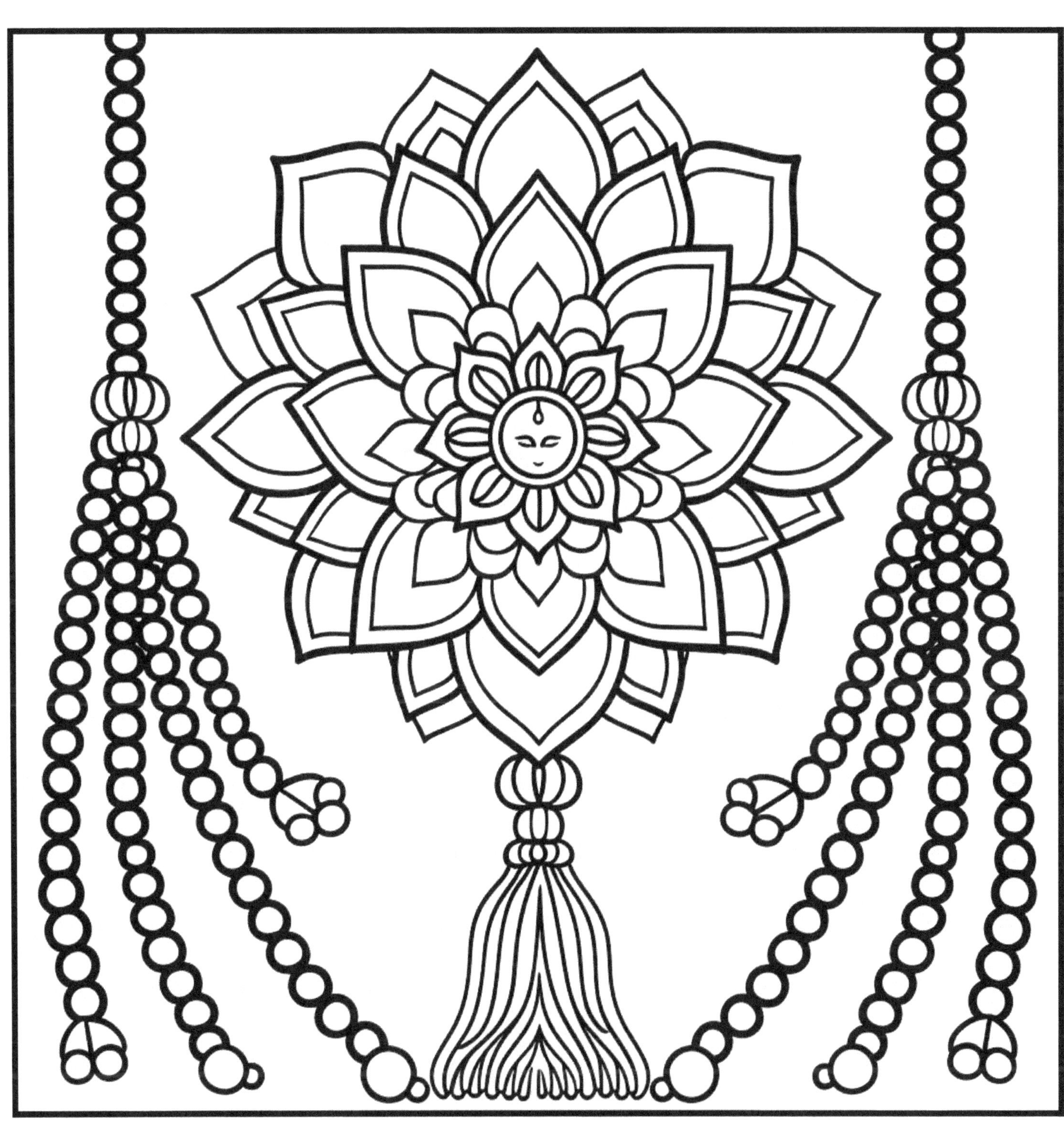

Day 51

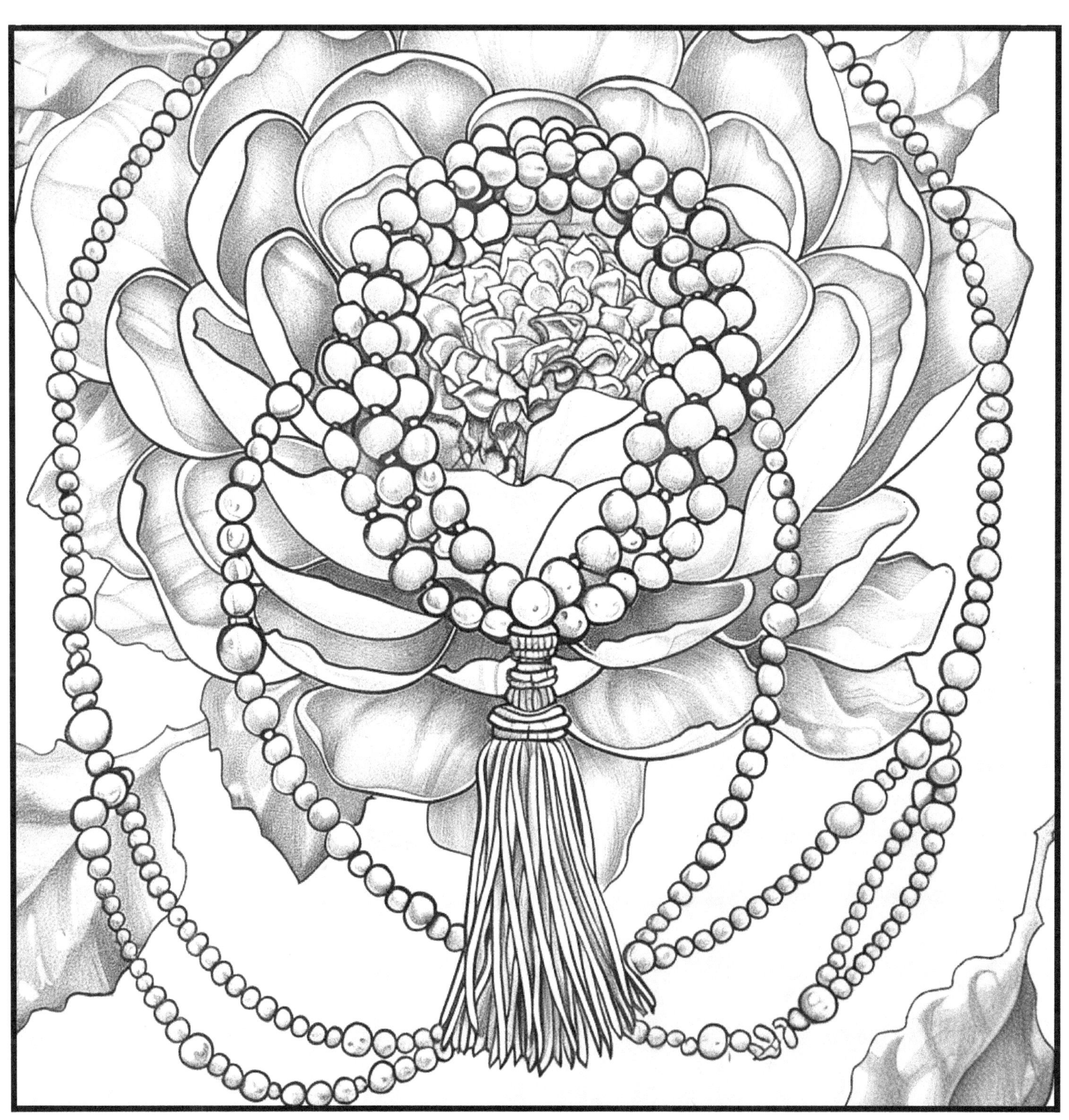

Day 52

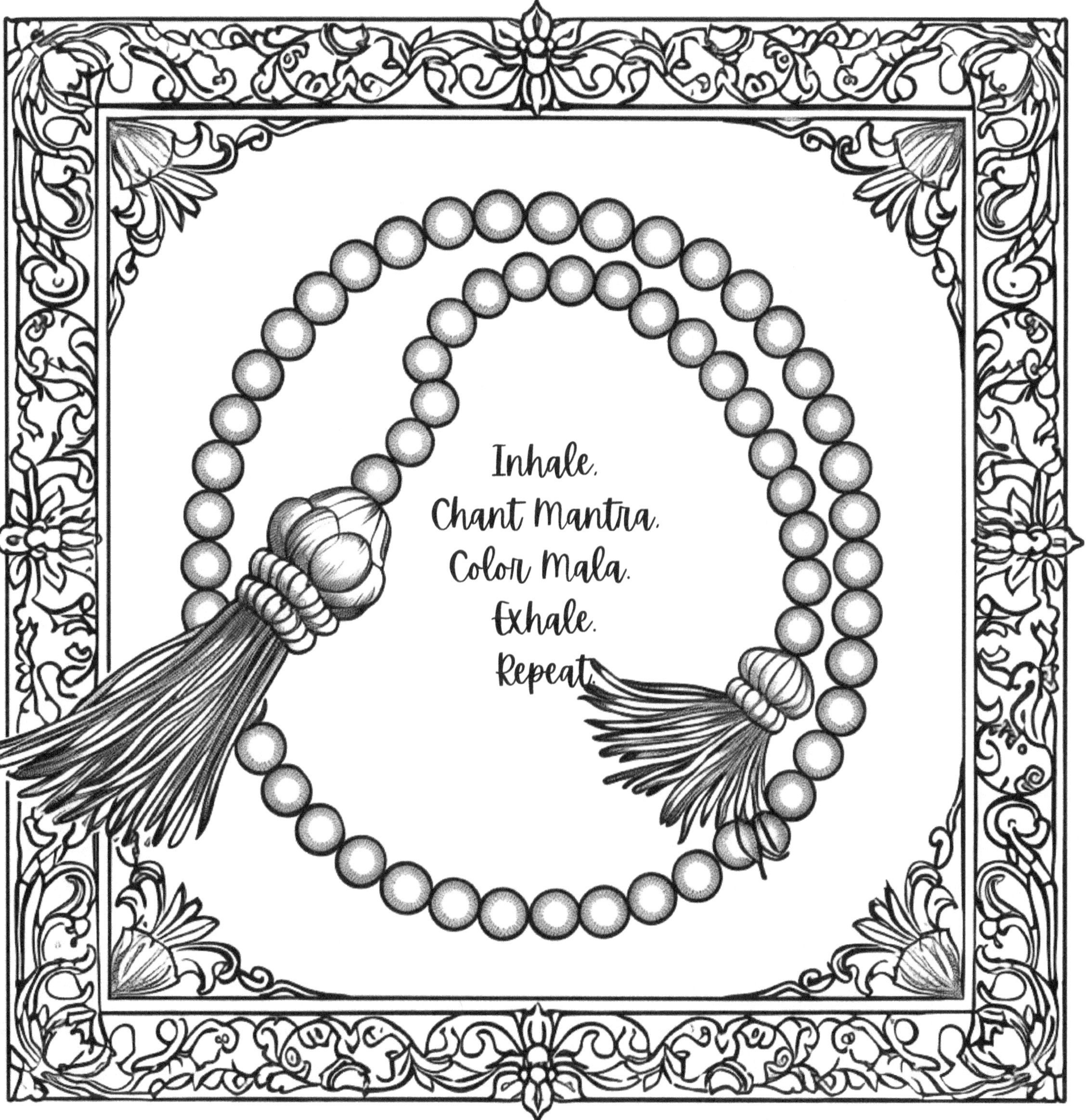
Inhale.
Chant Mantra.
Color Mala.
Exhale.
Repeat.

INHALE POSITIVITY
EXHALE POSSIBILITIES

Day 53

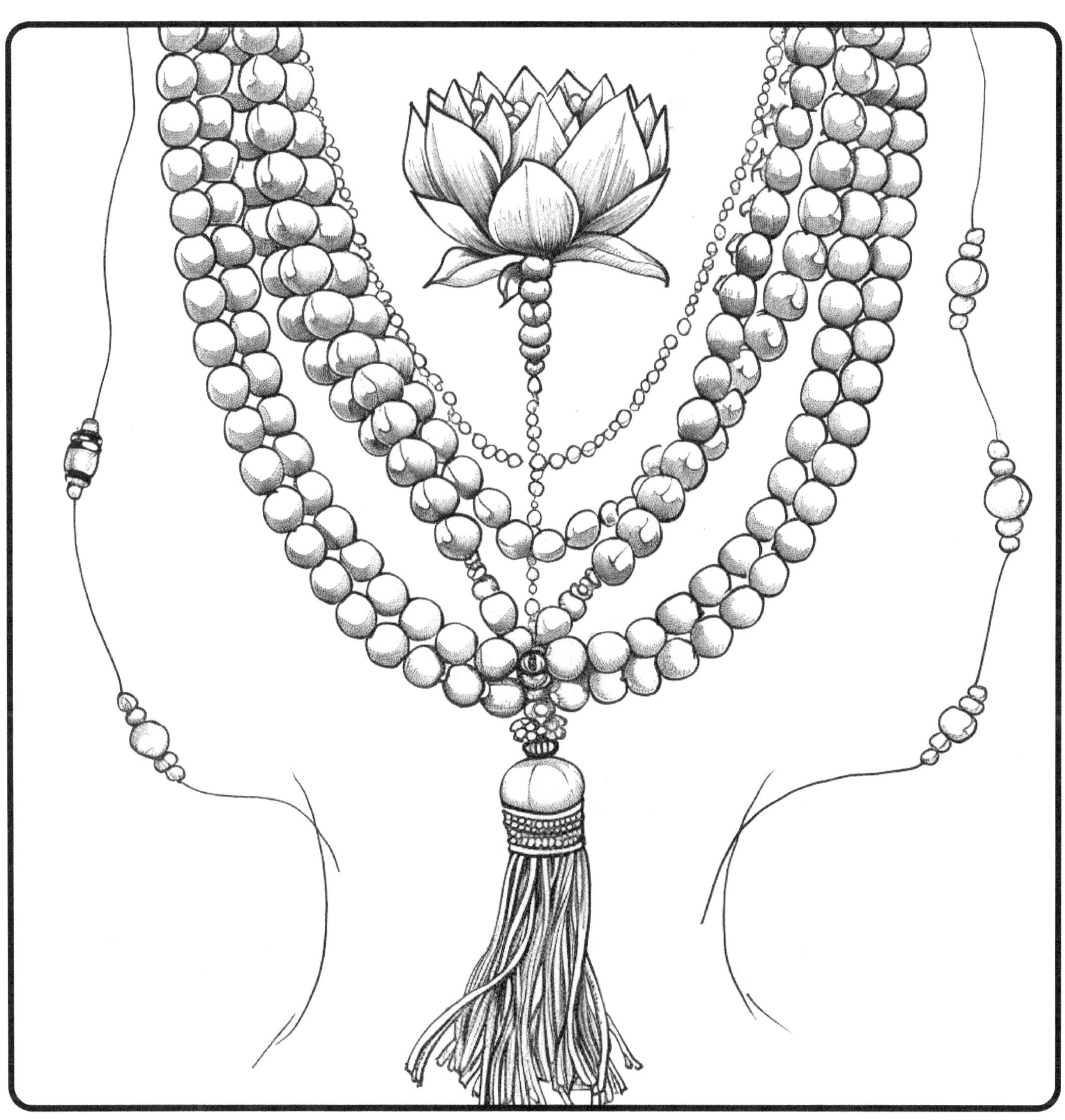

The Deeper the Breath

The Richer the Life

Day 54

You're halfway there!

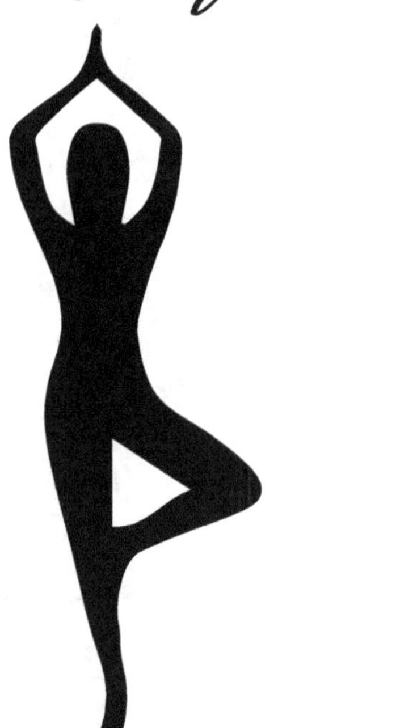

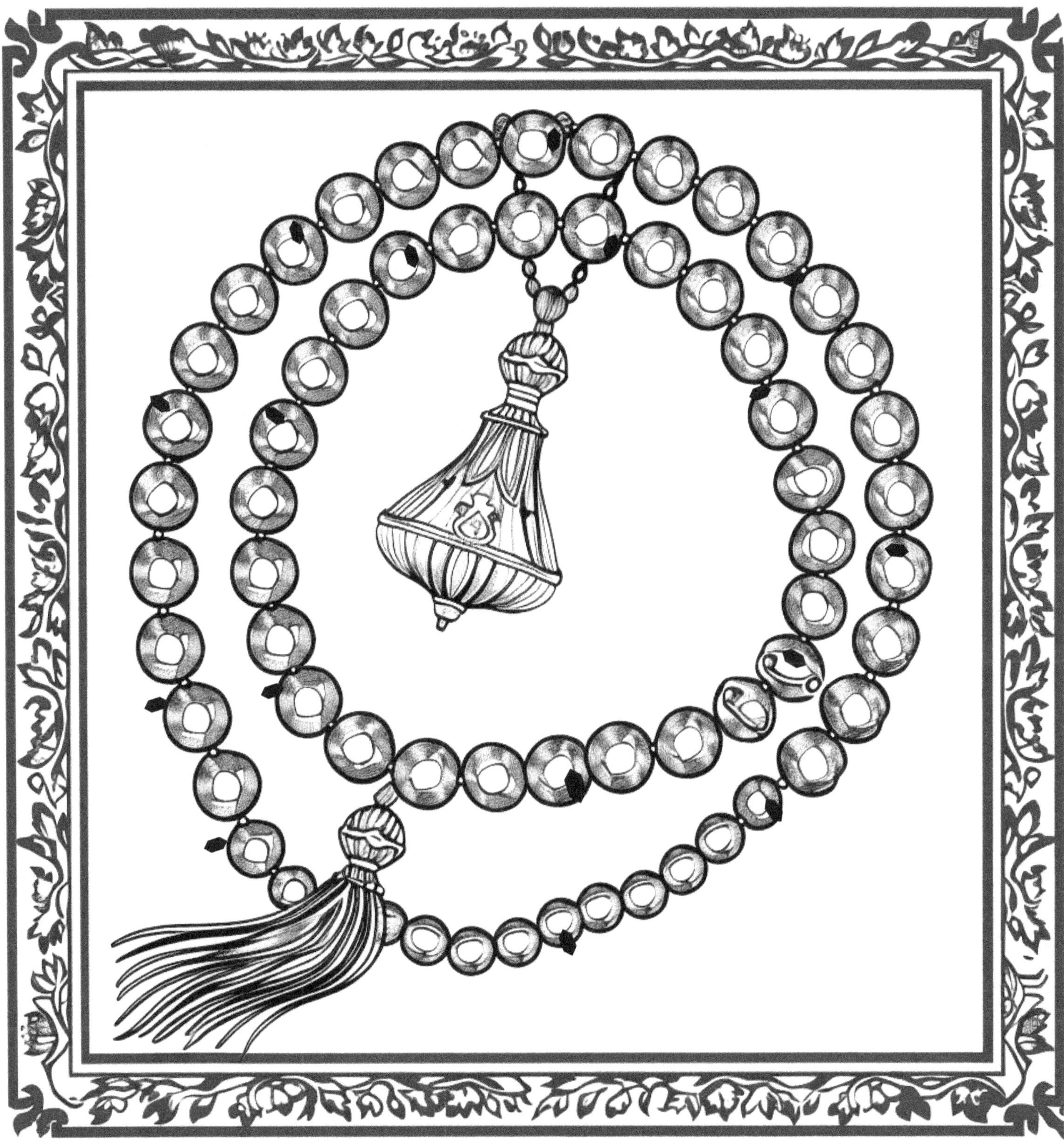

Day 55

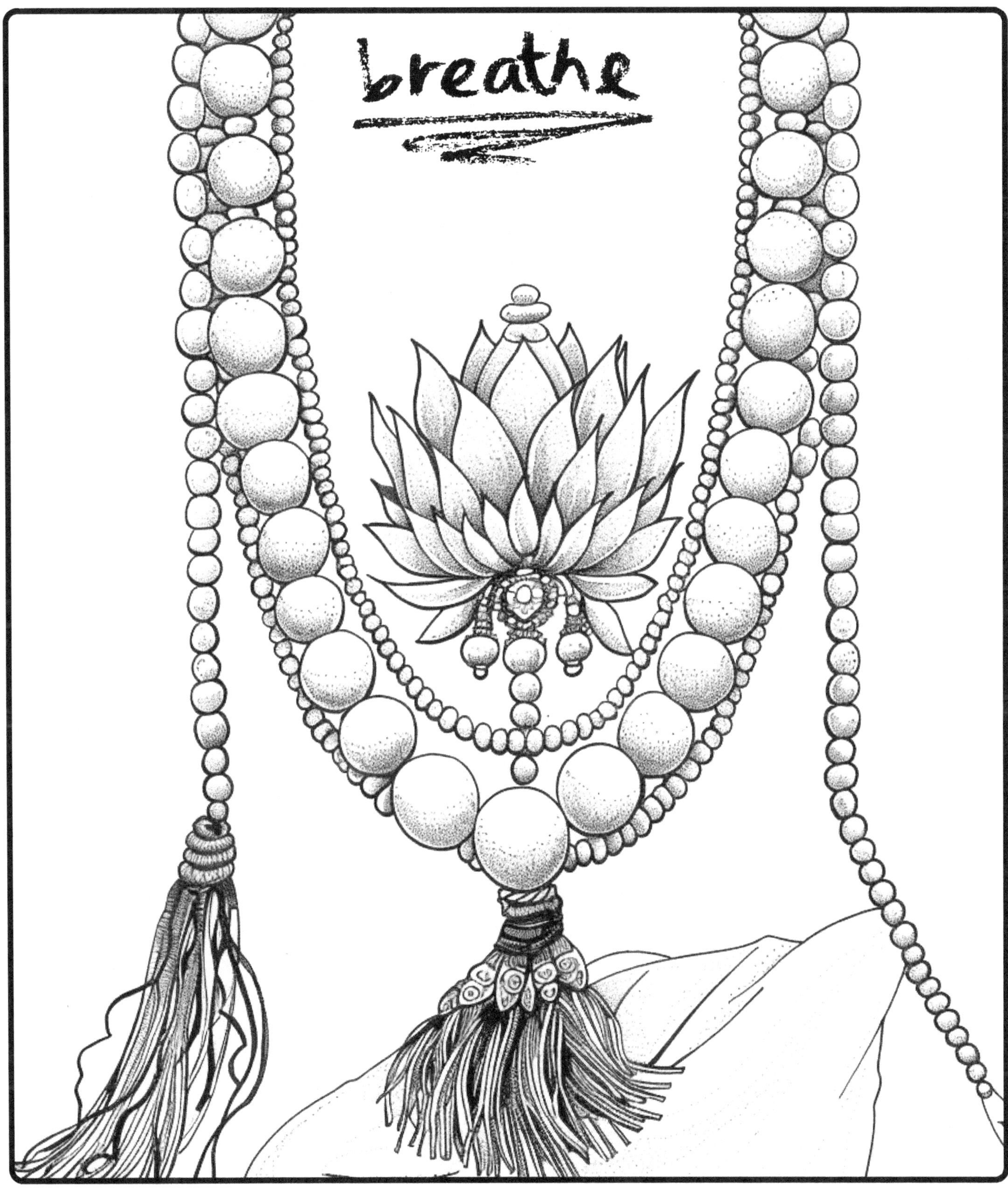
breathe

Day 56

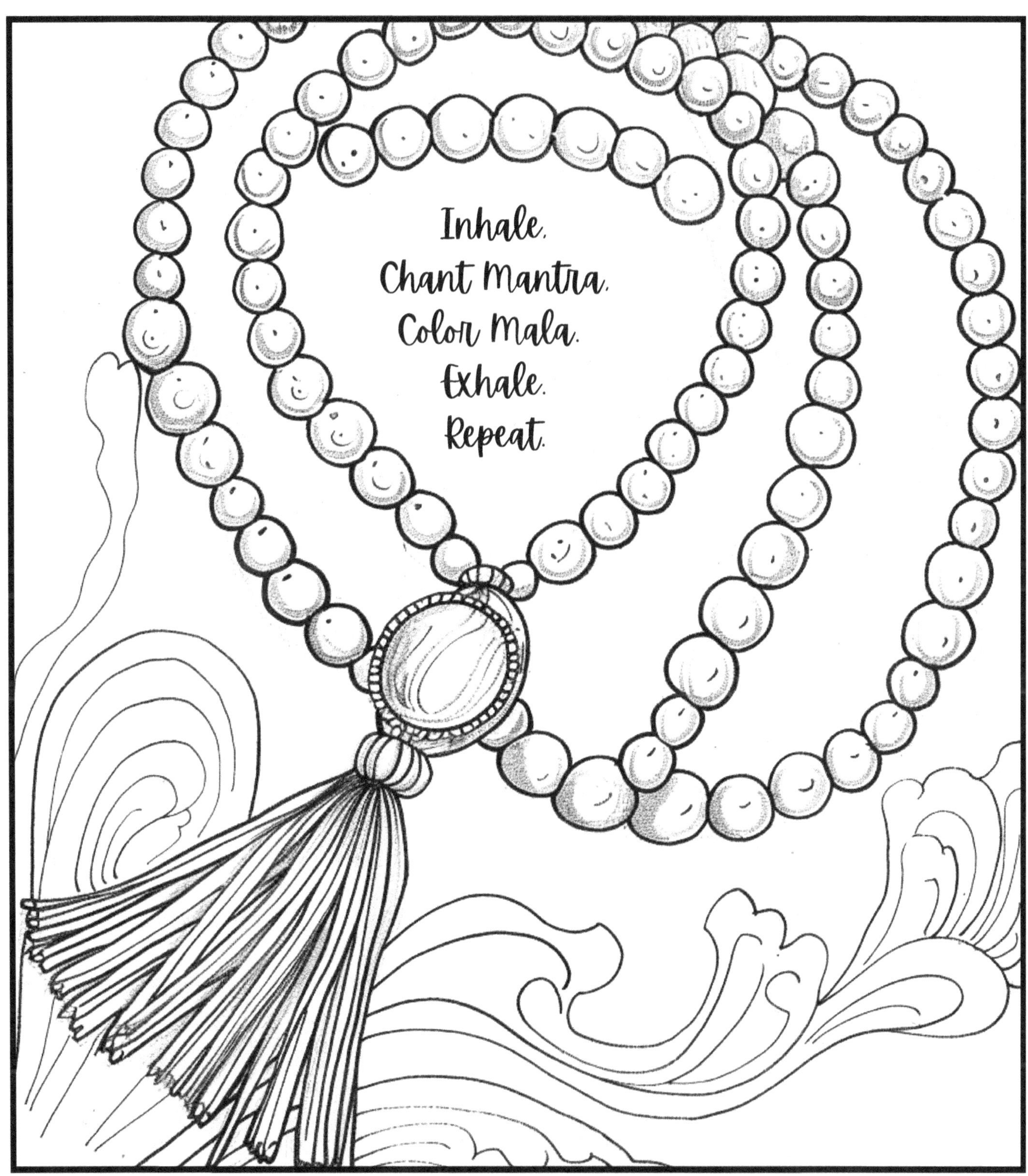

Inhale.
Chant Mantra.
Color Mala.
Exhale.
Repeat.

Day 57

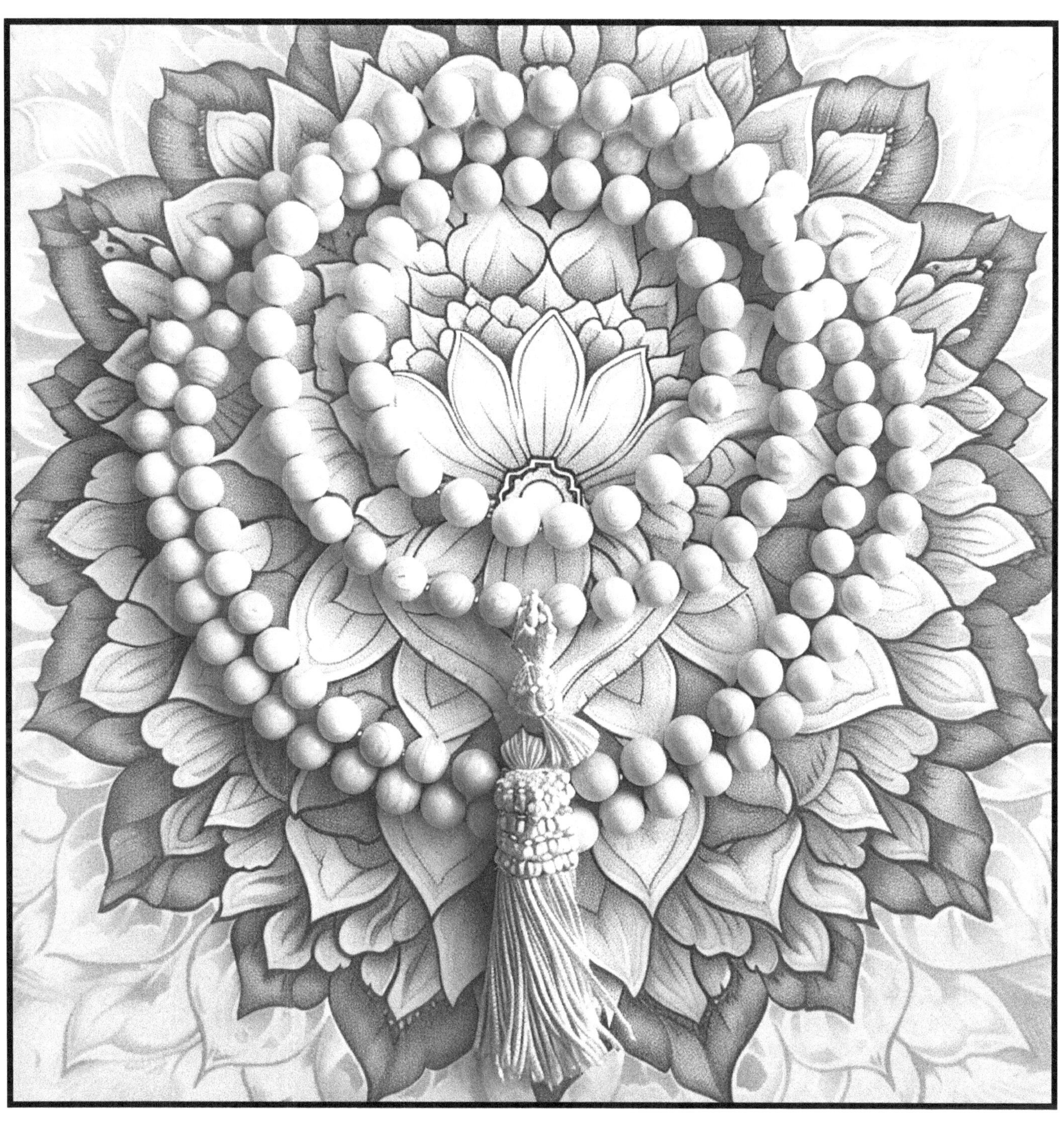

Peace &
BLESSINGS

Day 58

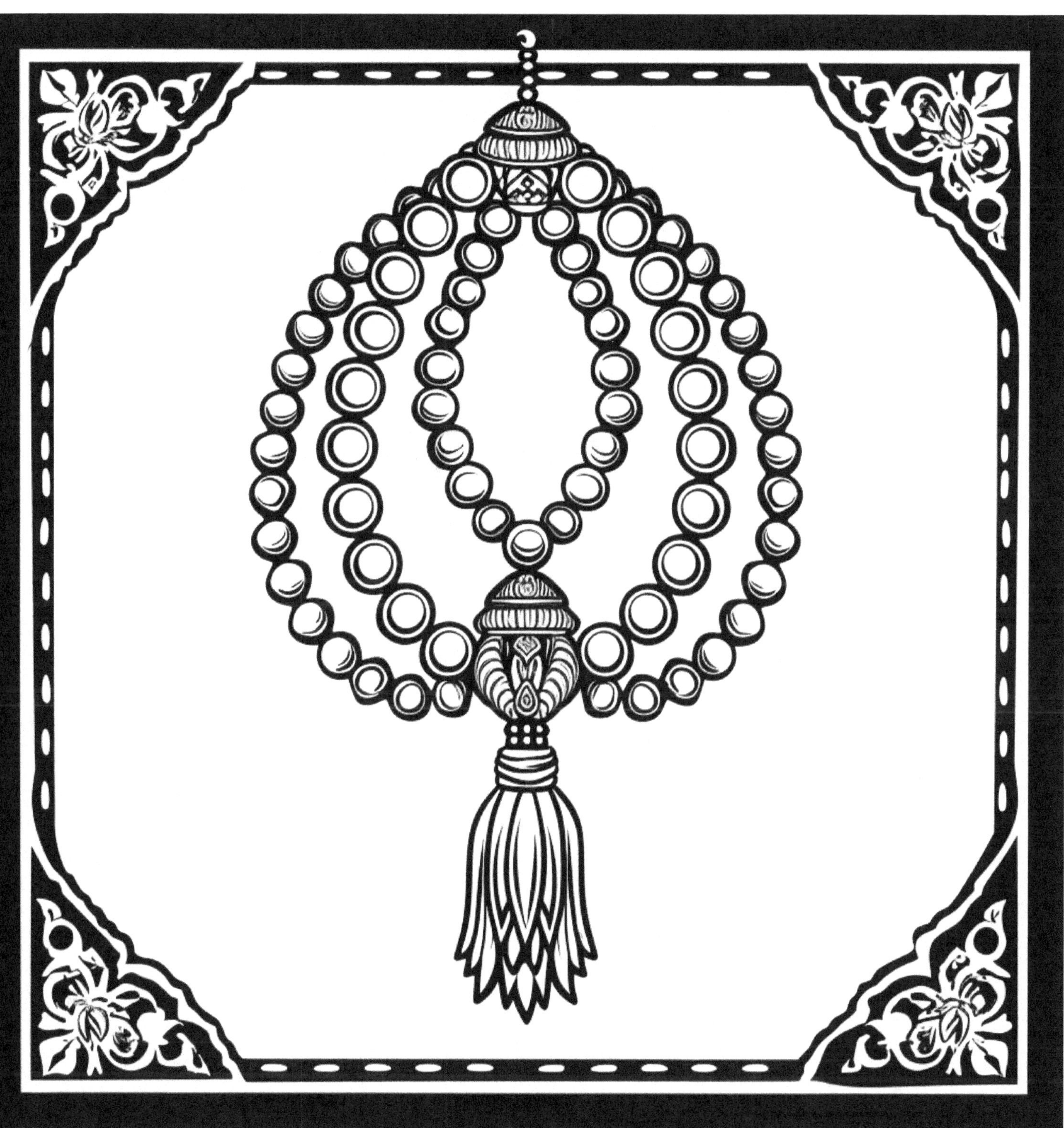

Day 59

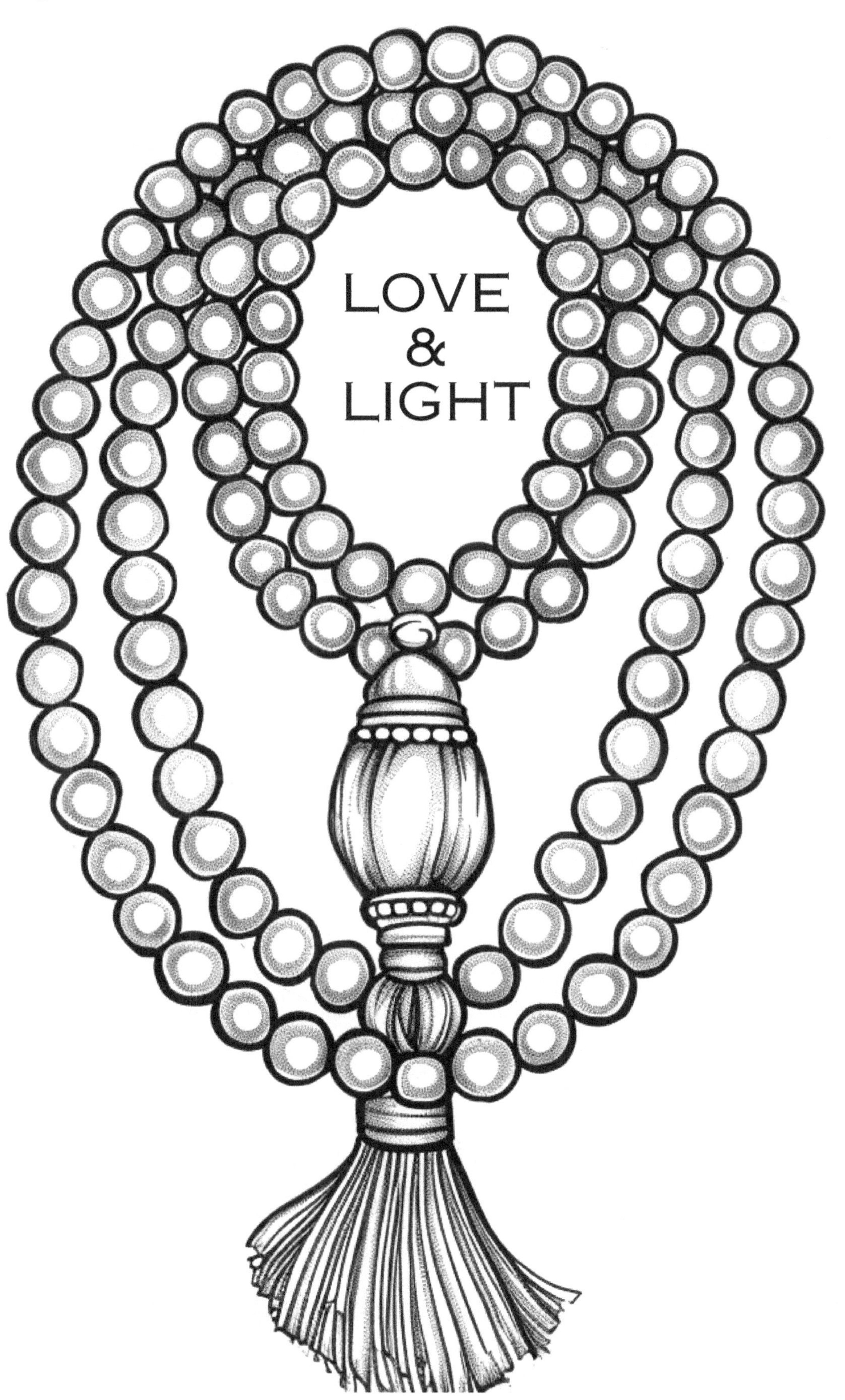

LOVE
&
LIGHT

Day 60

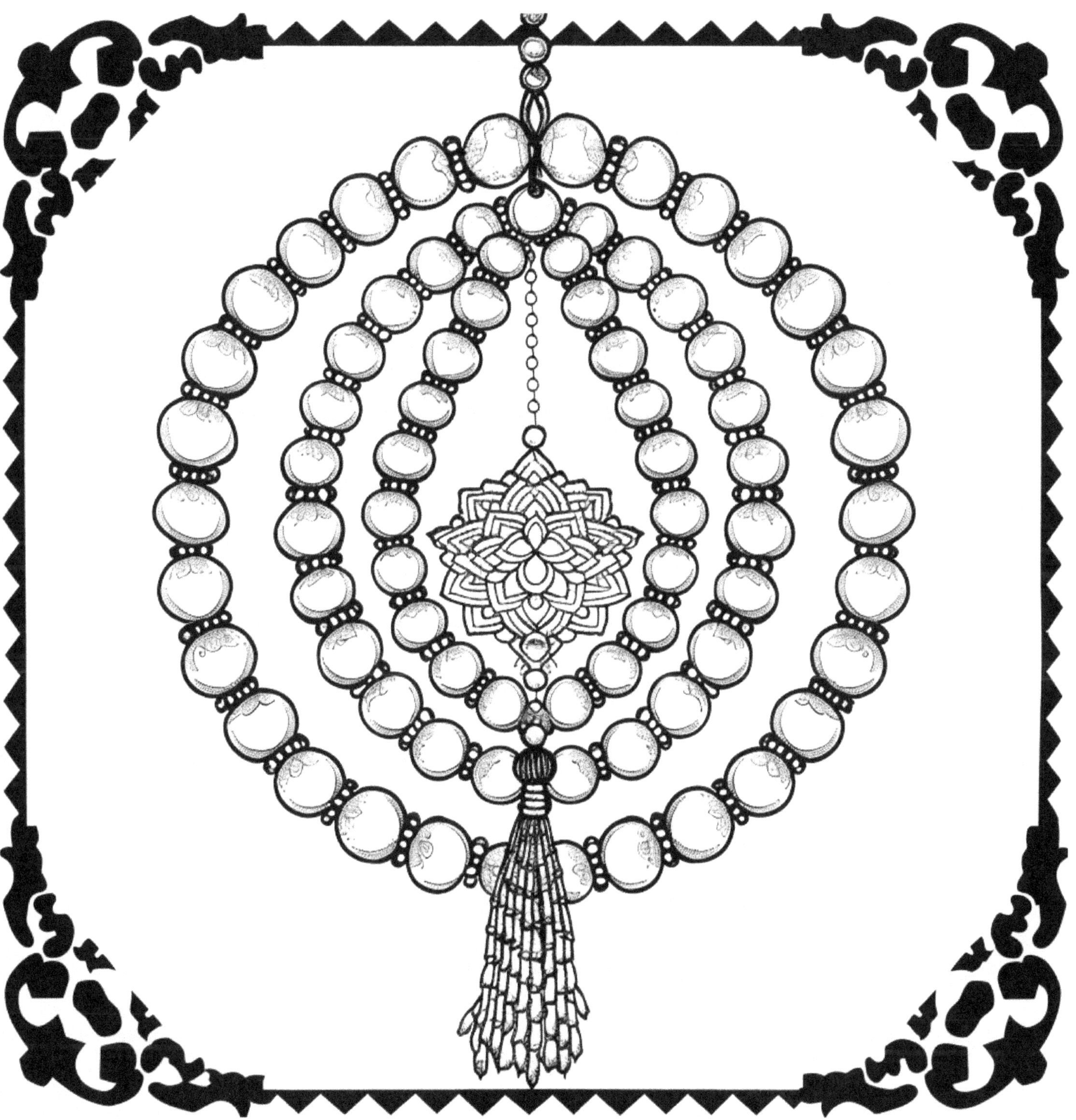

Day 61

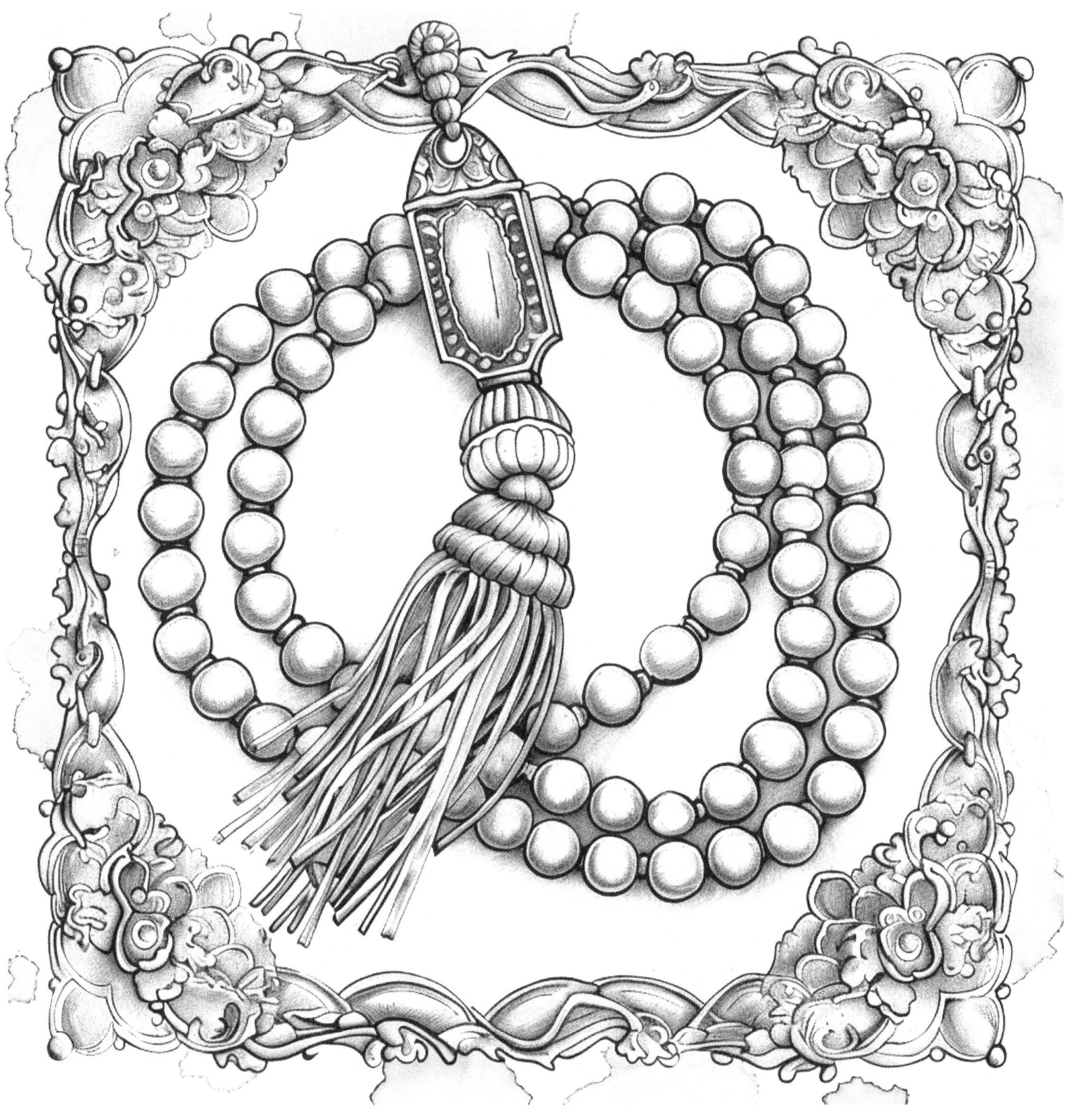

Day 62

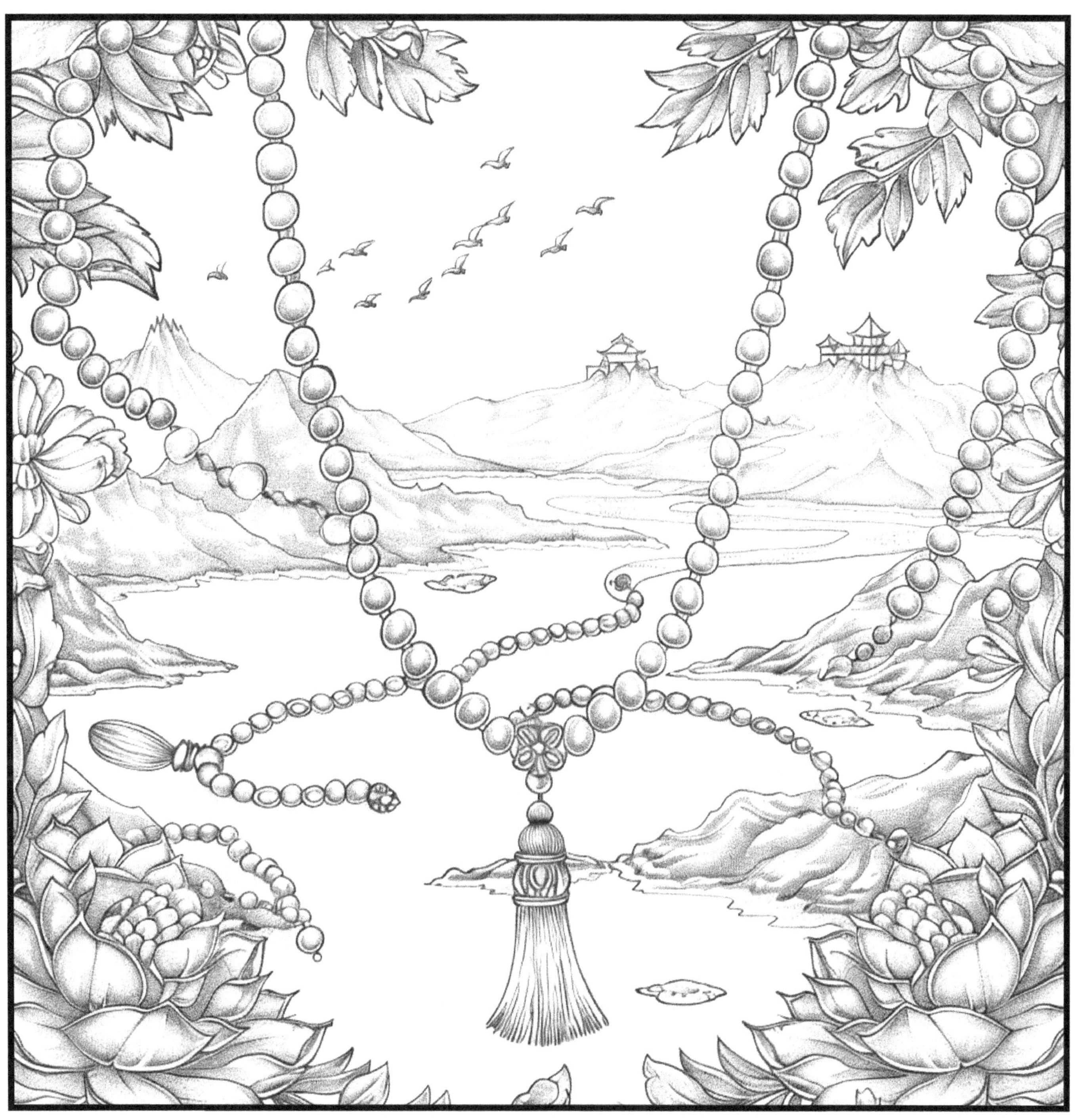

Breath deep like a breeze,
exhale stress with ease.

Day 63

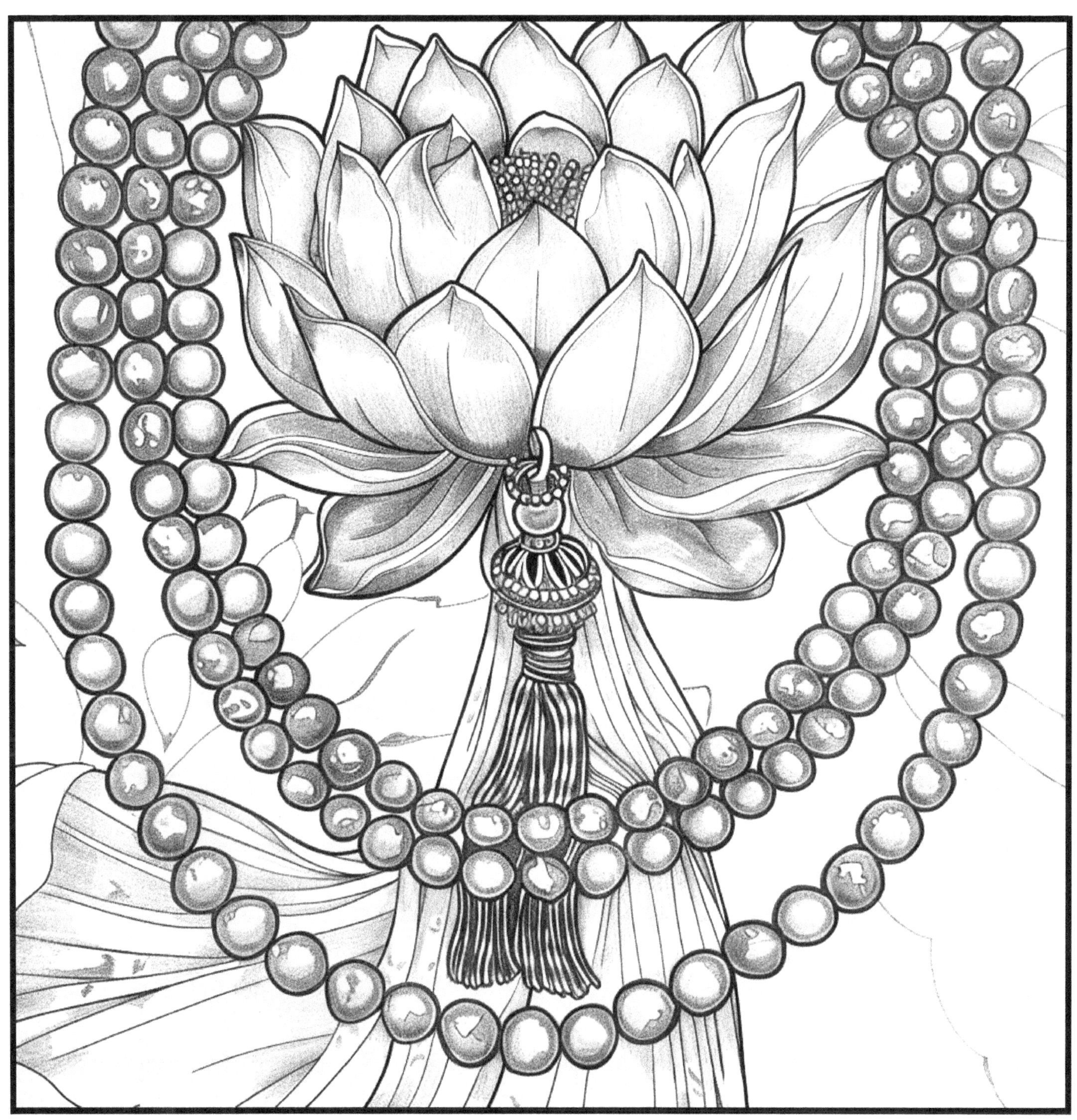

The lotus flower symbolizes purity and spiritual awakening as it emerges pristine from the muddy waters, reflecting resilience and enlightenment.

Day 64

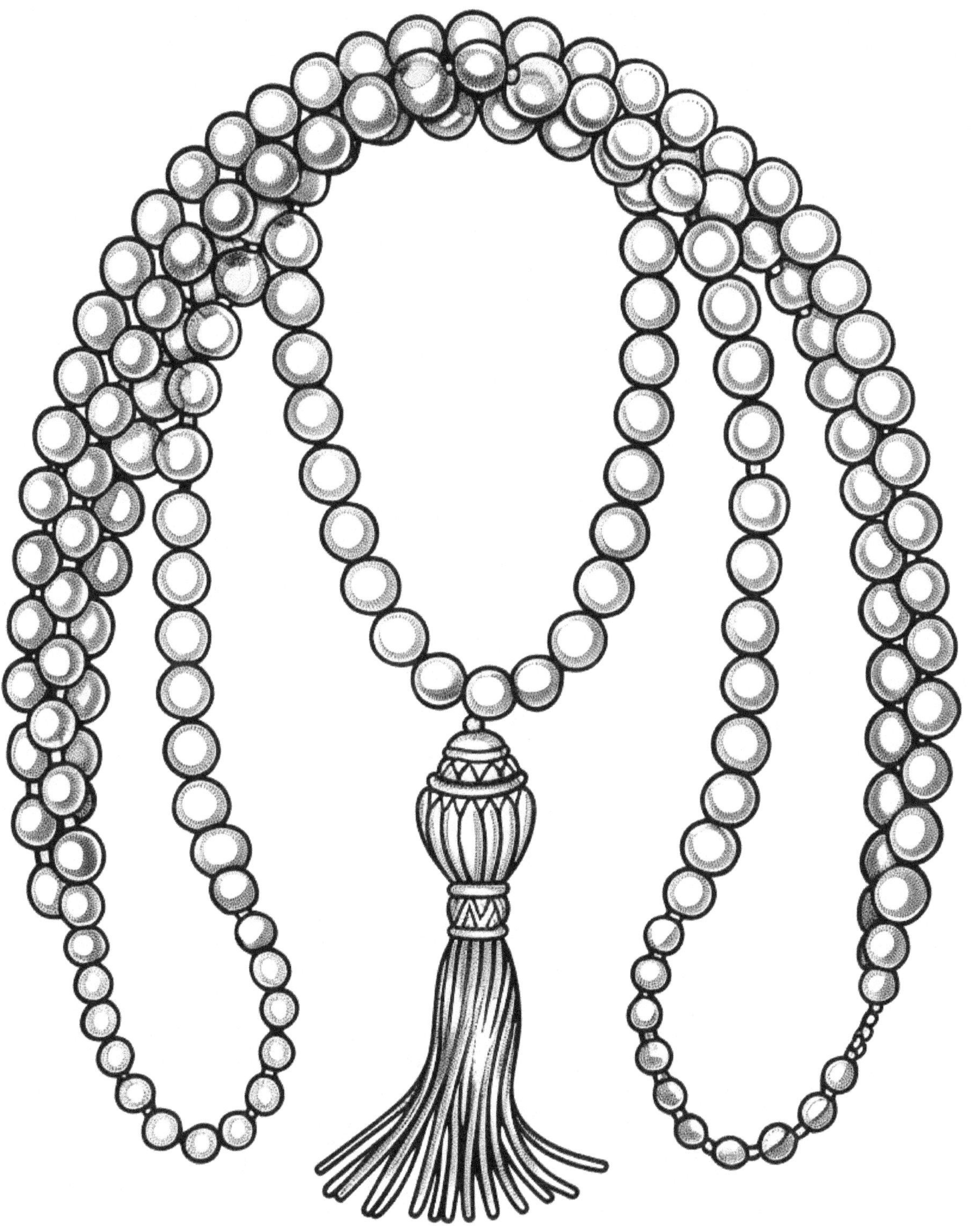

Day 65

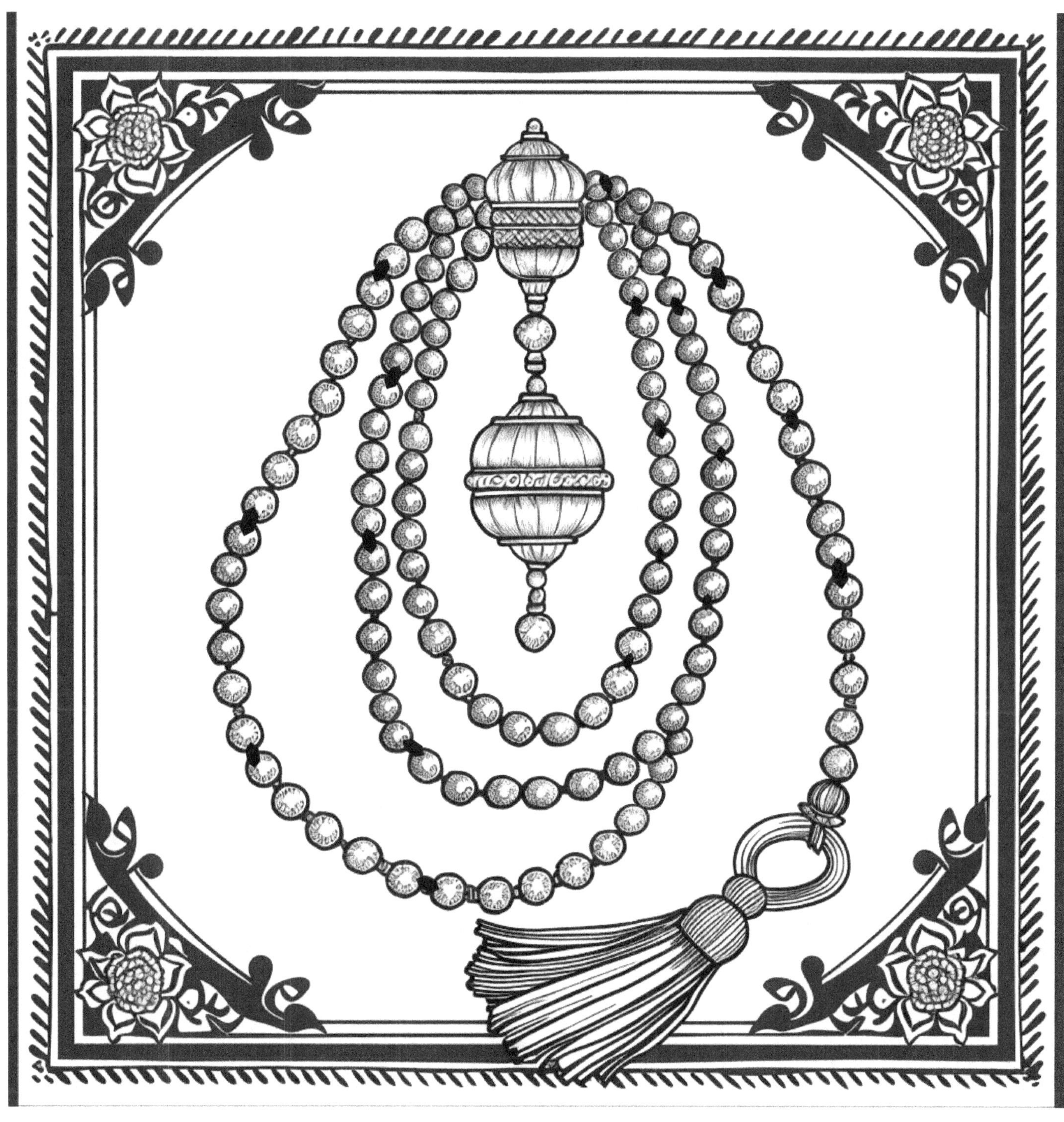

Day 66

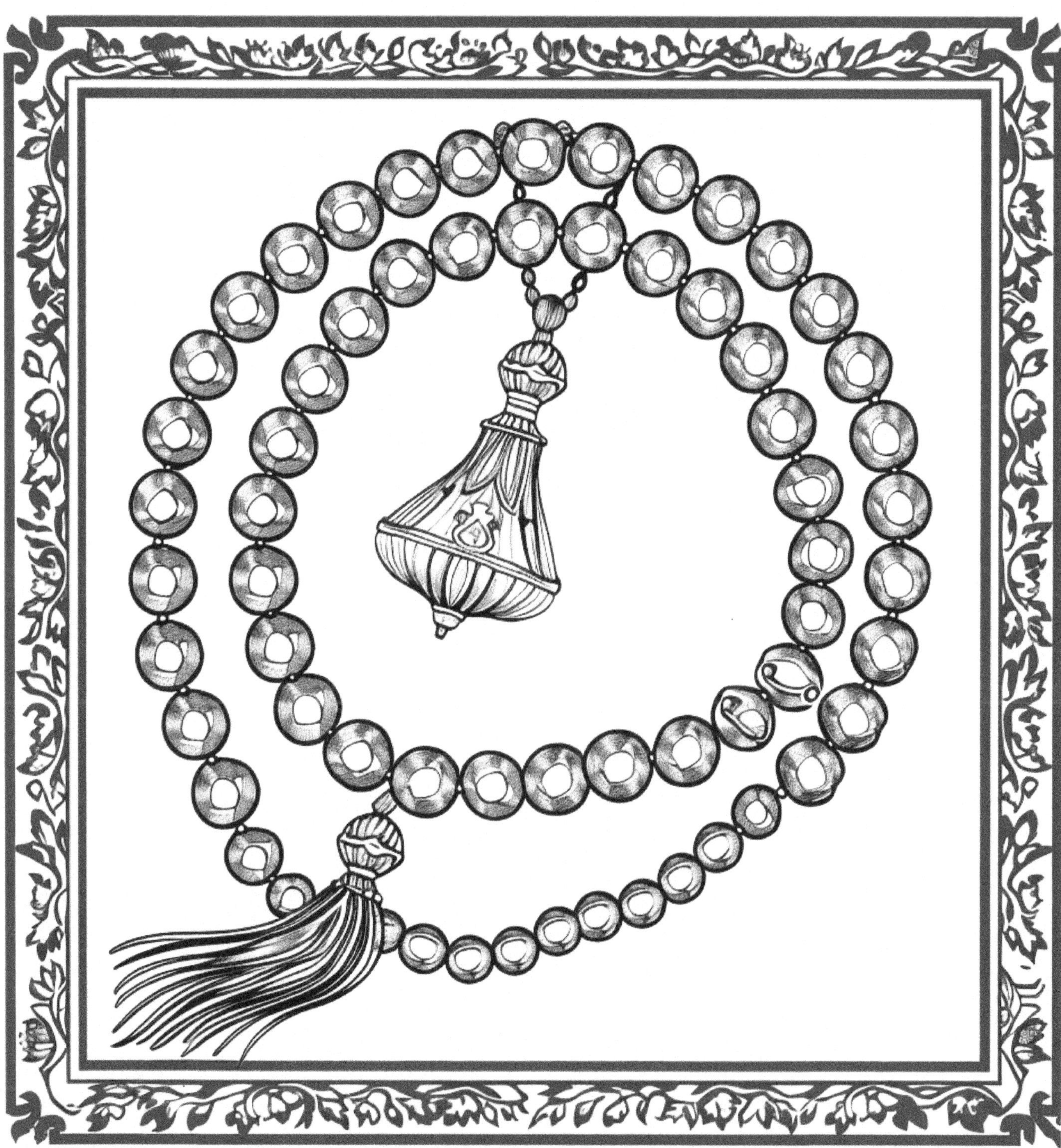

Day 67

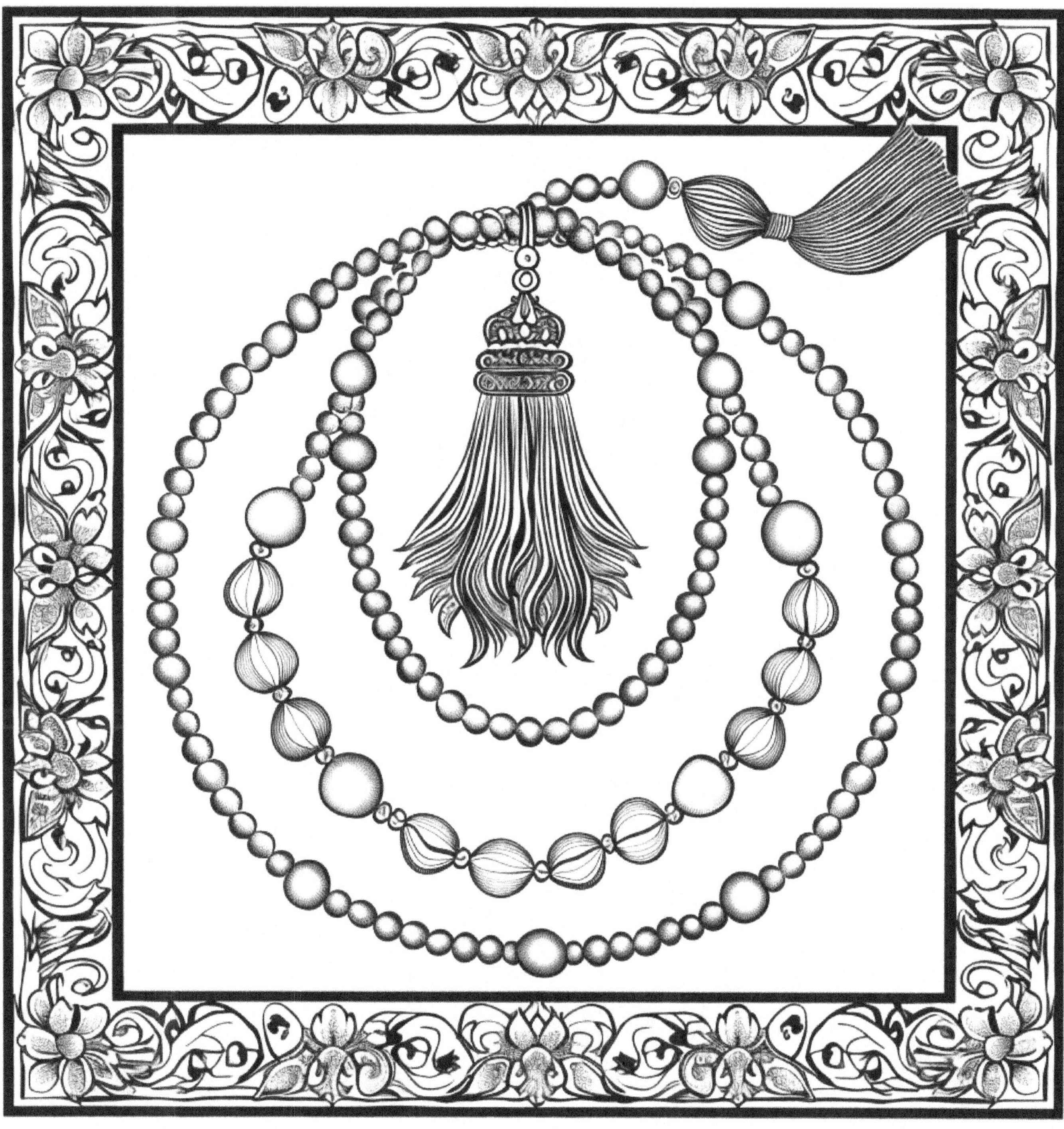

Day 68

Now is a great time to close your eyes, take deep breaths, and simply smile.

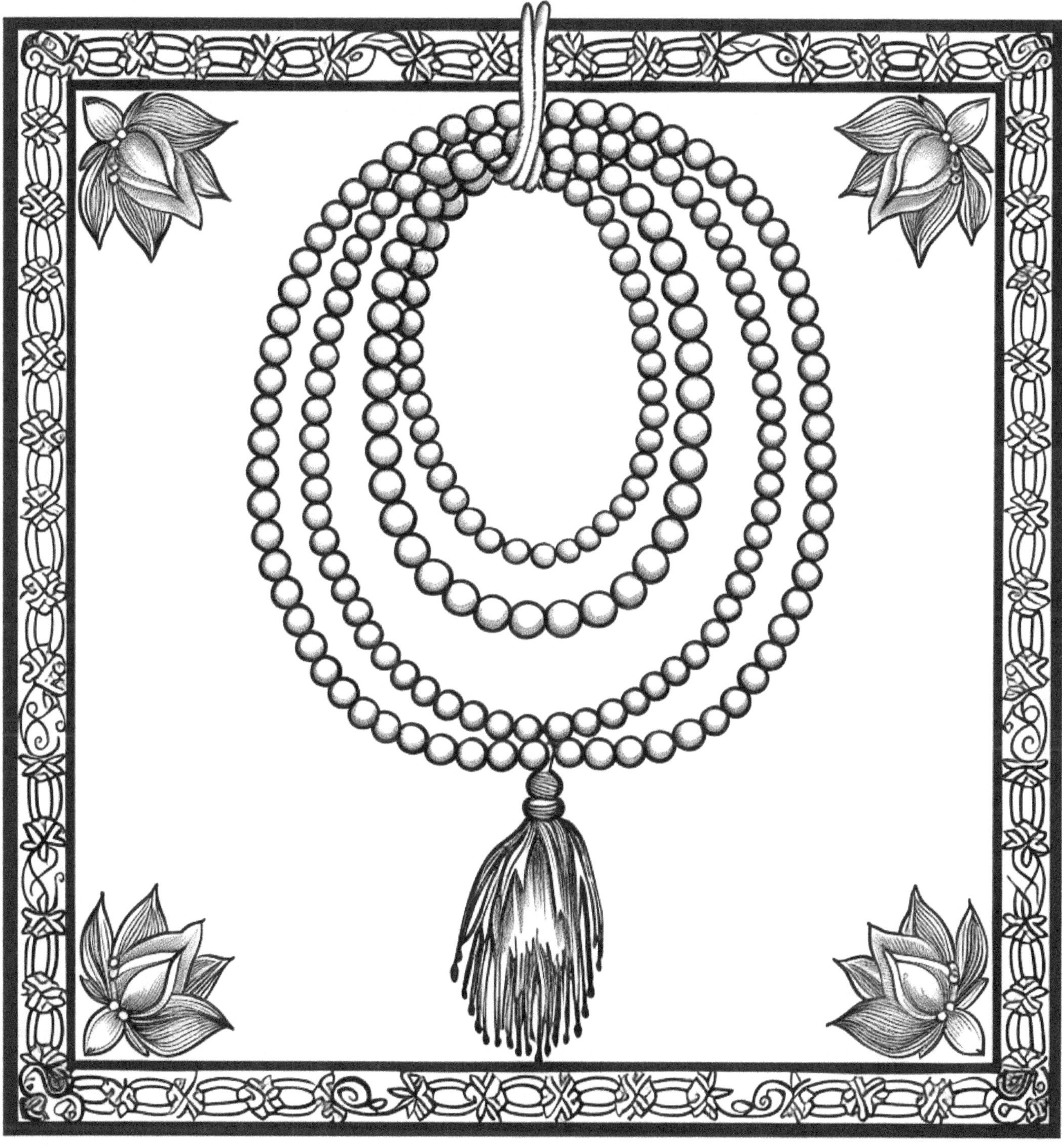

Day 69

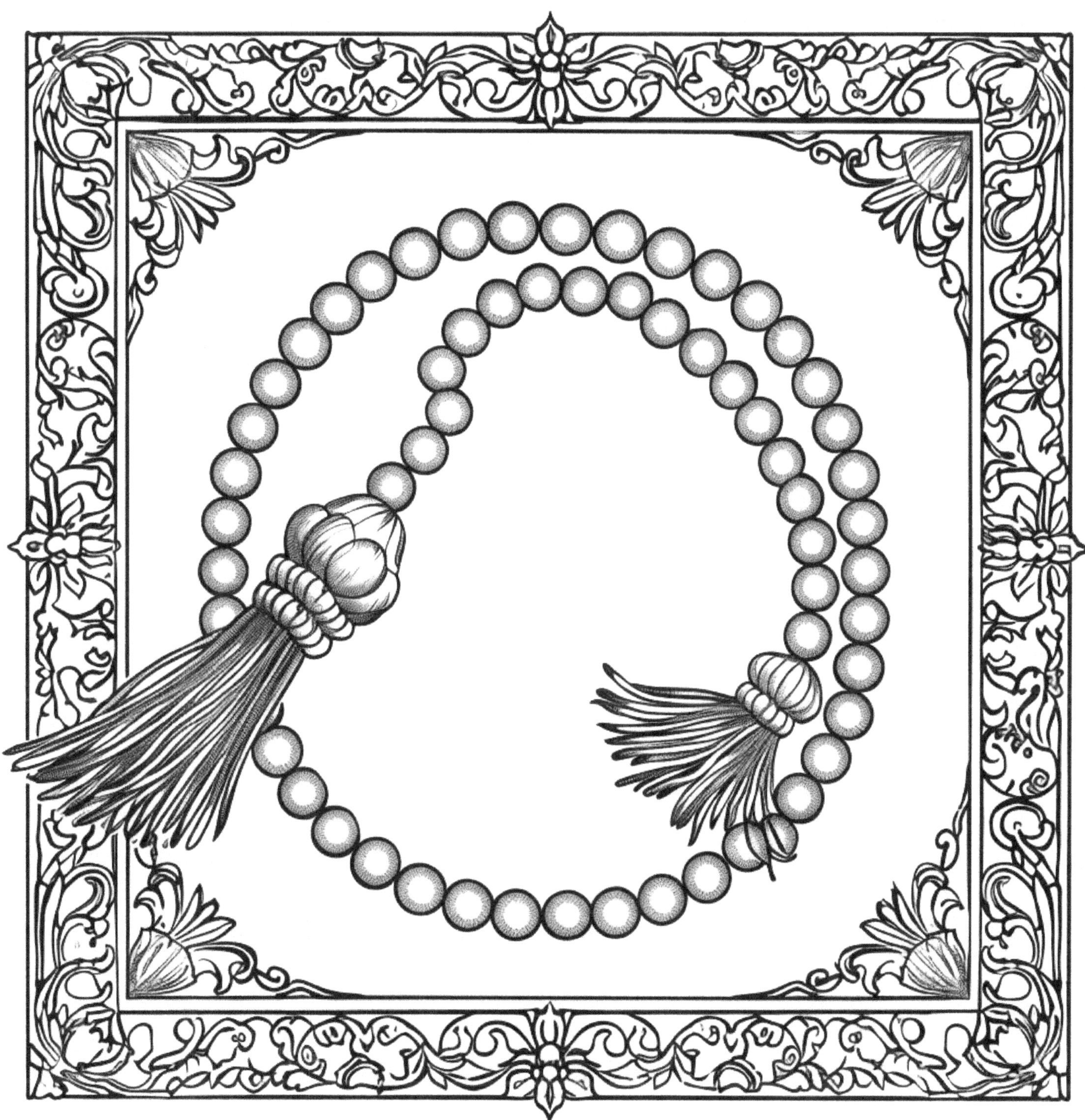

Day 70

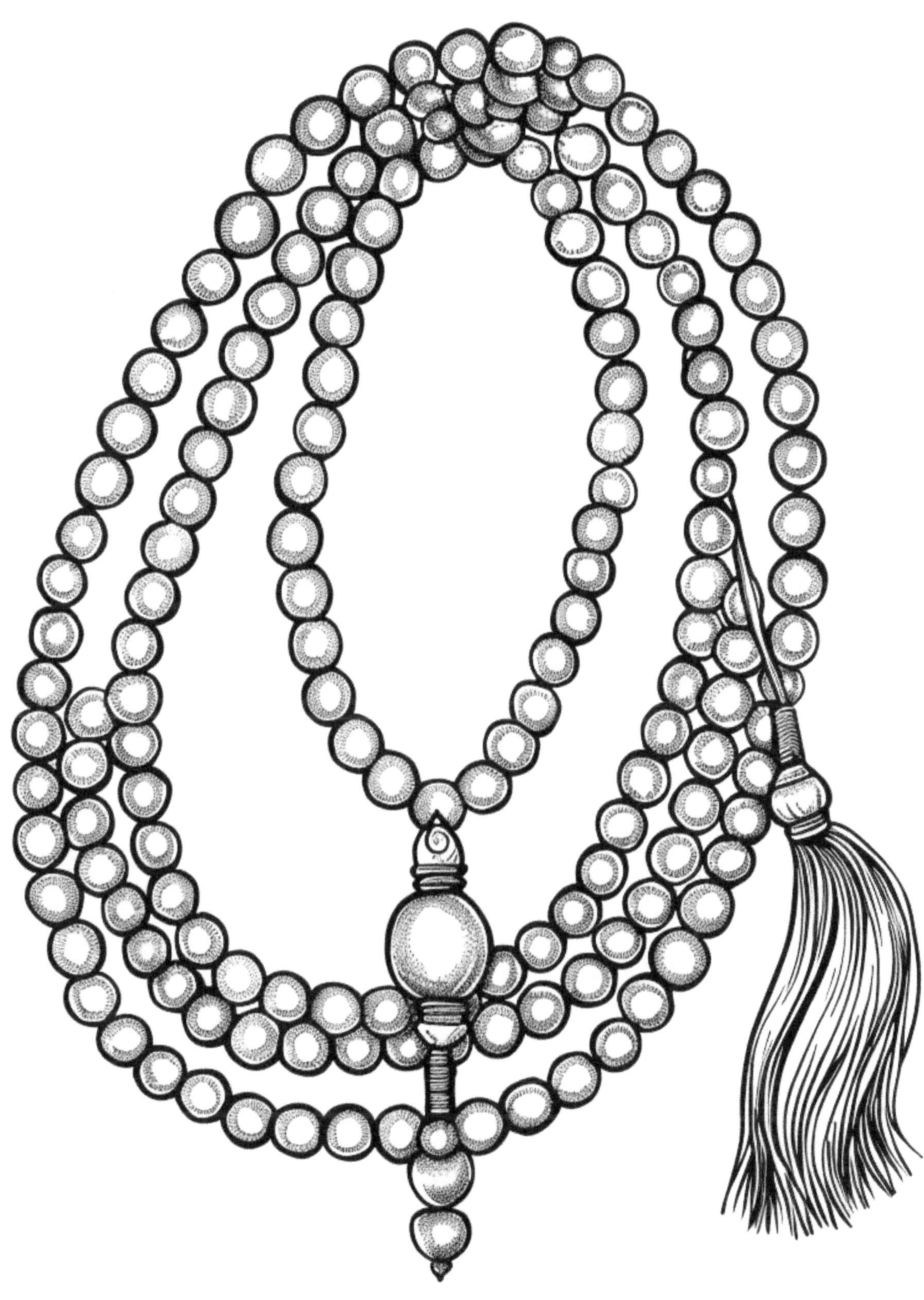

Day 71

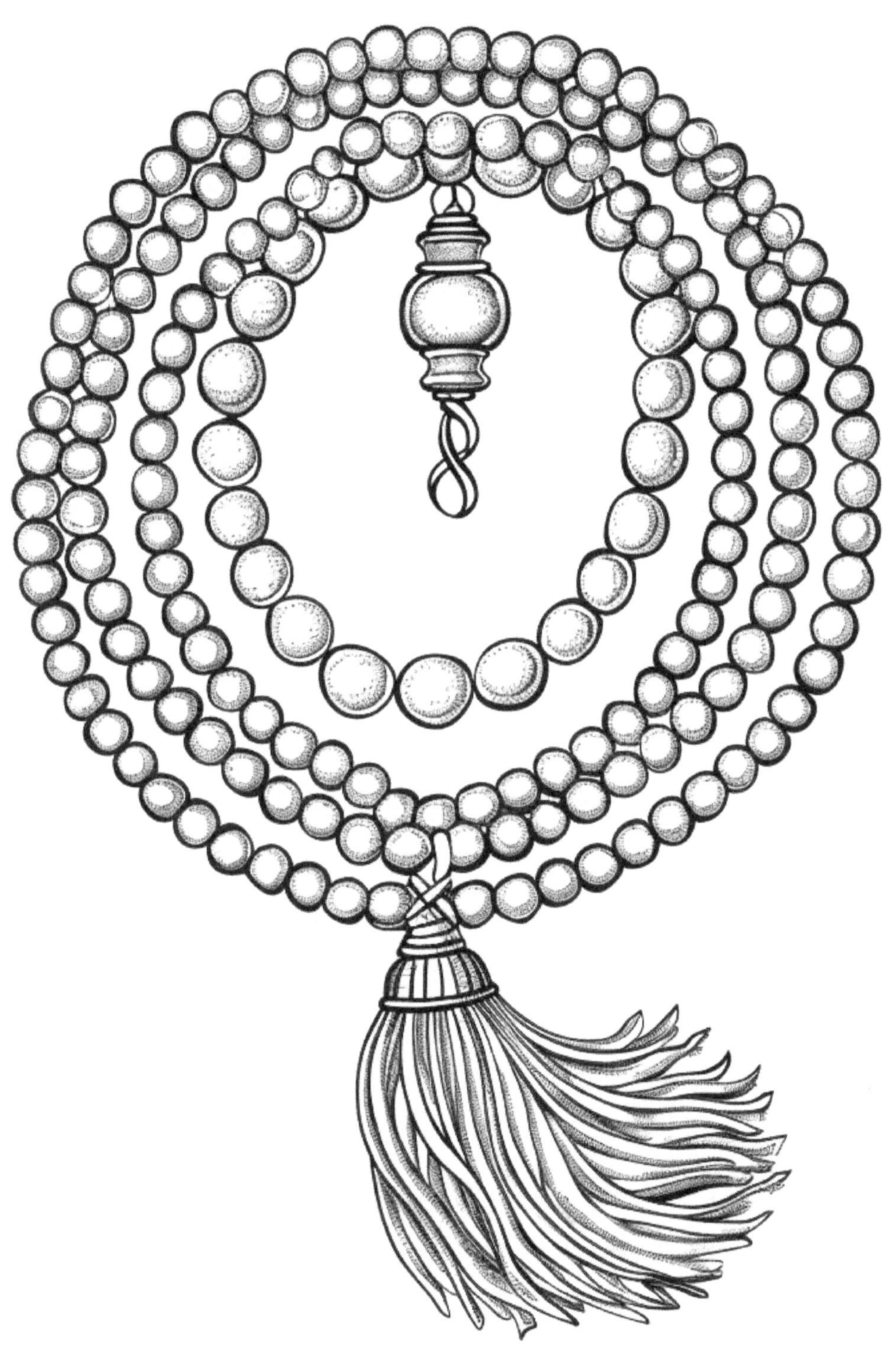

Day 72

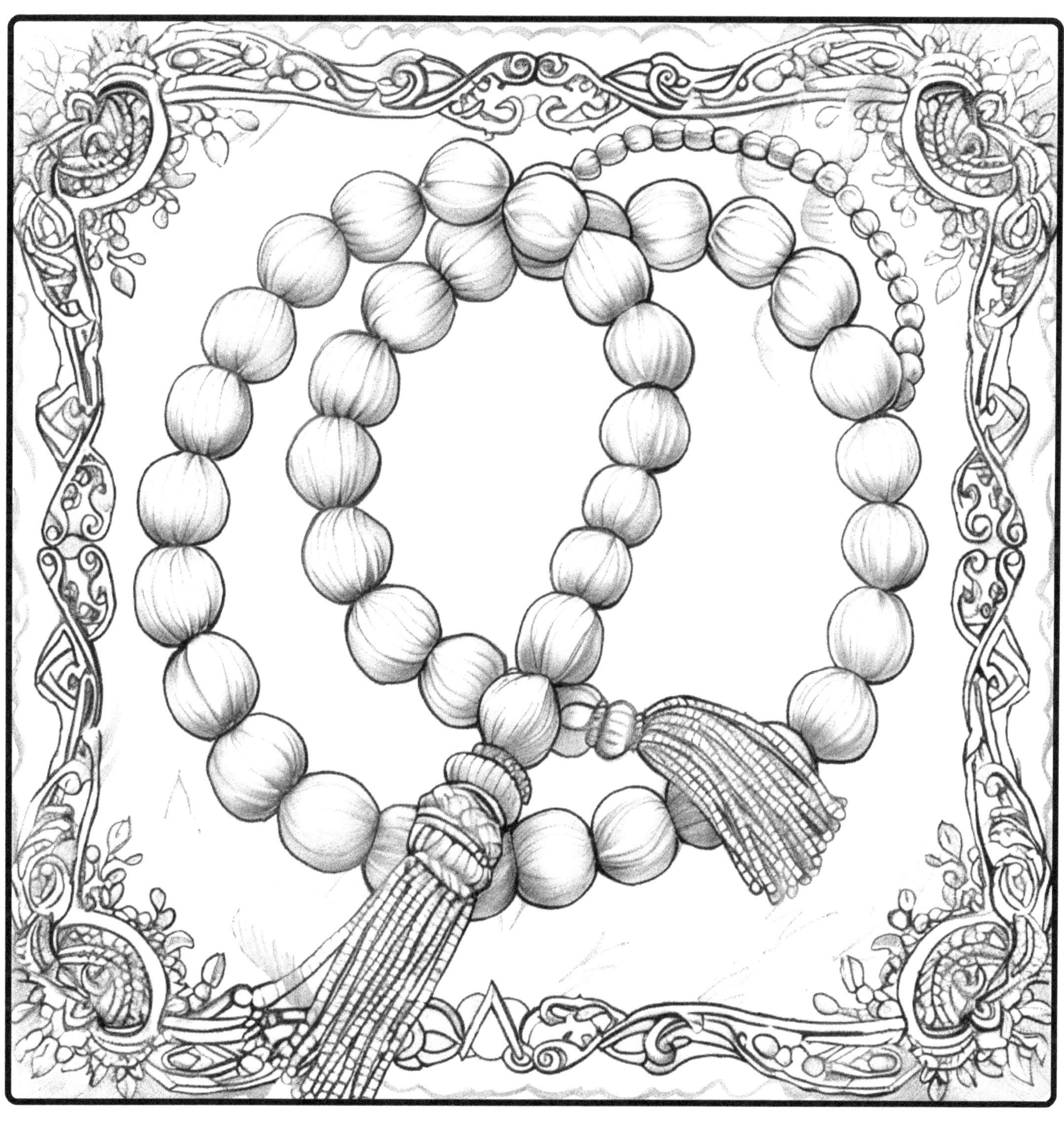

Day 73

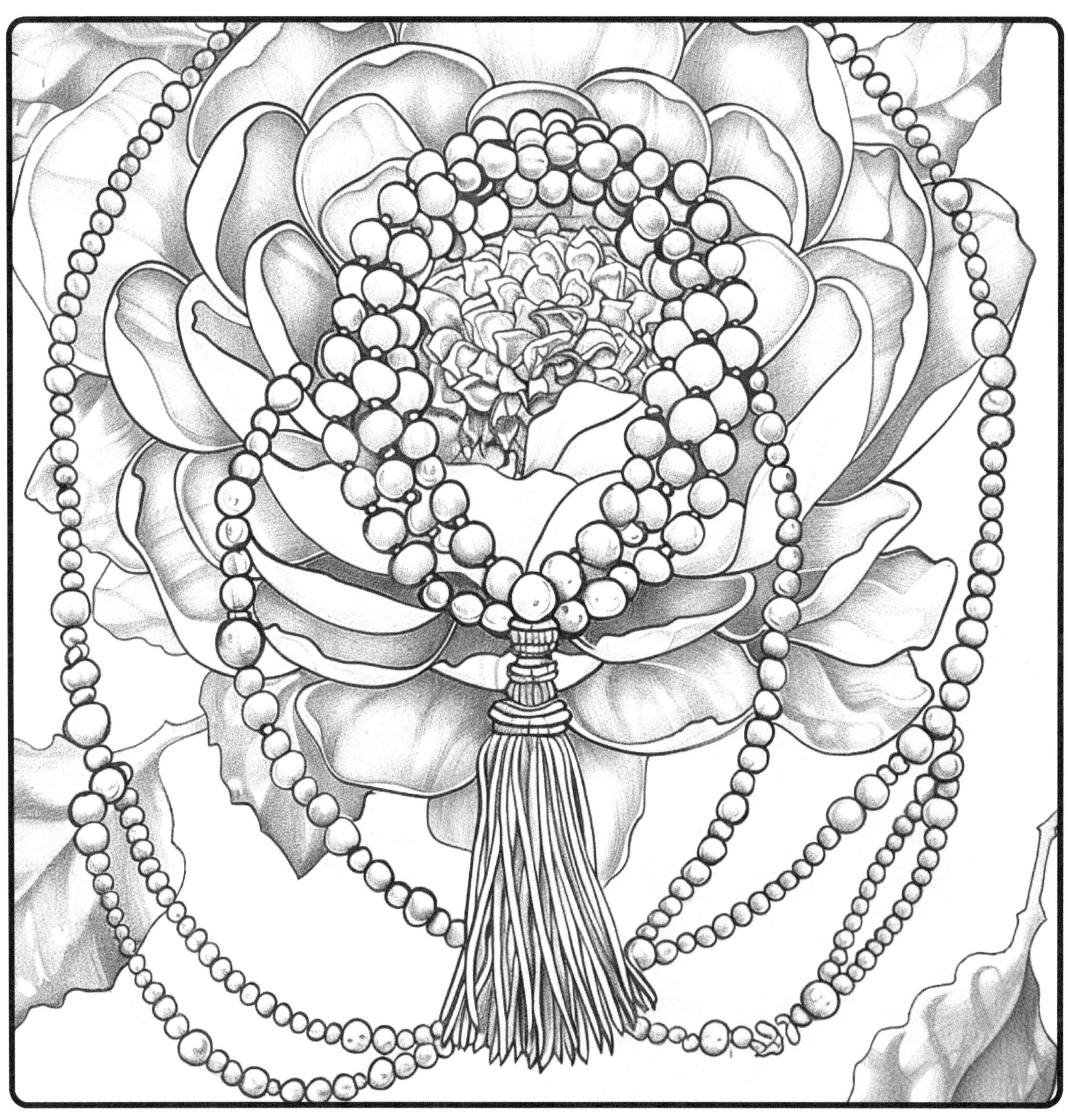

Day 74

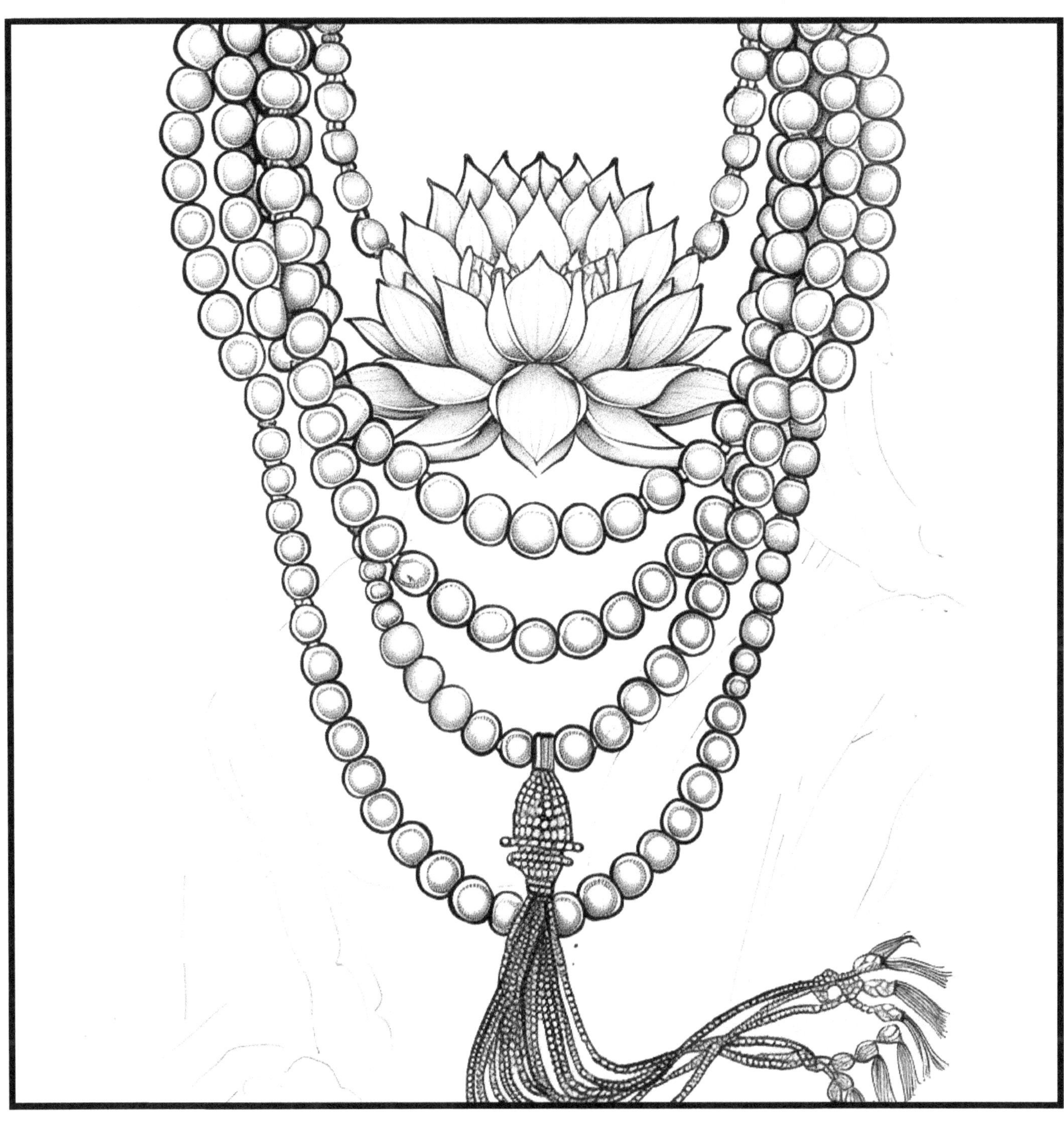

Day 75

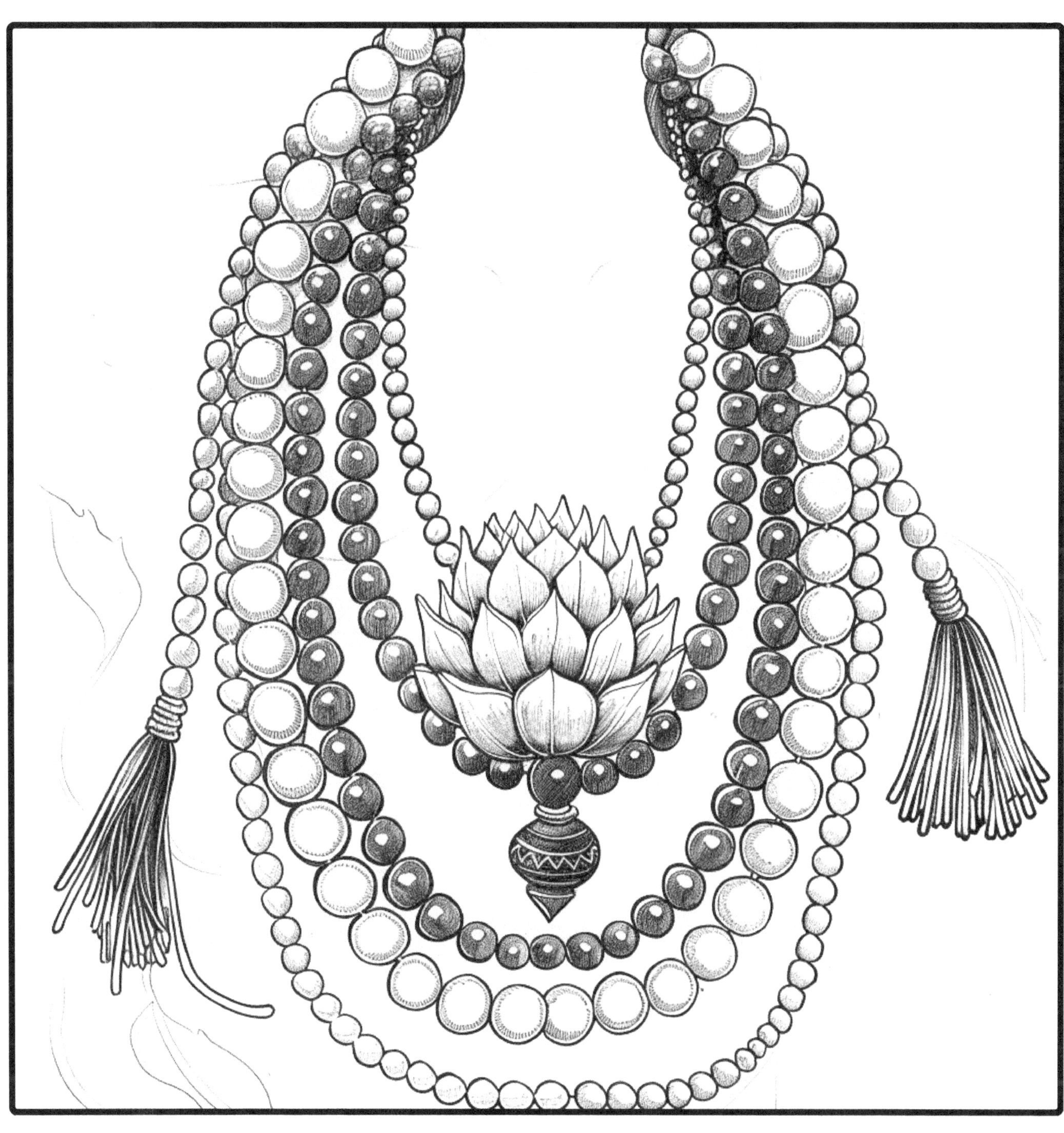

Day 76

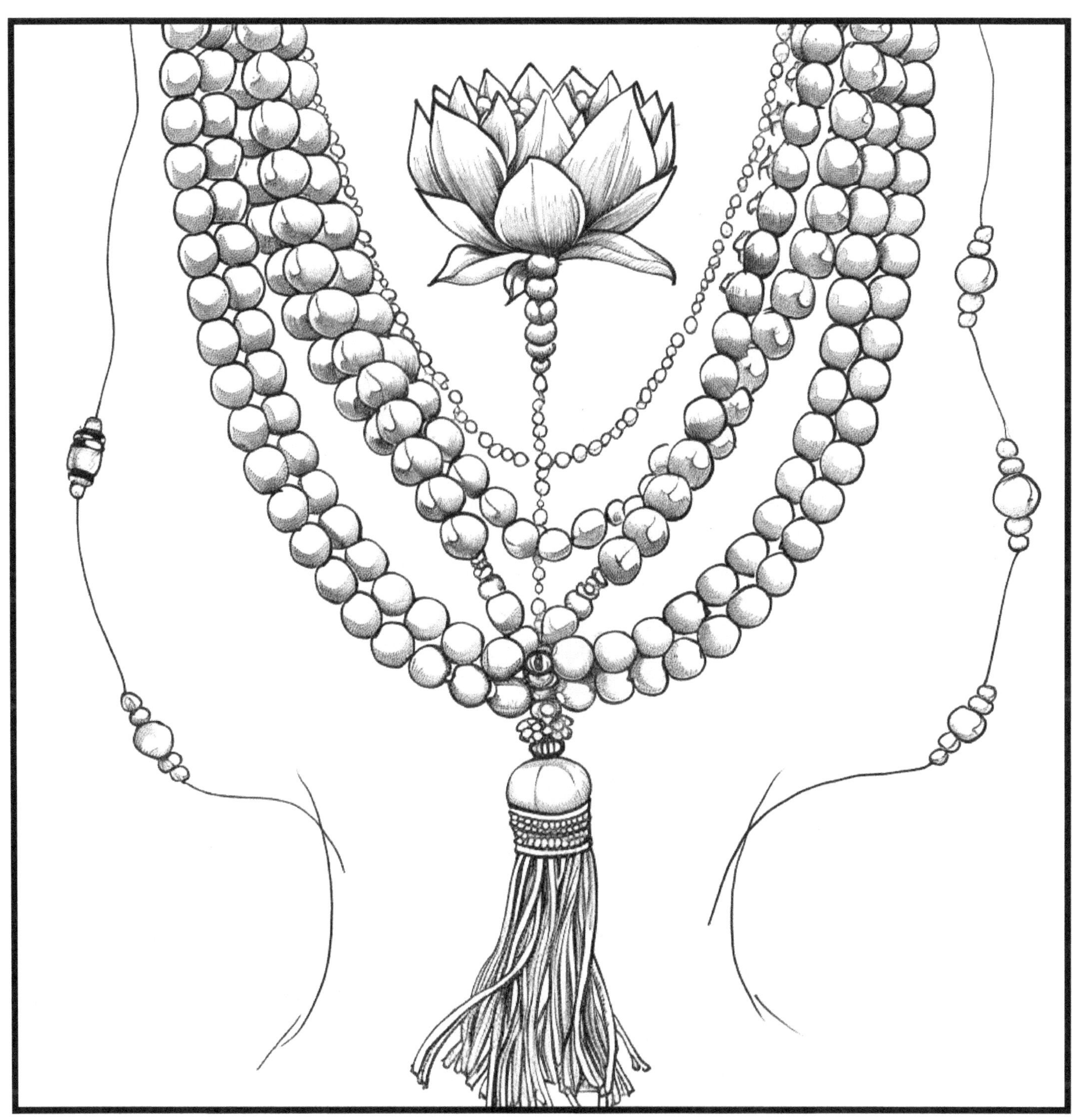

The Deeper the Breath
The Richer the Life

Day 77

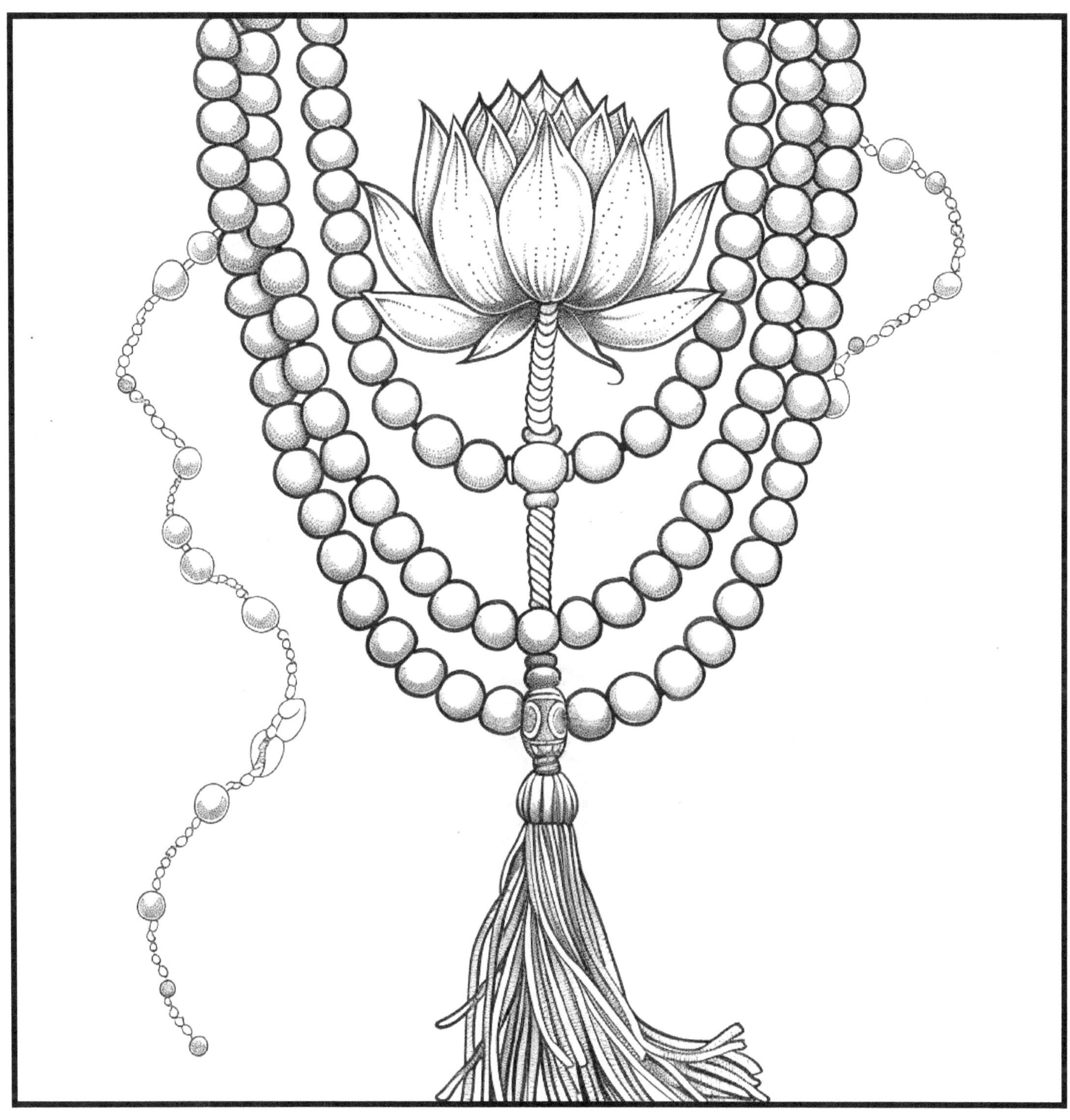

Day 78

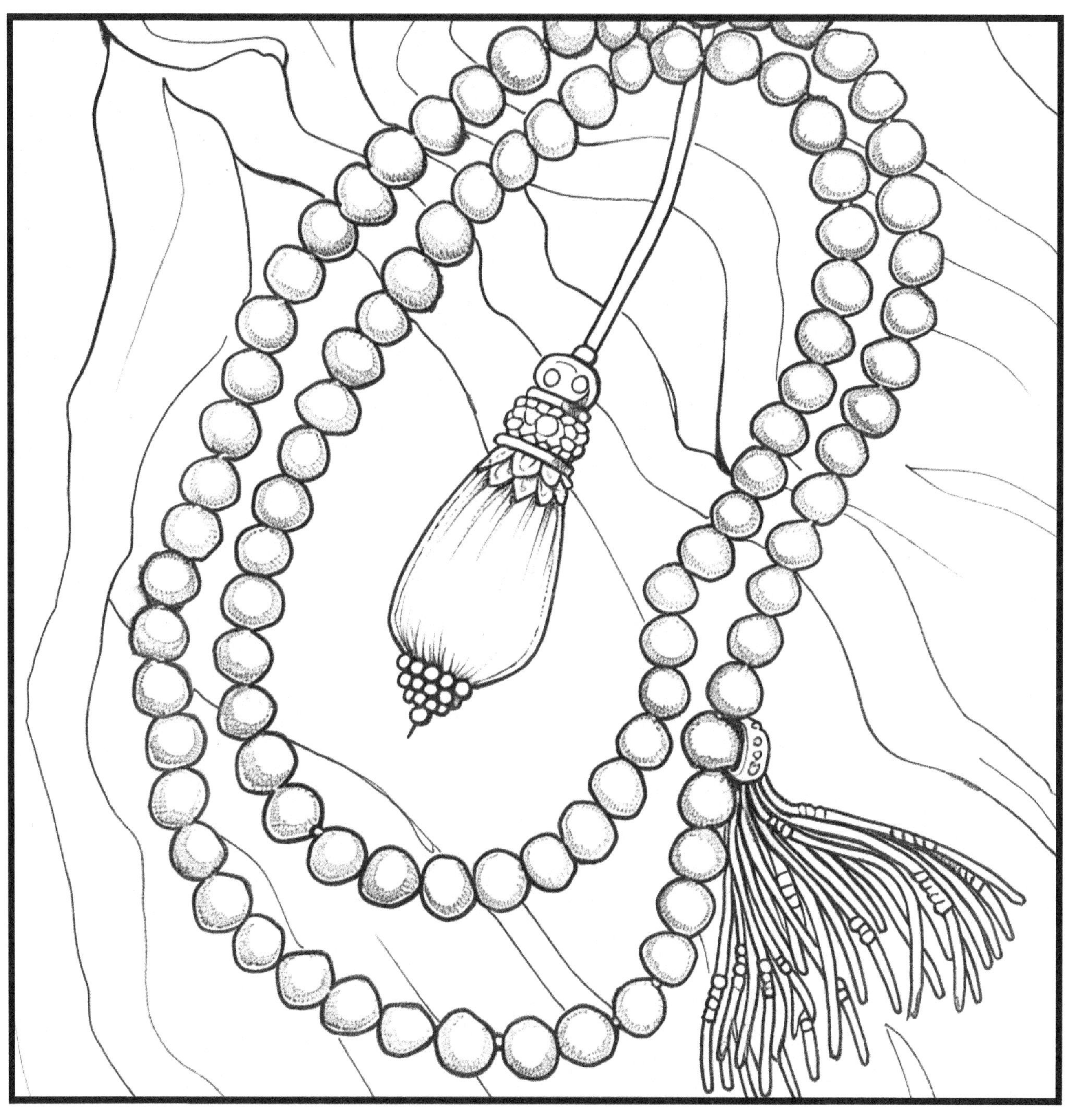

Day 79

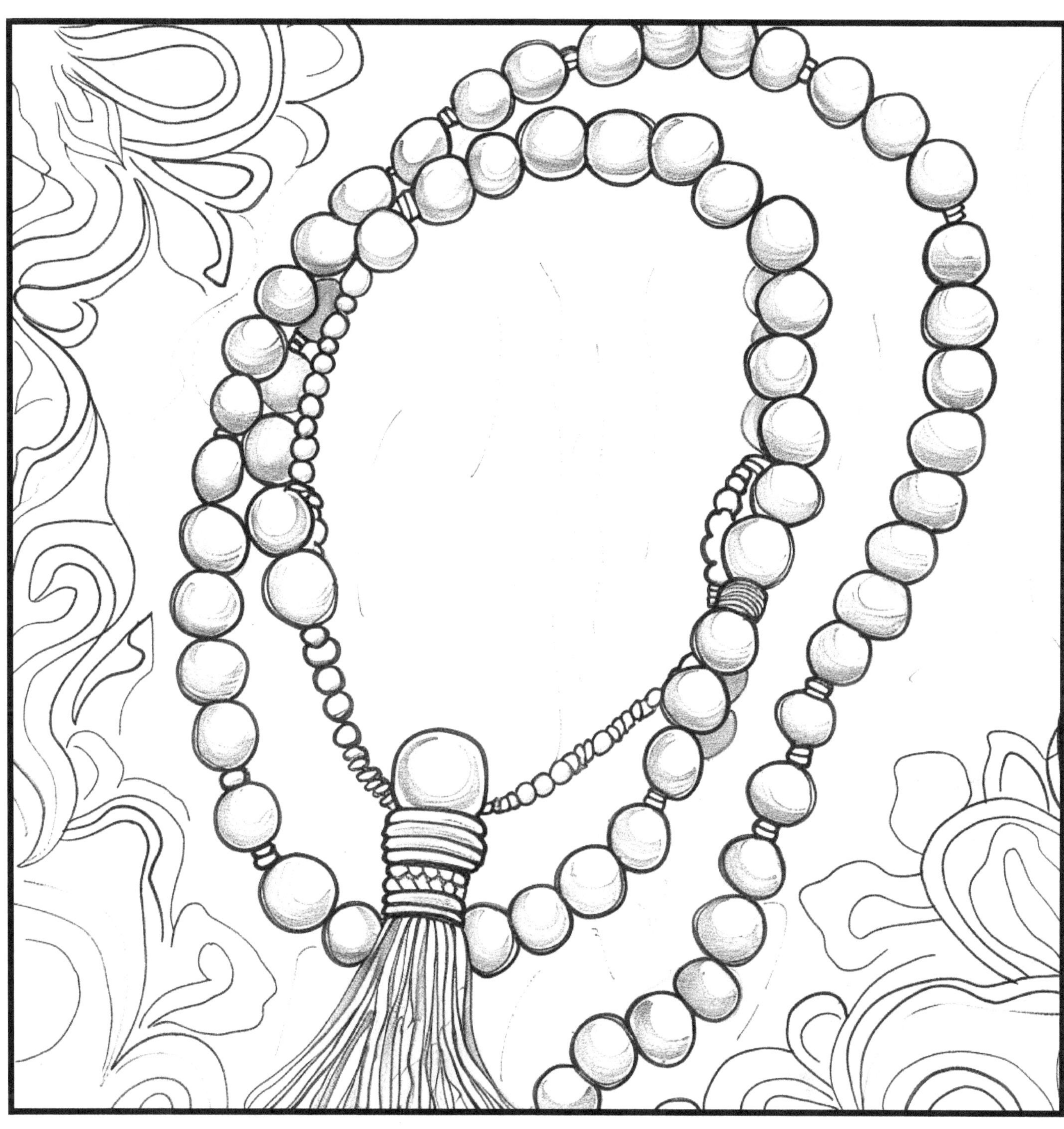

Day 80

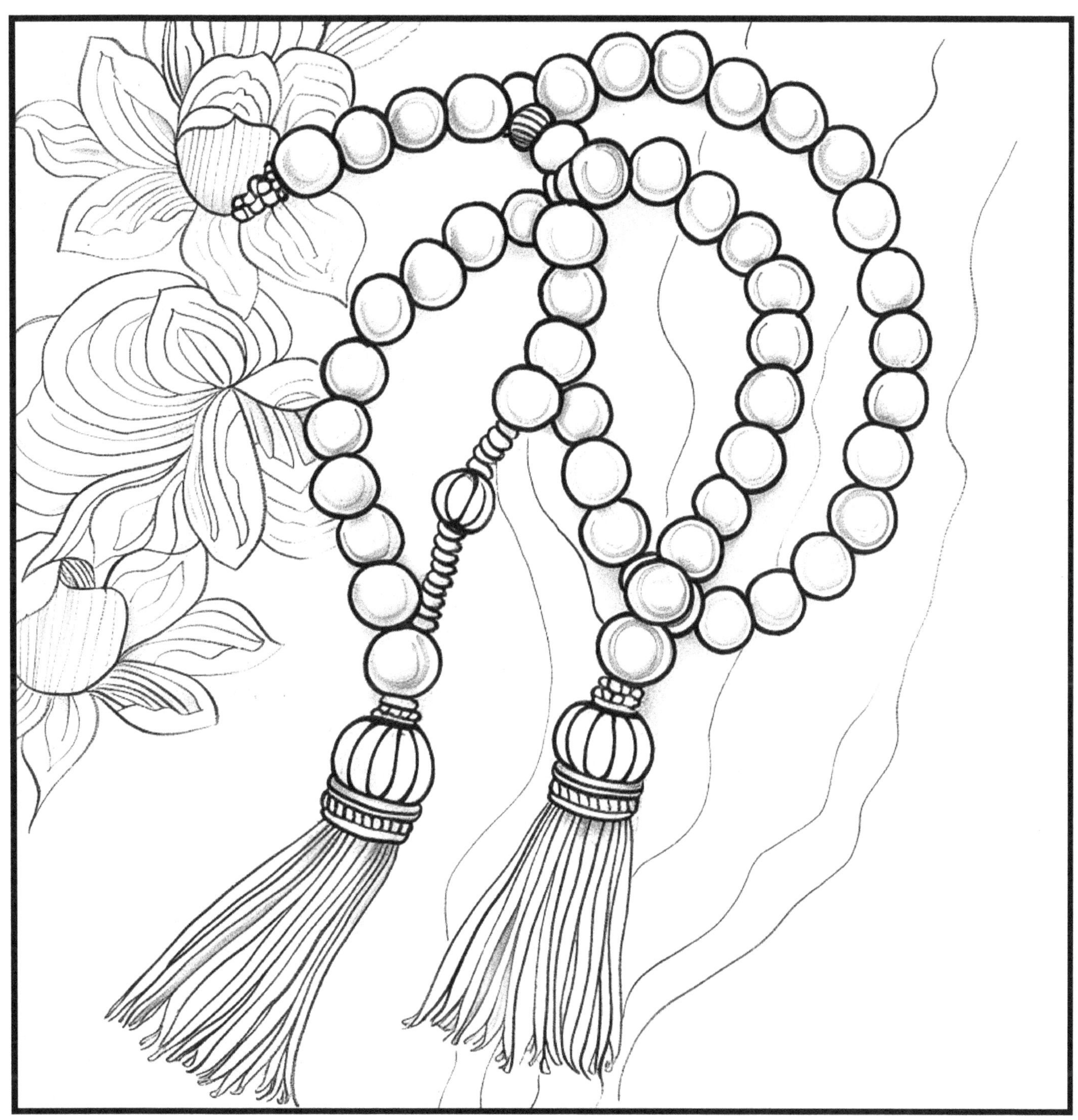

Day 81

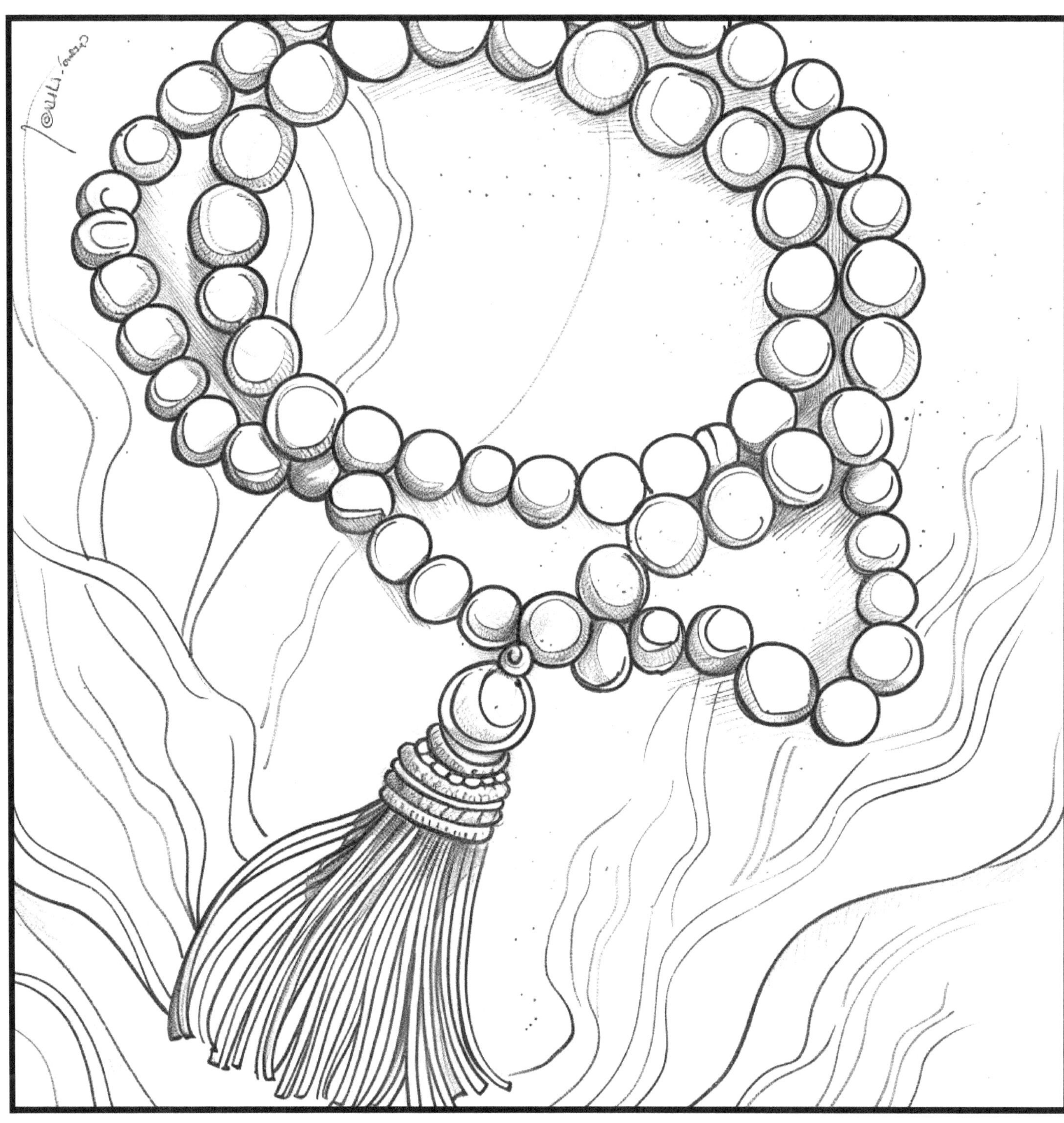

Day 82

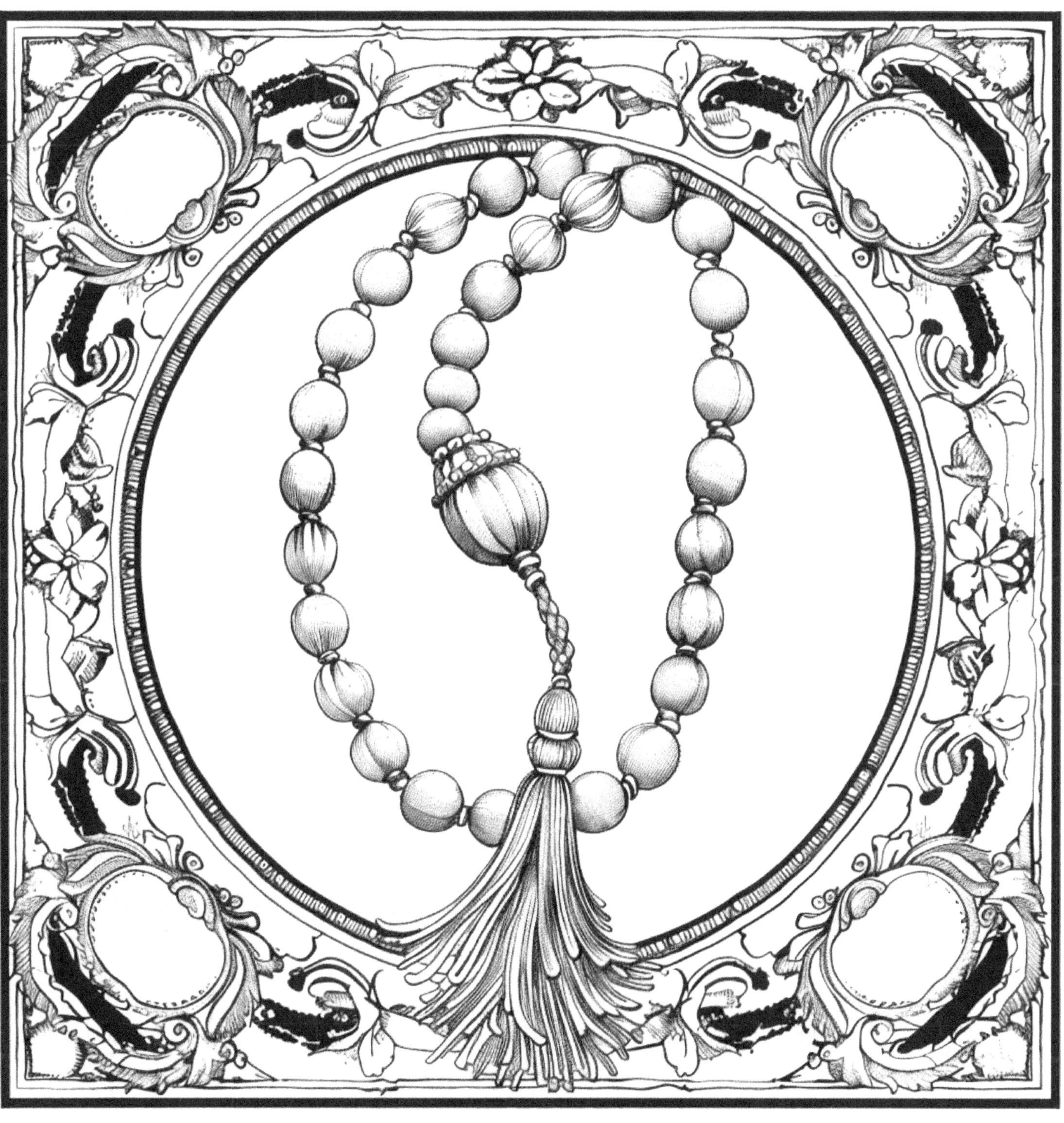

Day 83

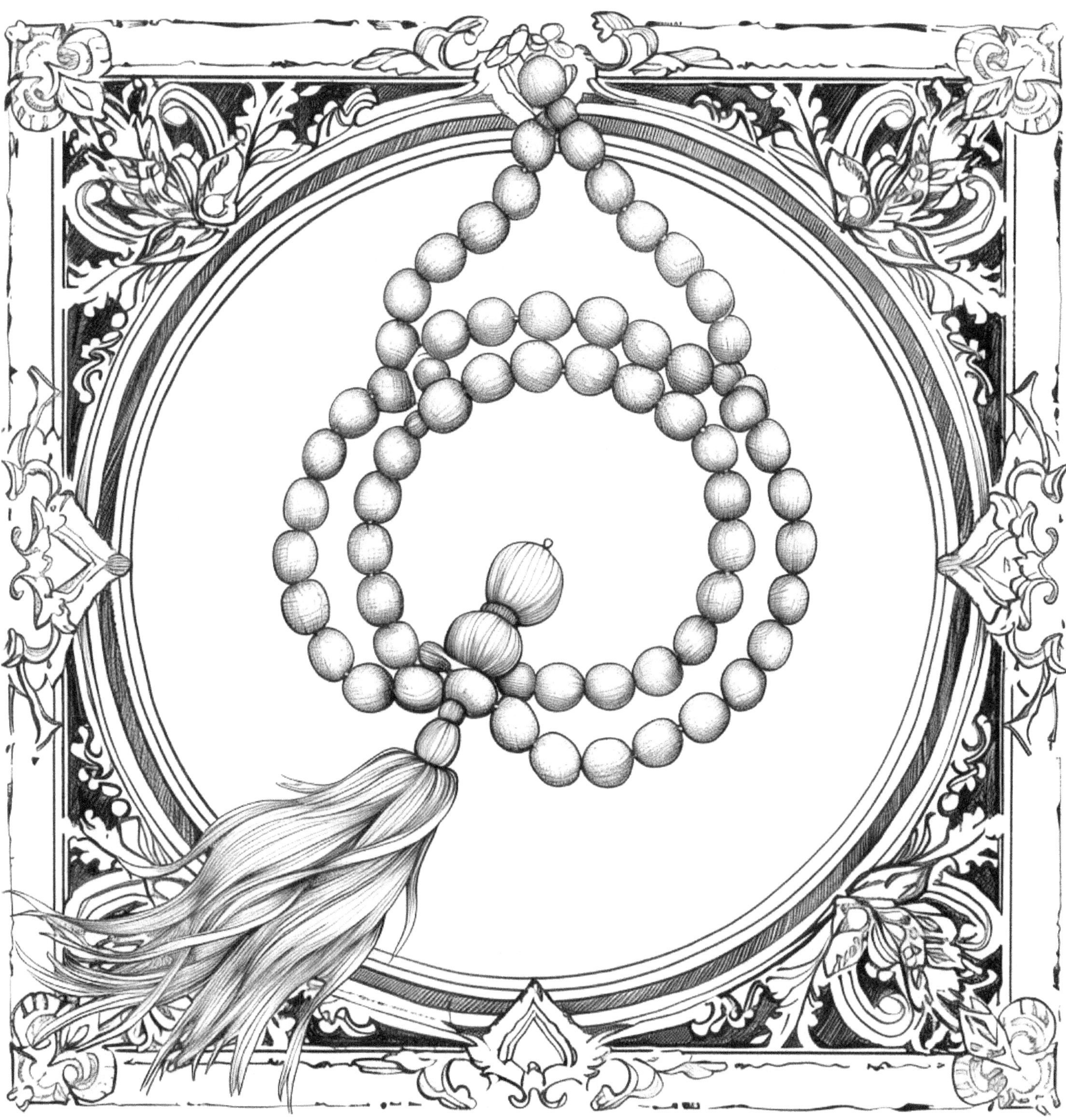

Day 84

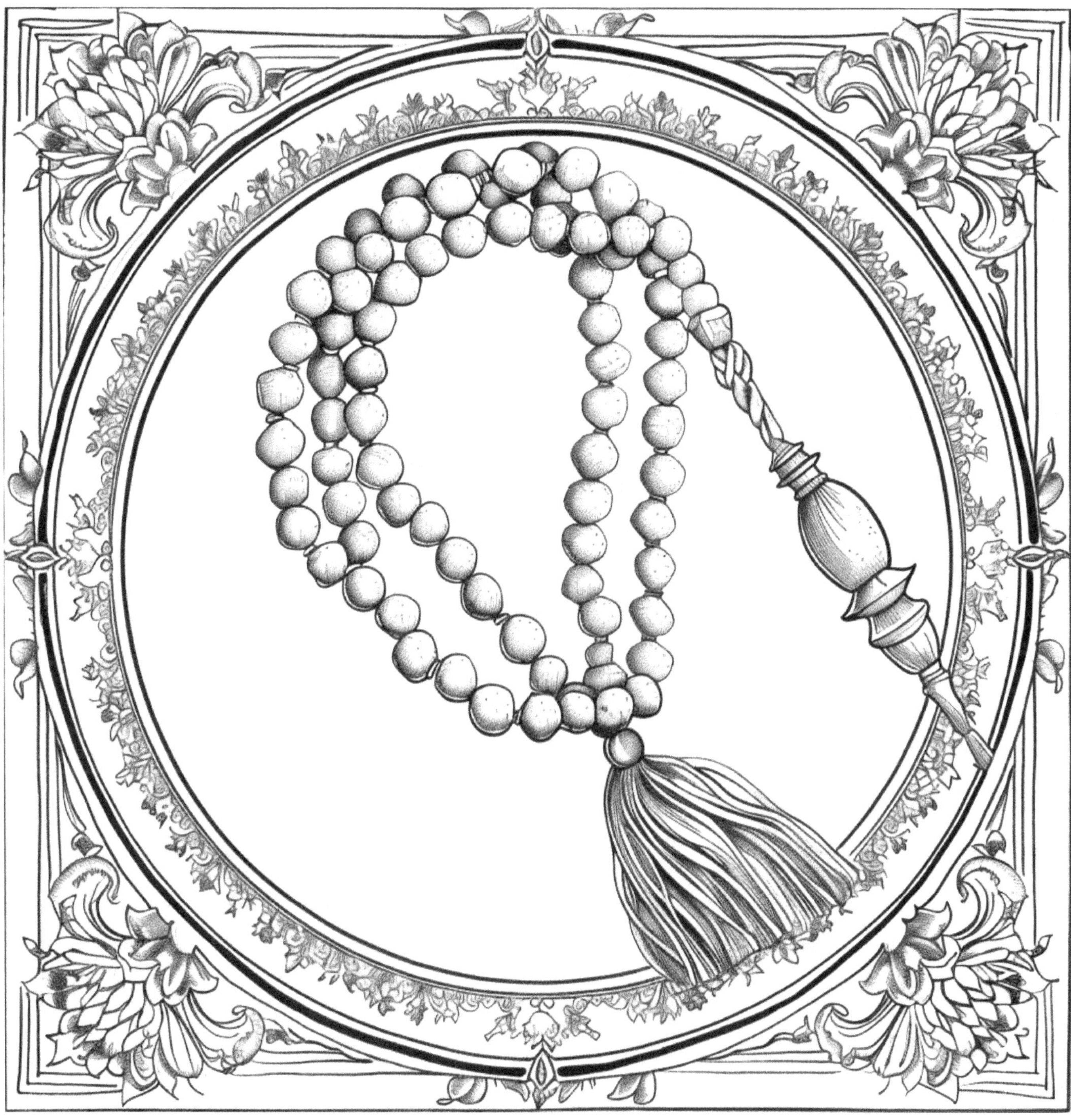

Day 85

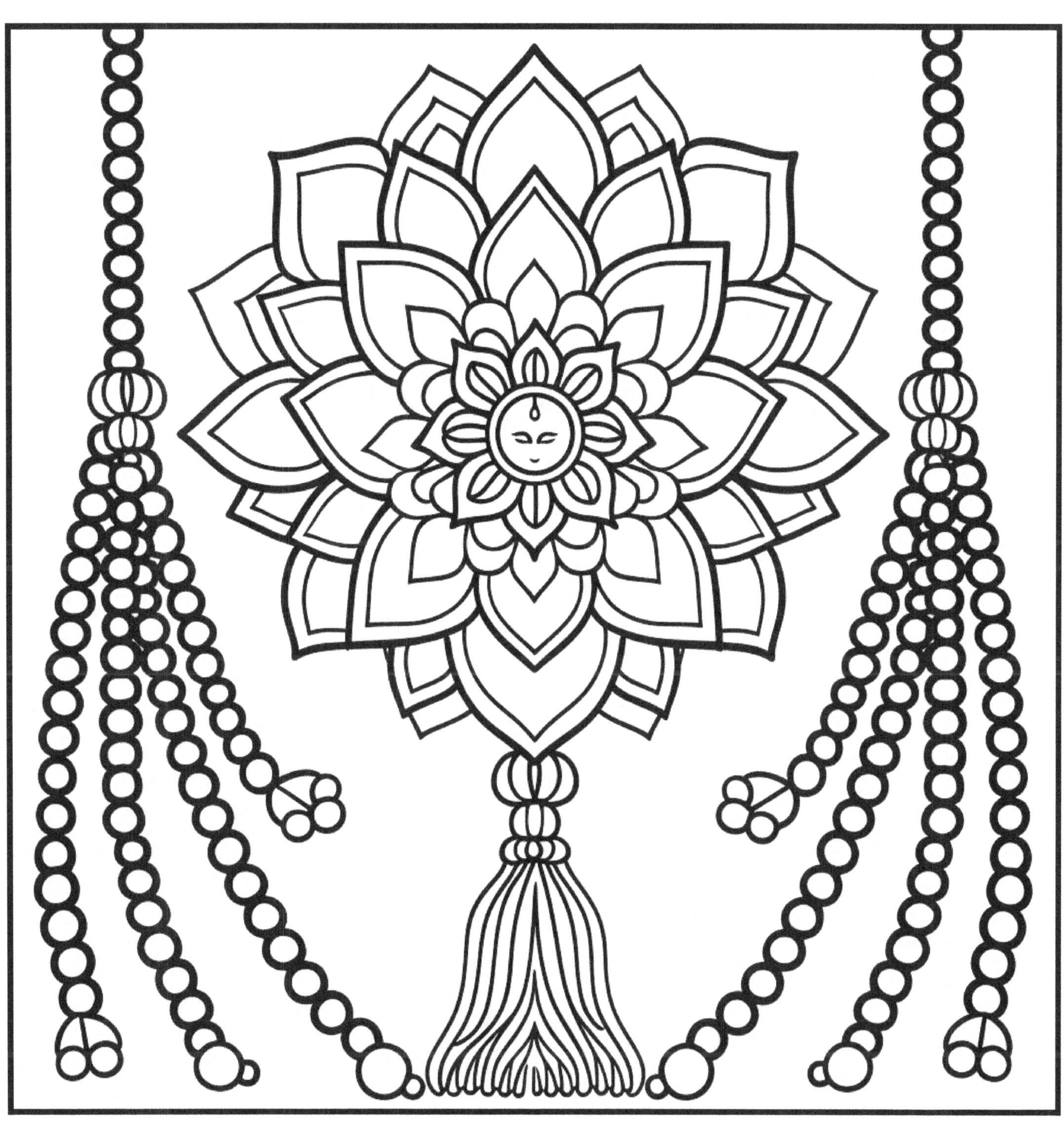

Day 86

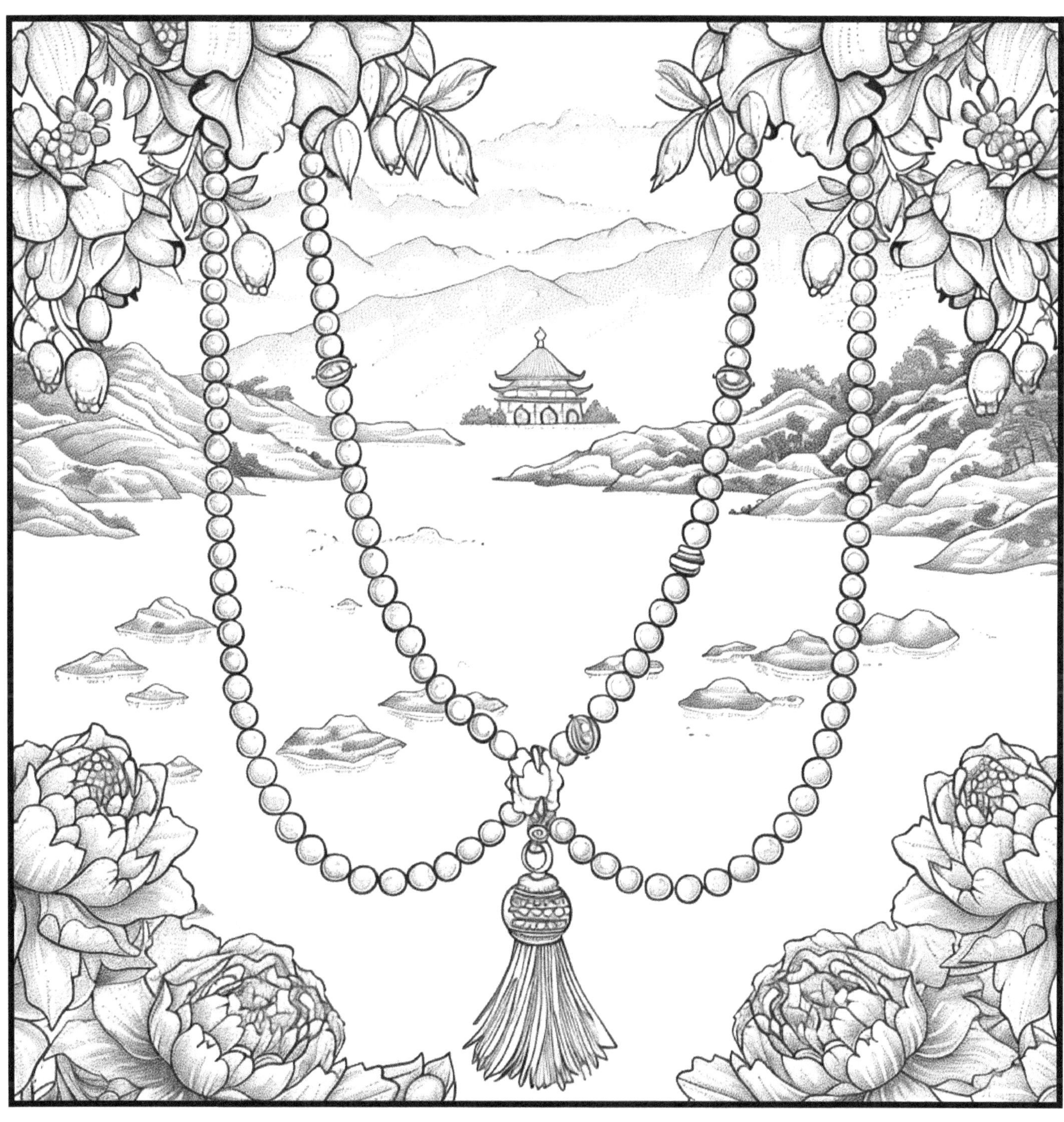

Day 87

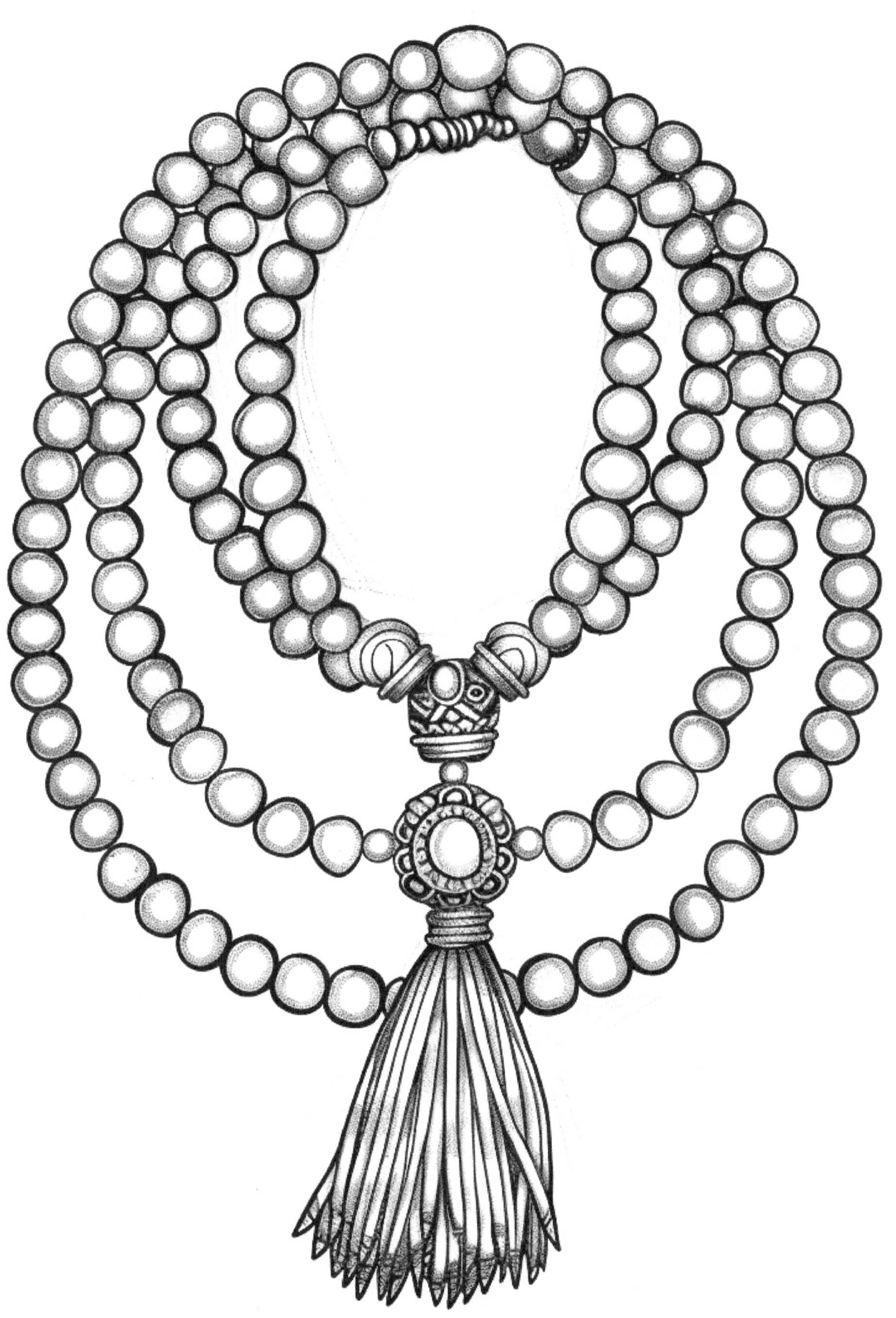

Day 88

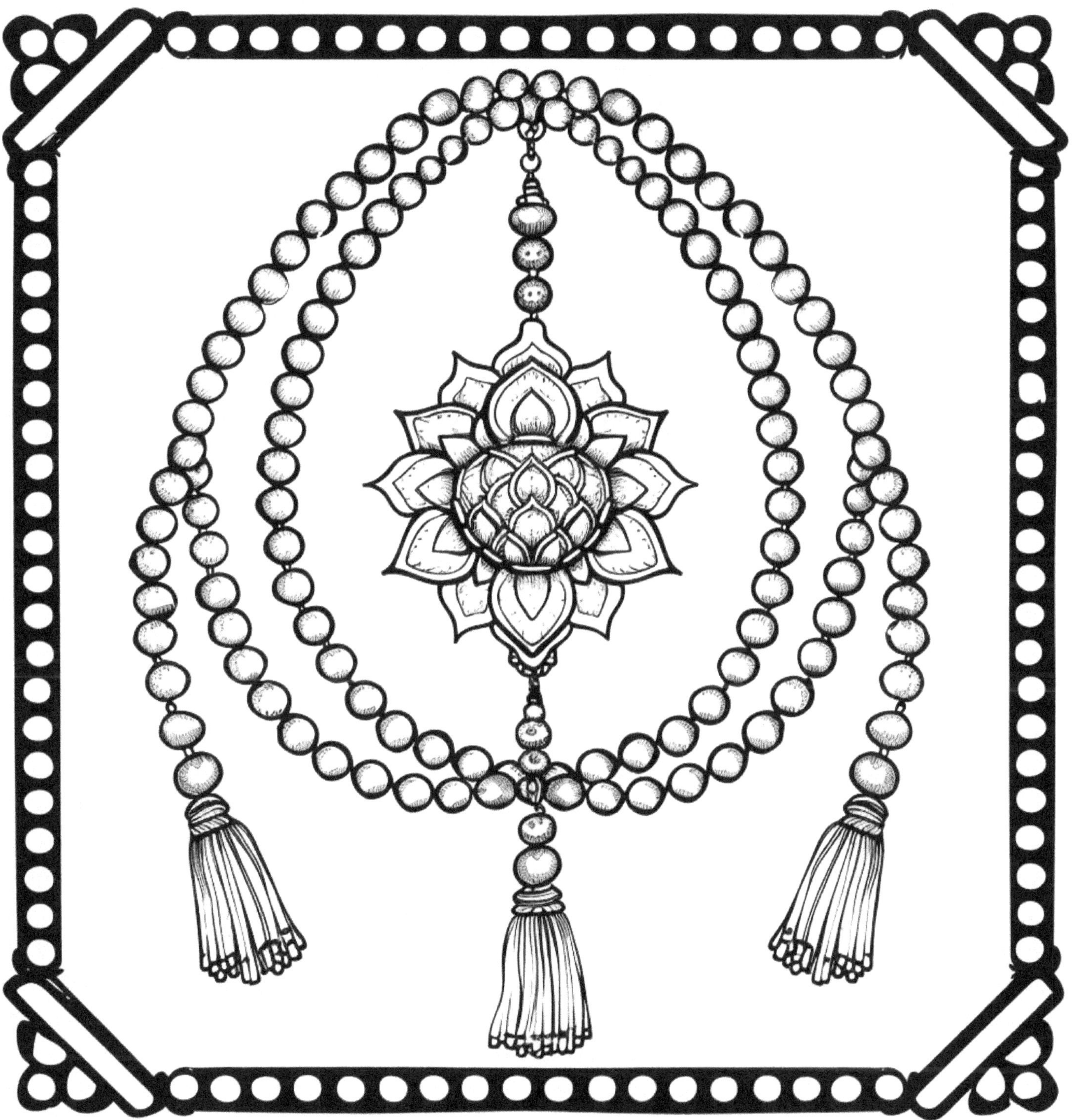

Day 89

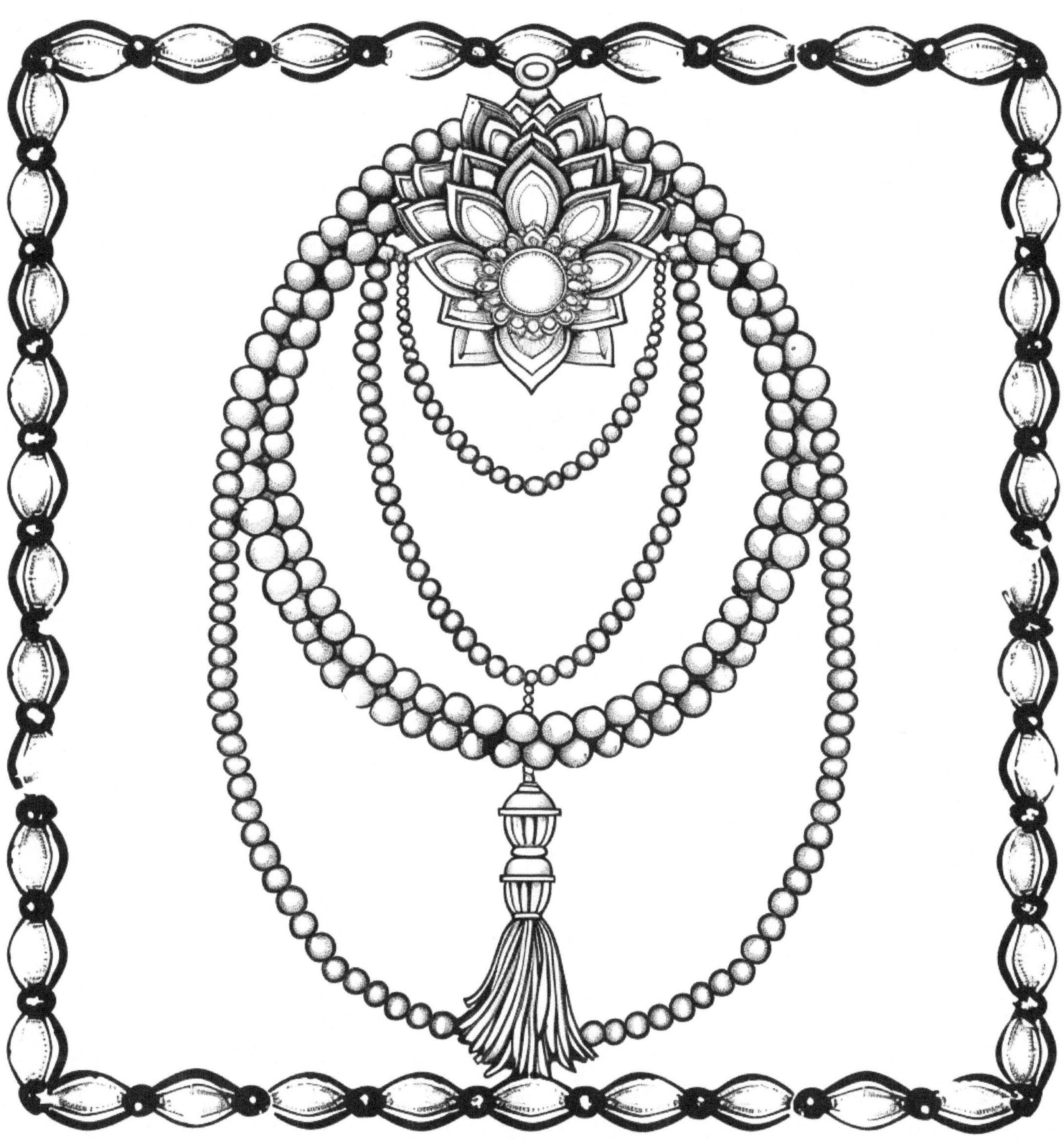

Day 90

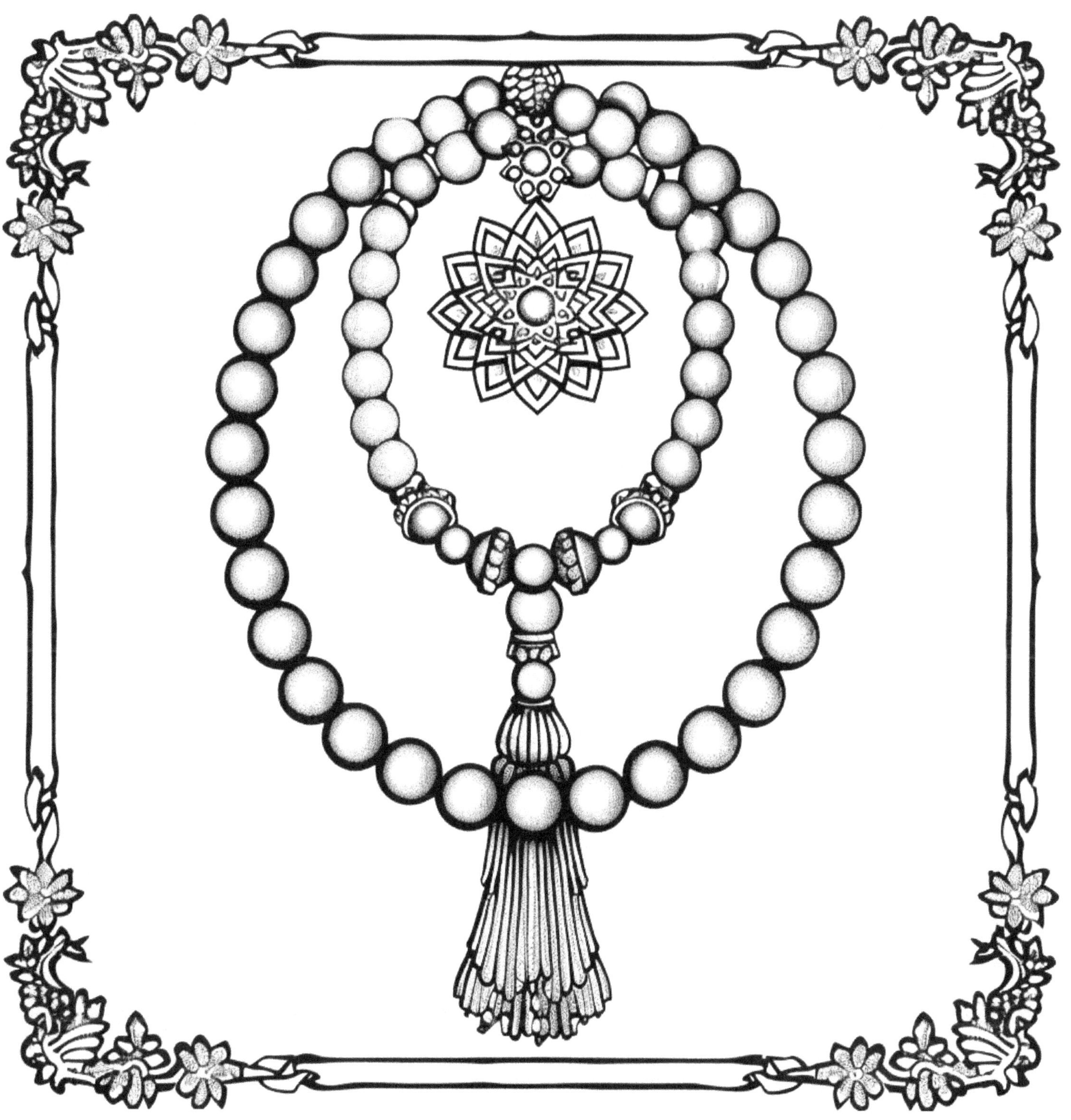

Day 91

LOVE
&
LIGHT

Day 92

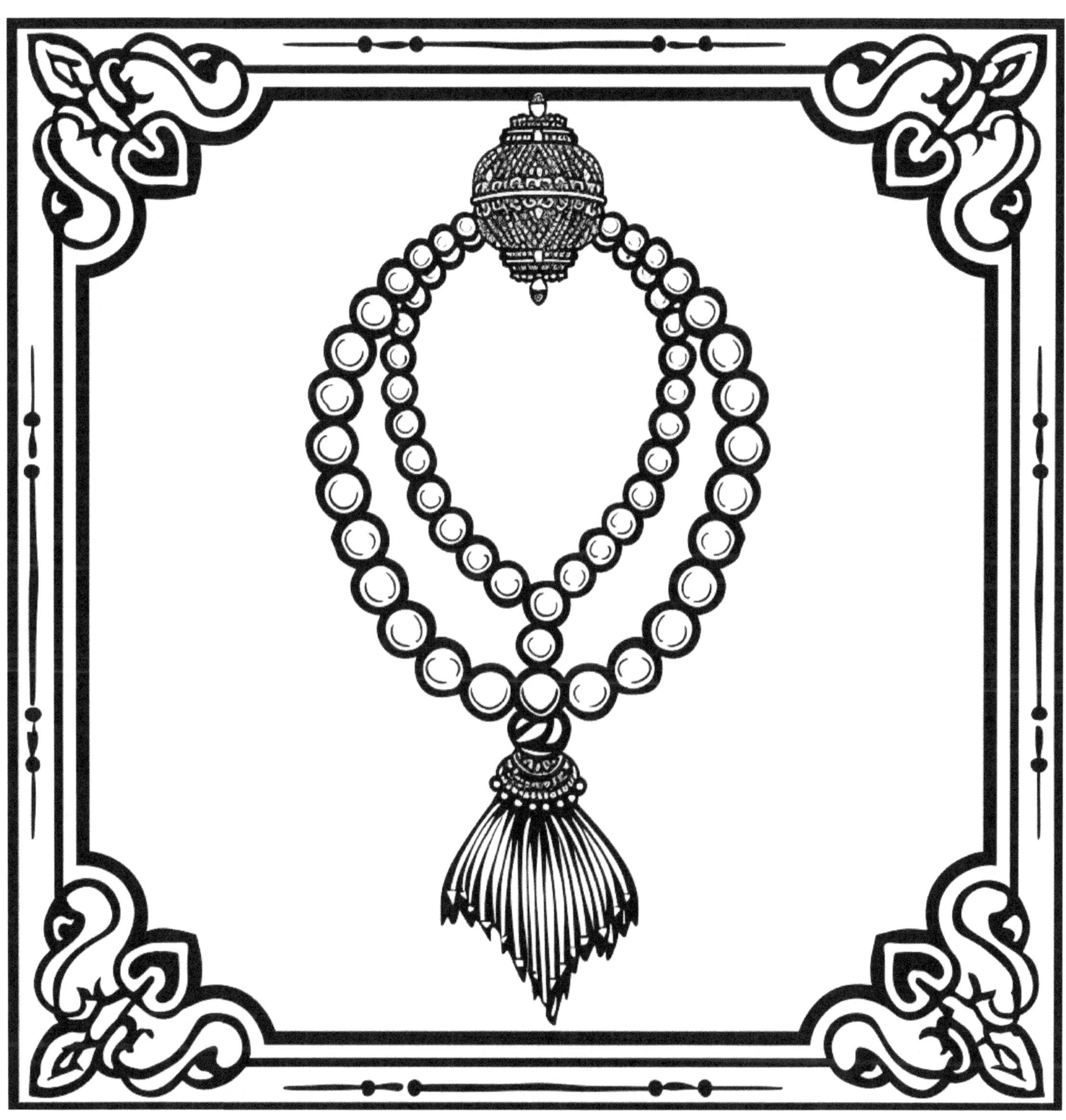

Day 93

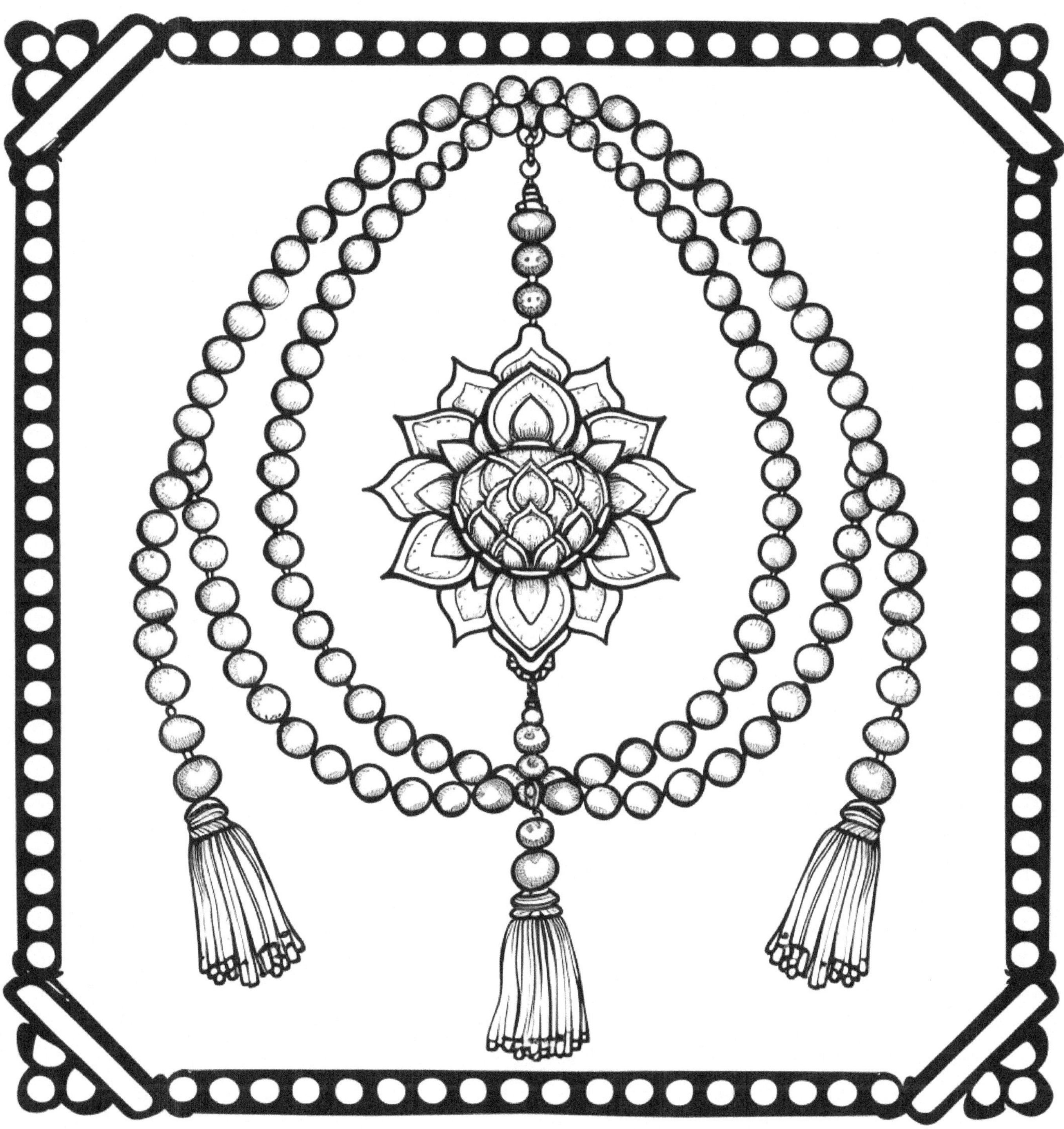

Day 94

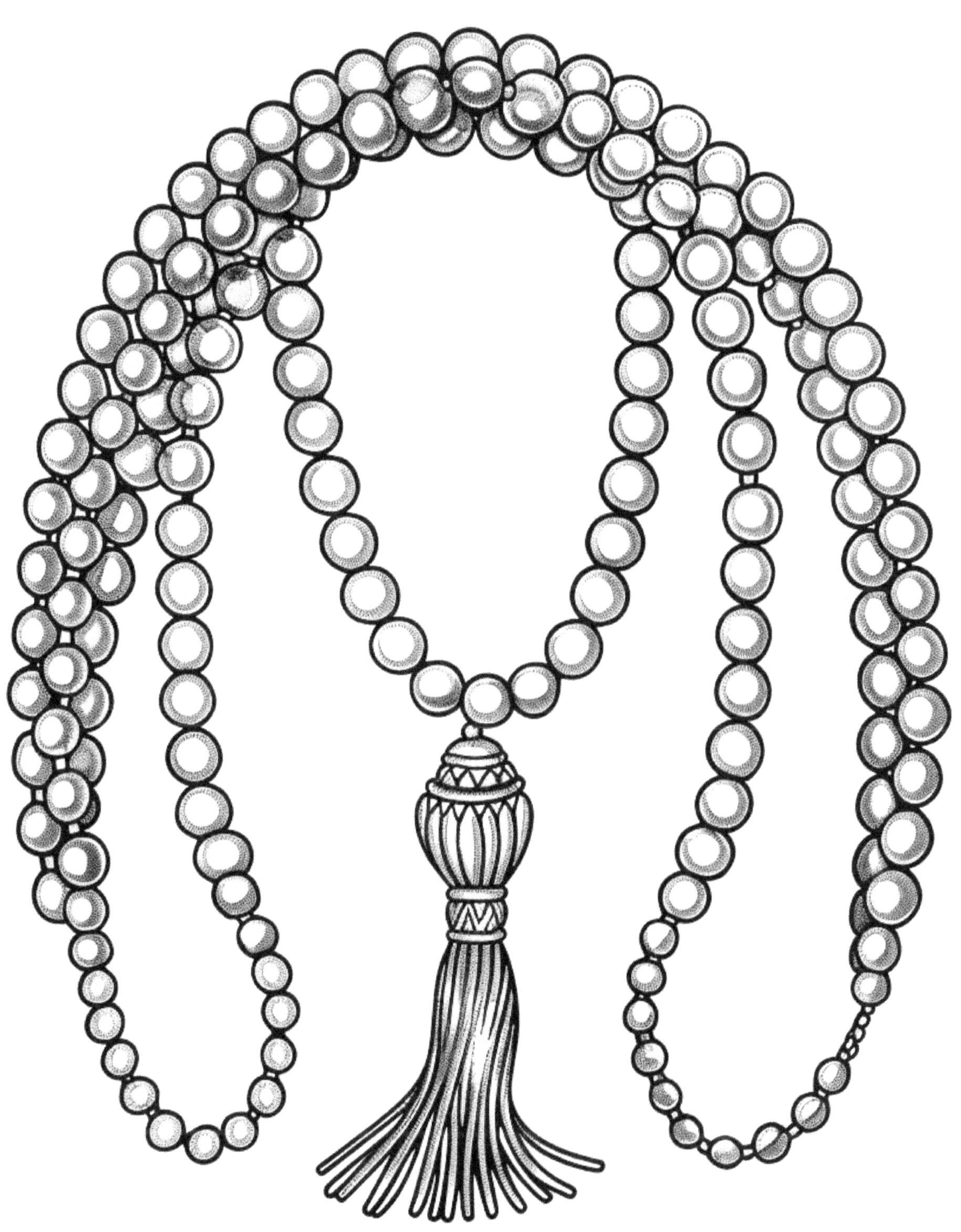

Day 95

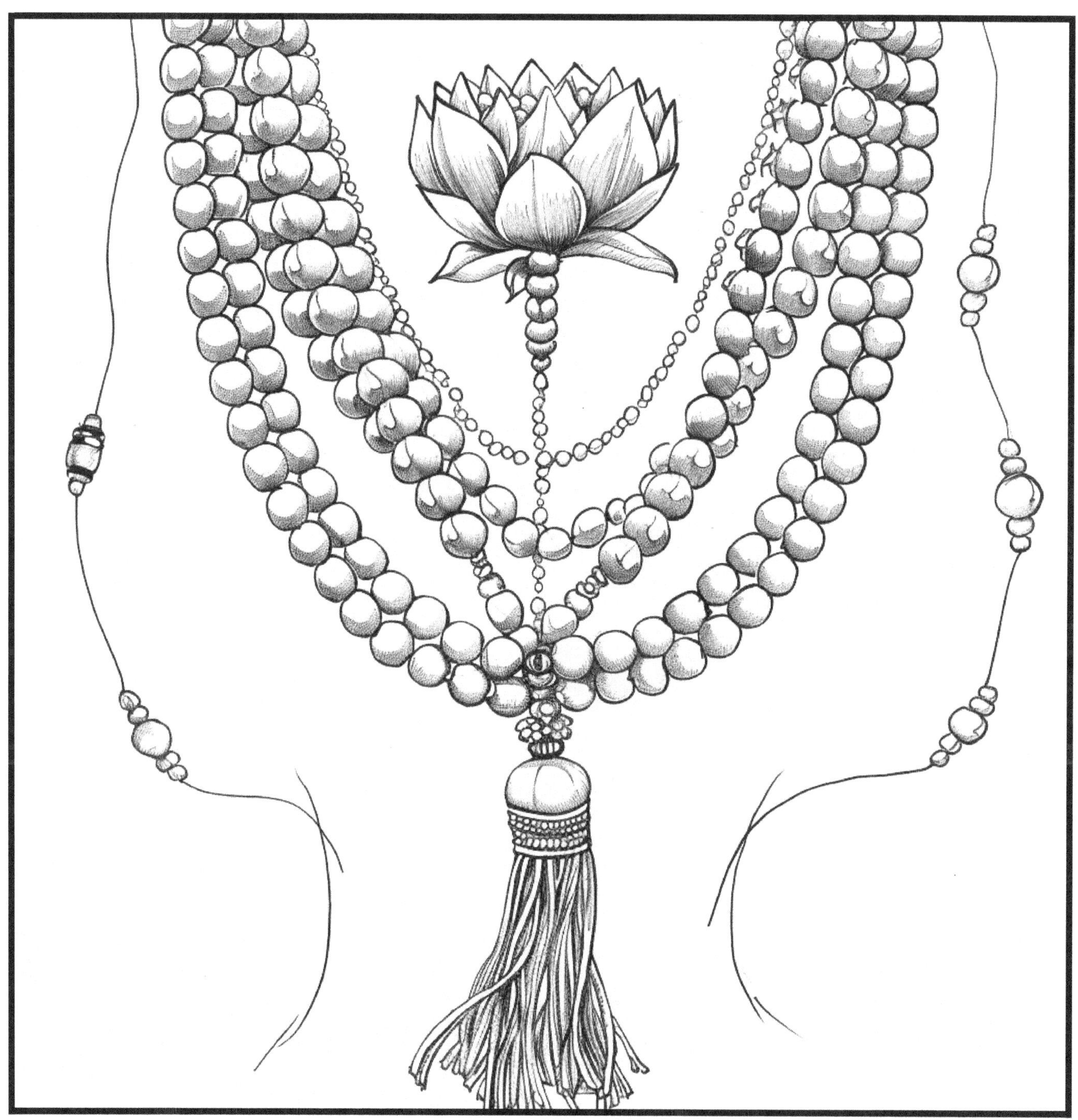

The Deeper the Breath

The Richer the Life

Day 96

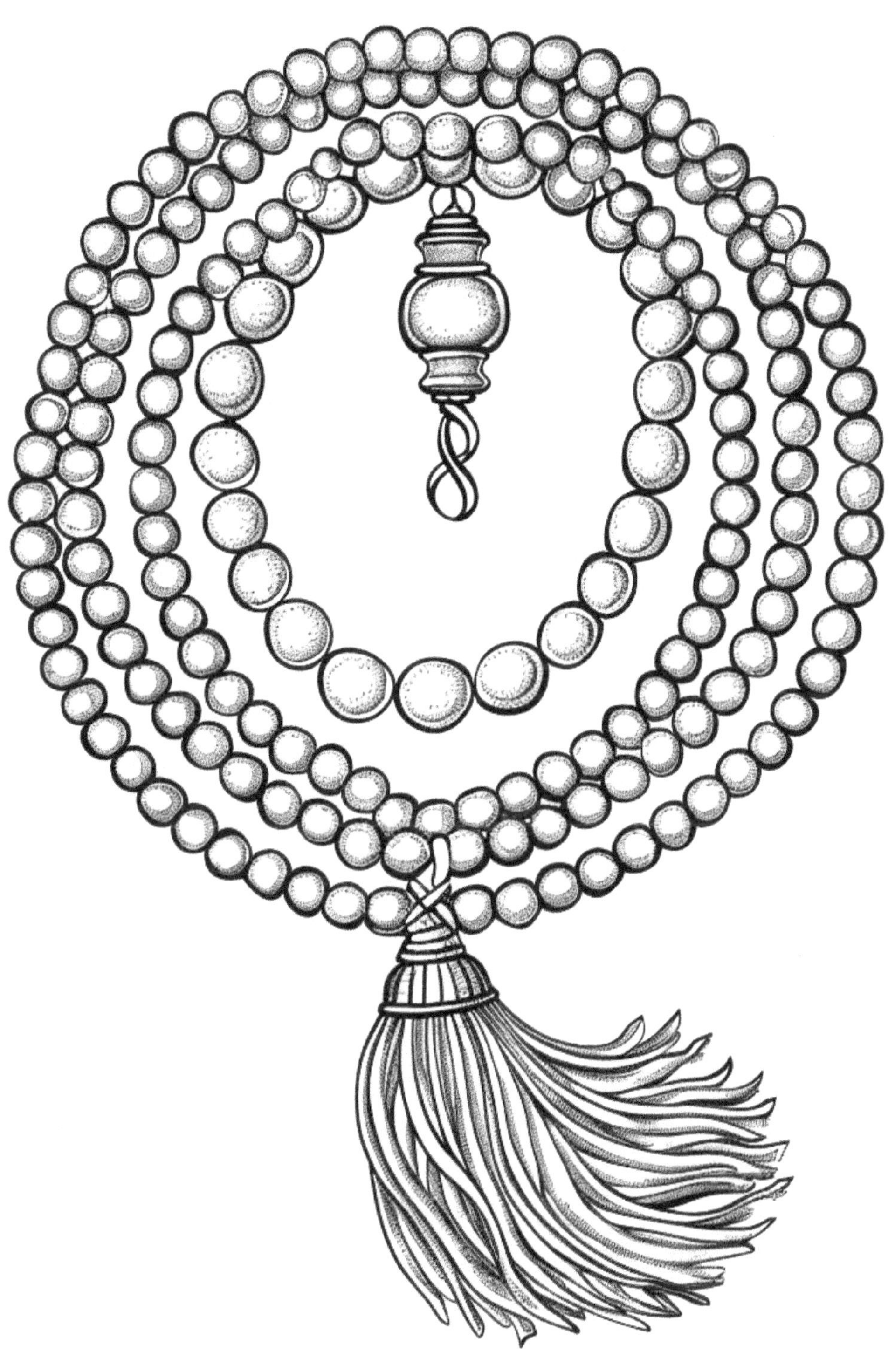

Day 97

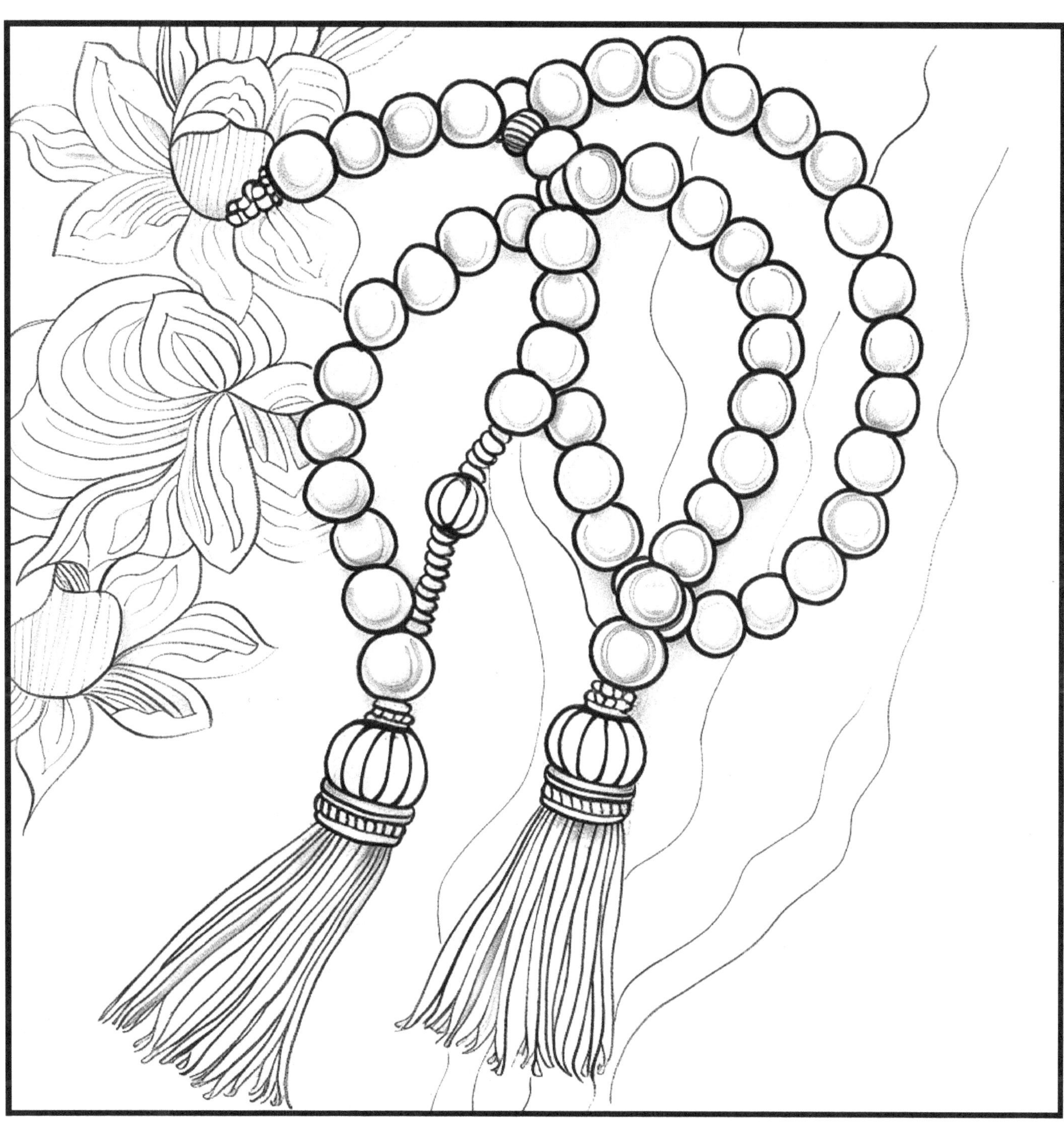

Day 98

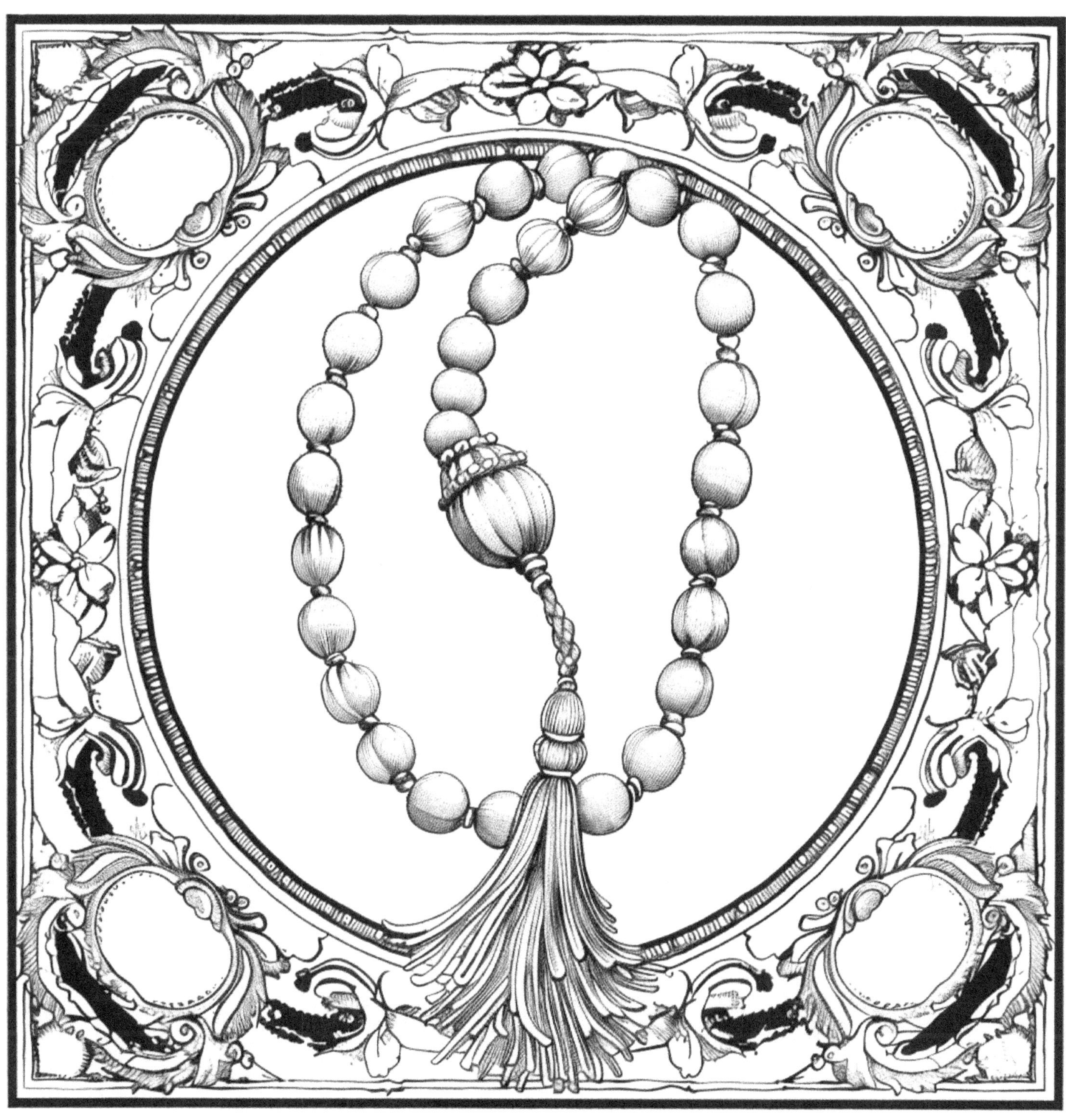

Day 99

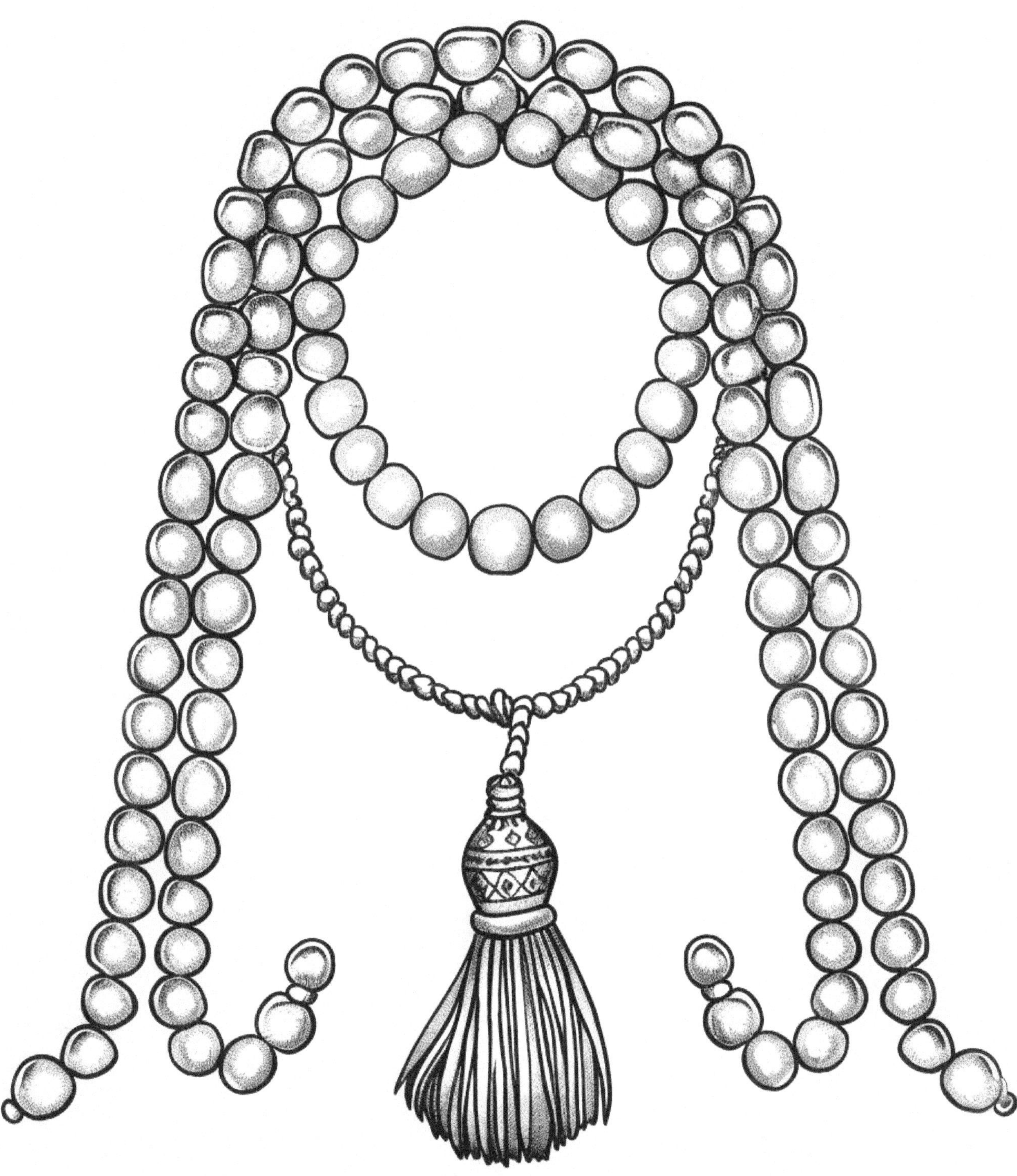

Day 100

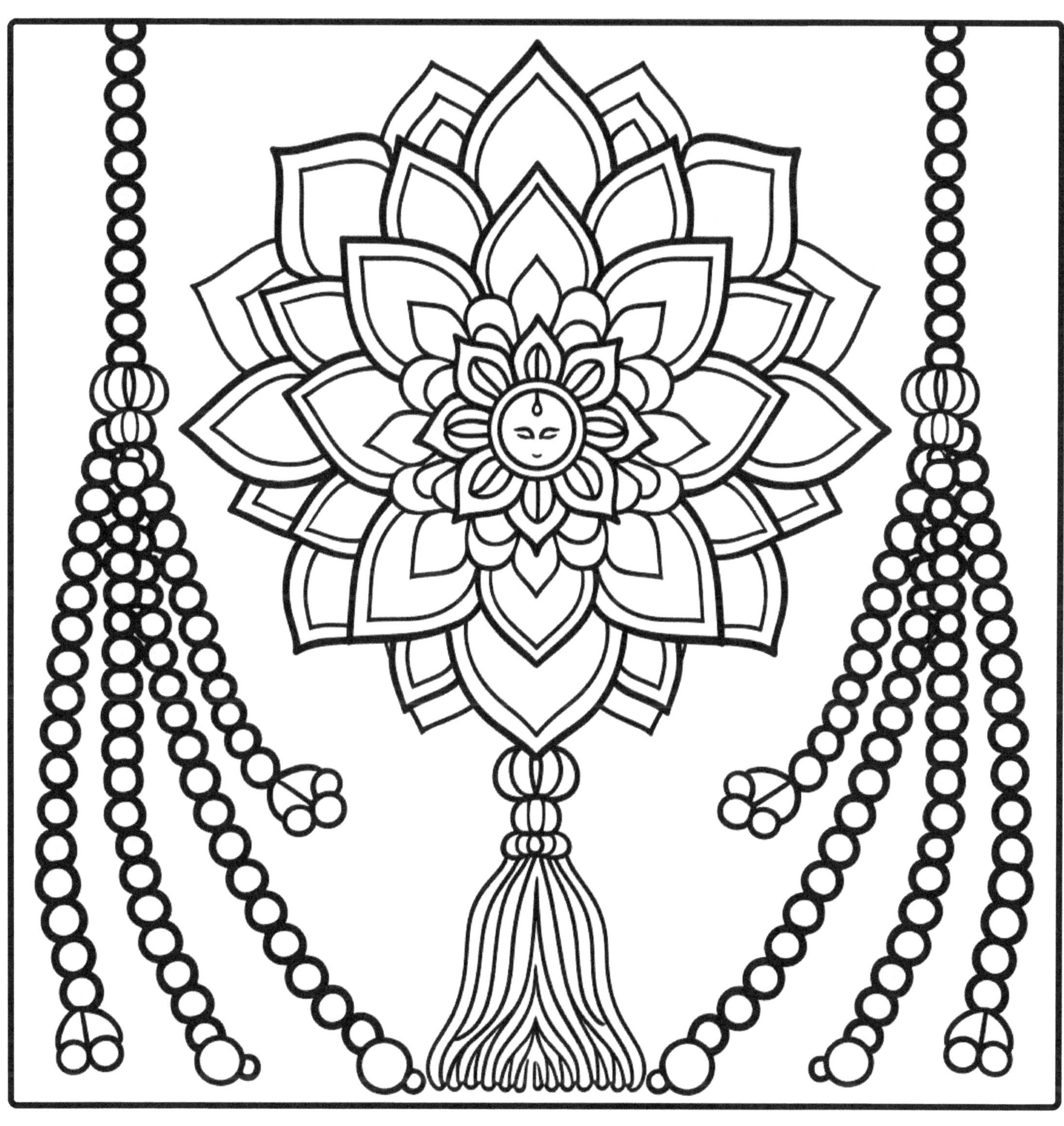

Day 101

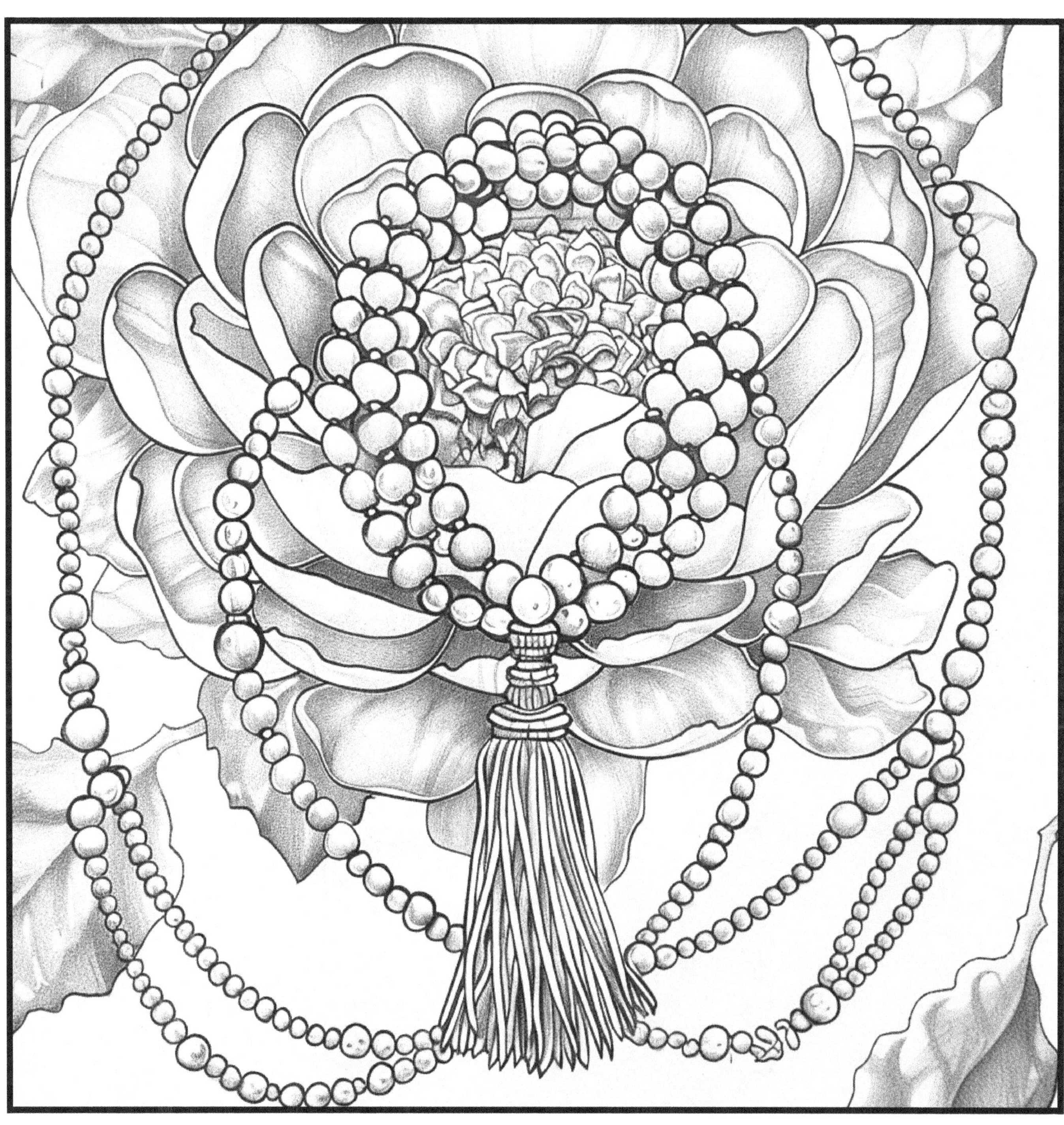

Day 102

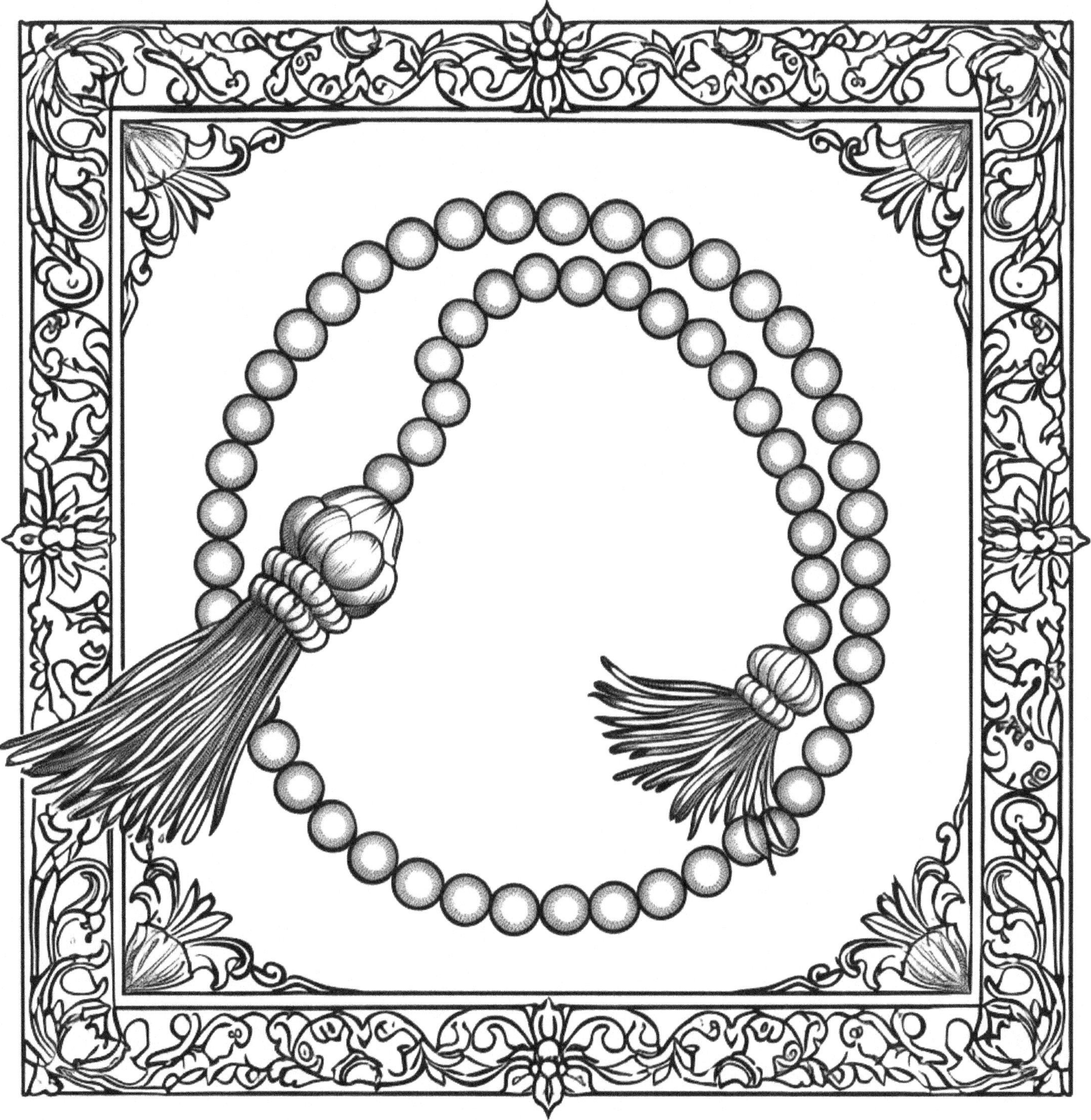

Day 103

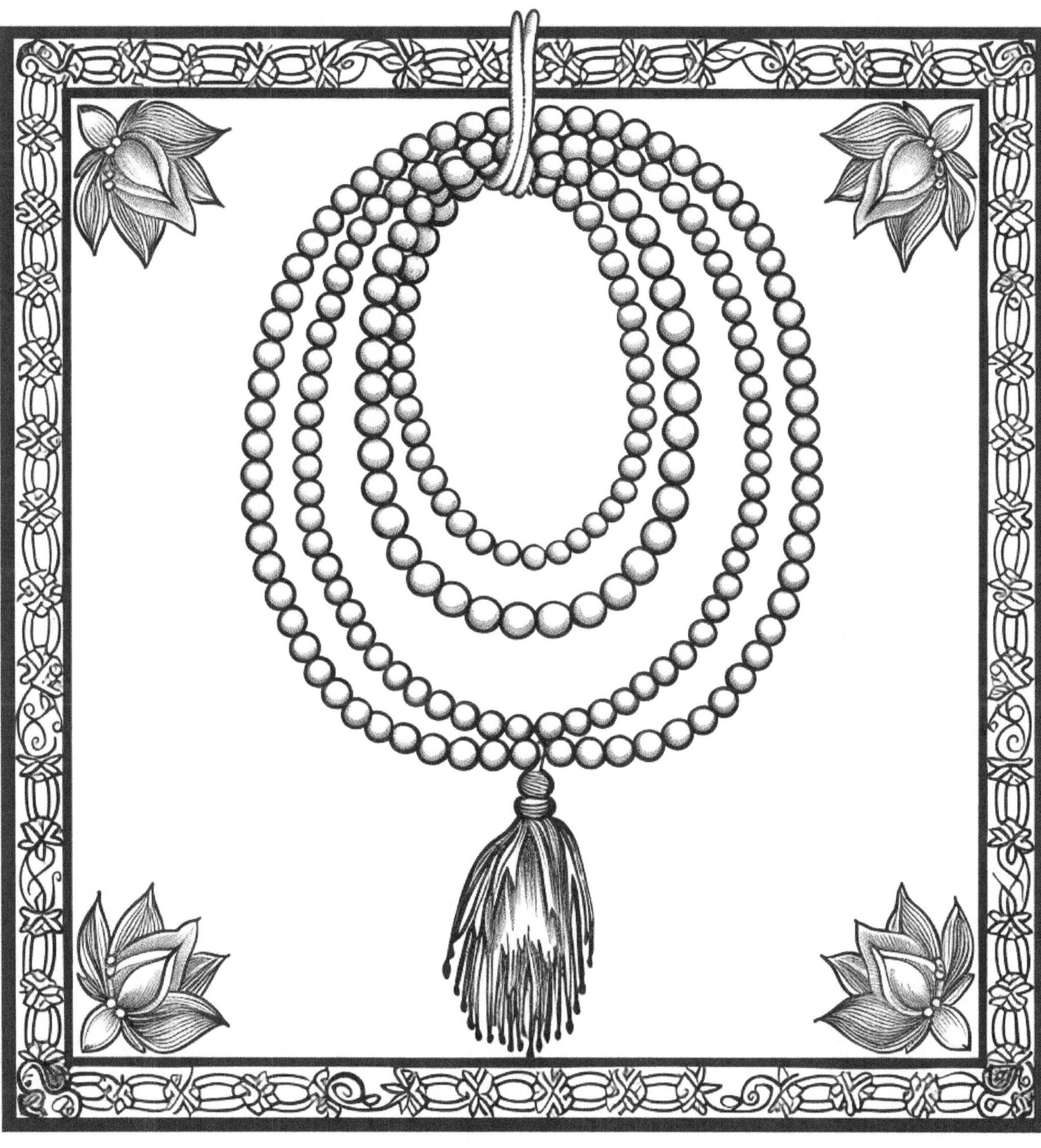

Day 104

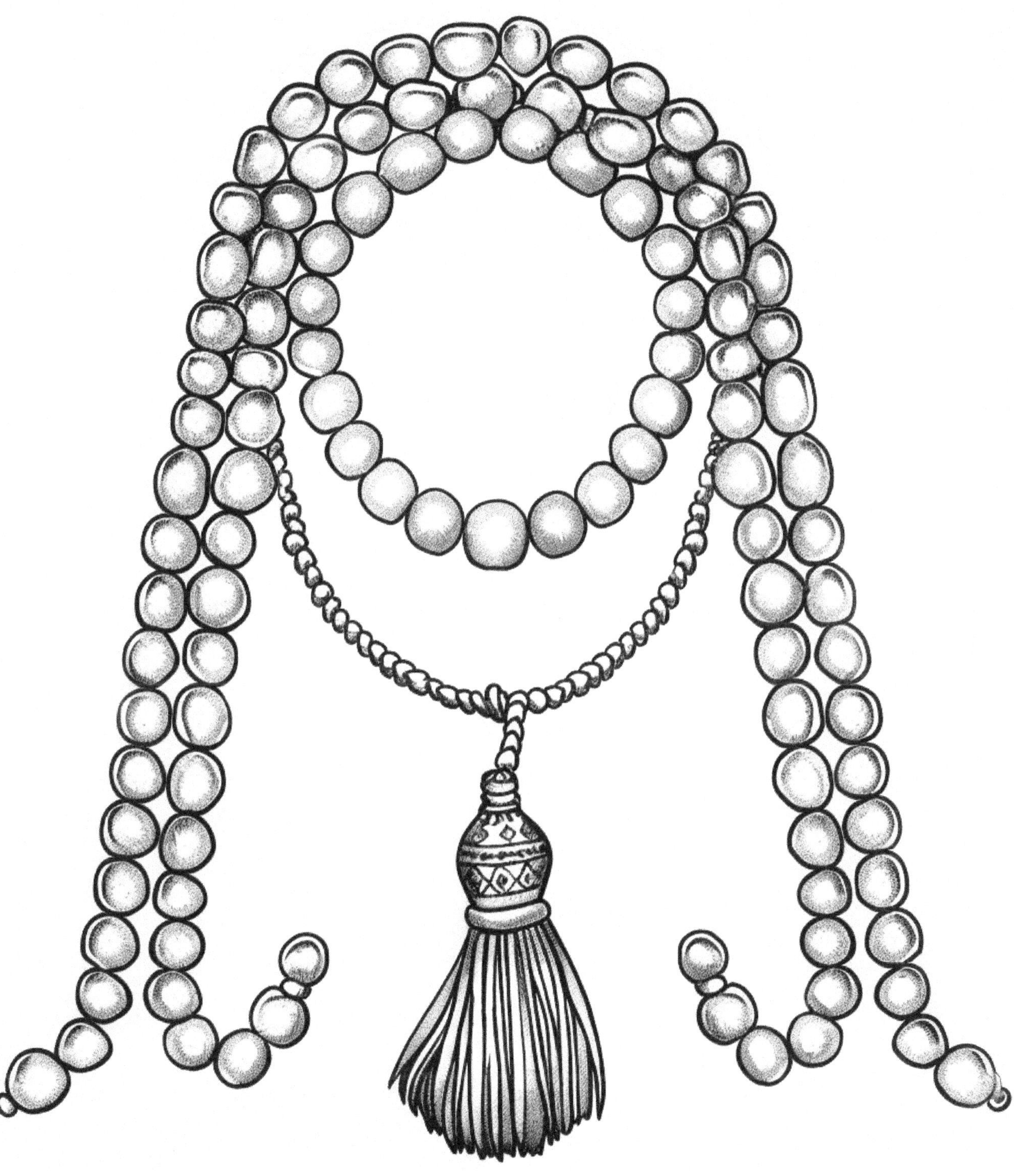

Day 105

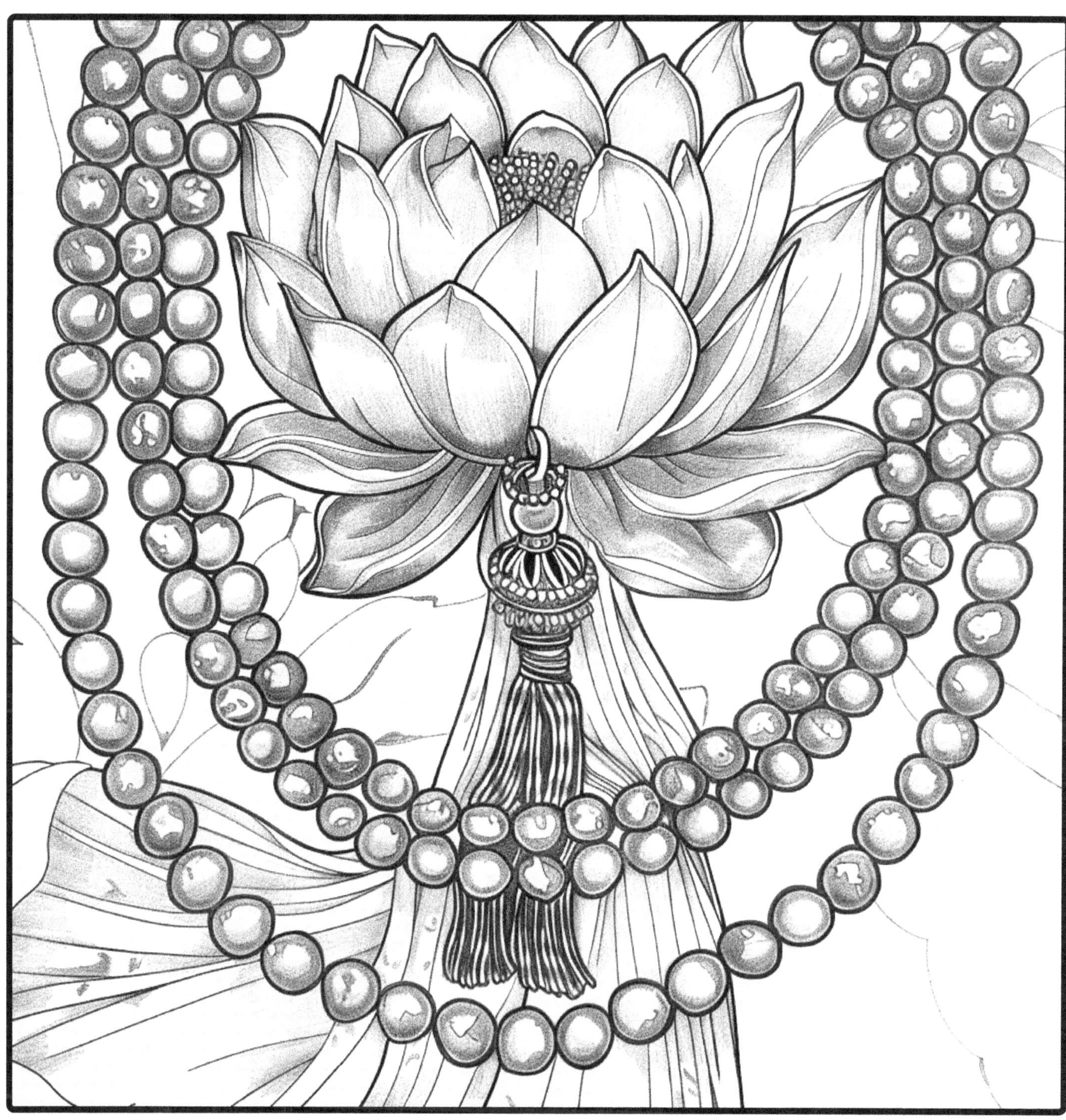

Day 106

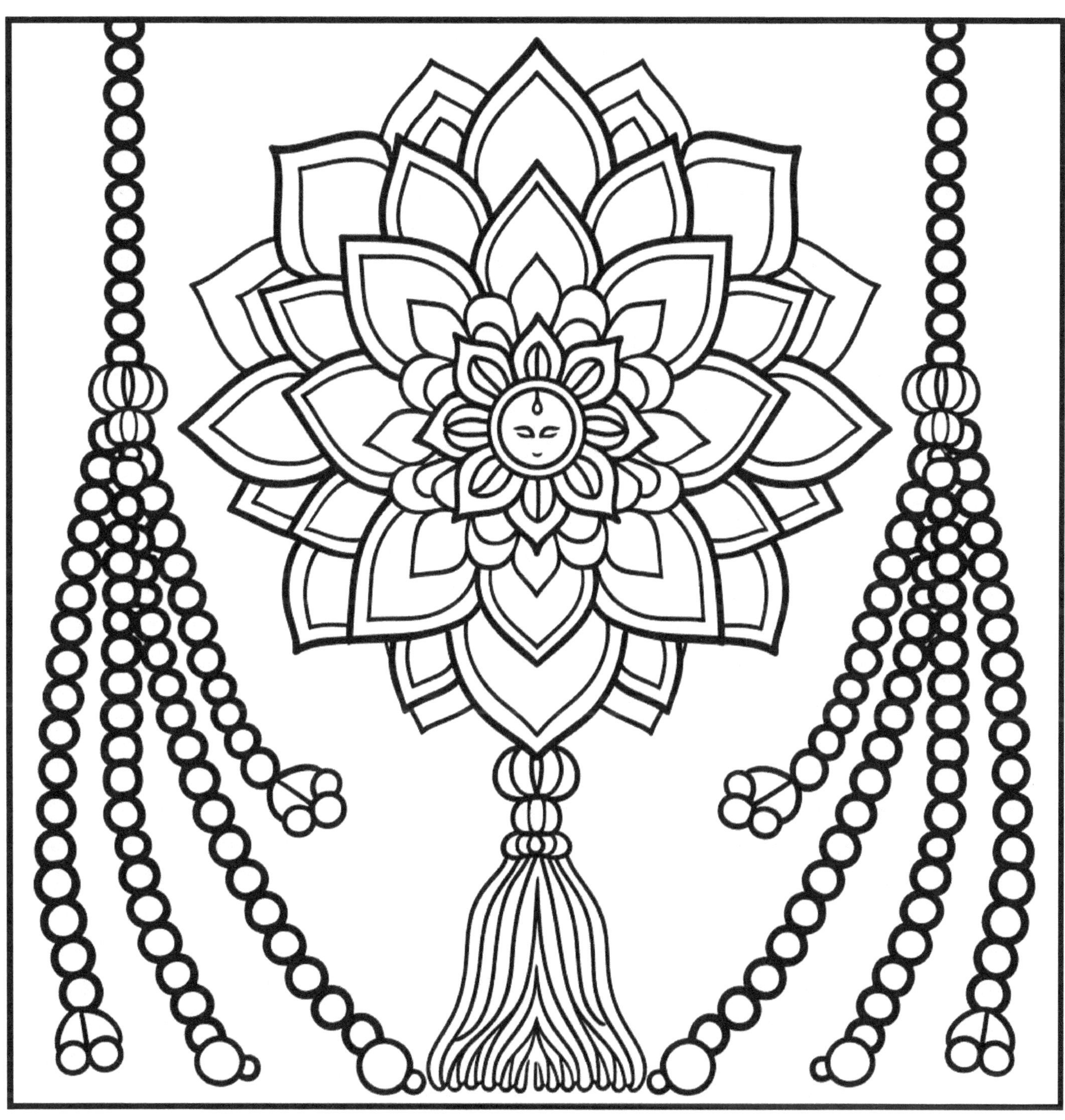

Day 107

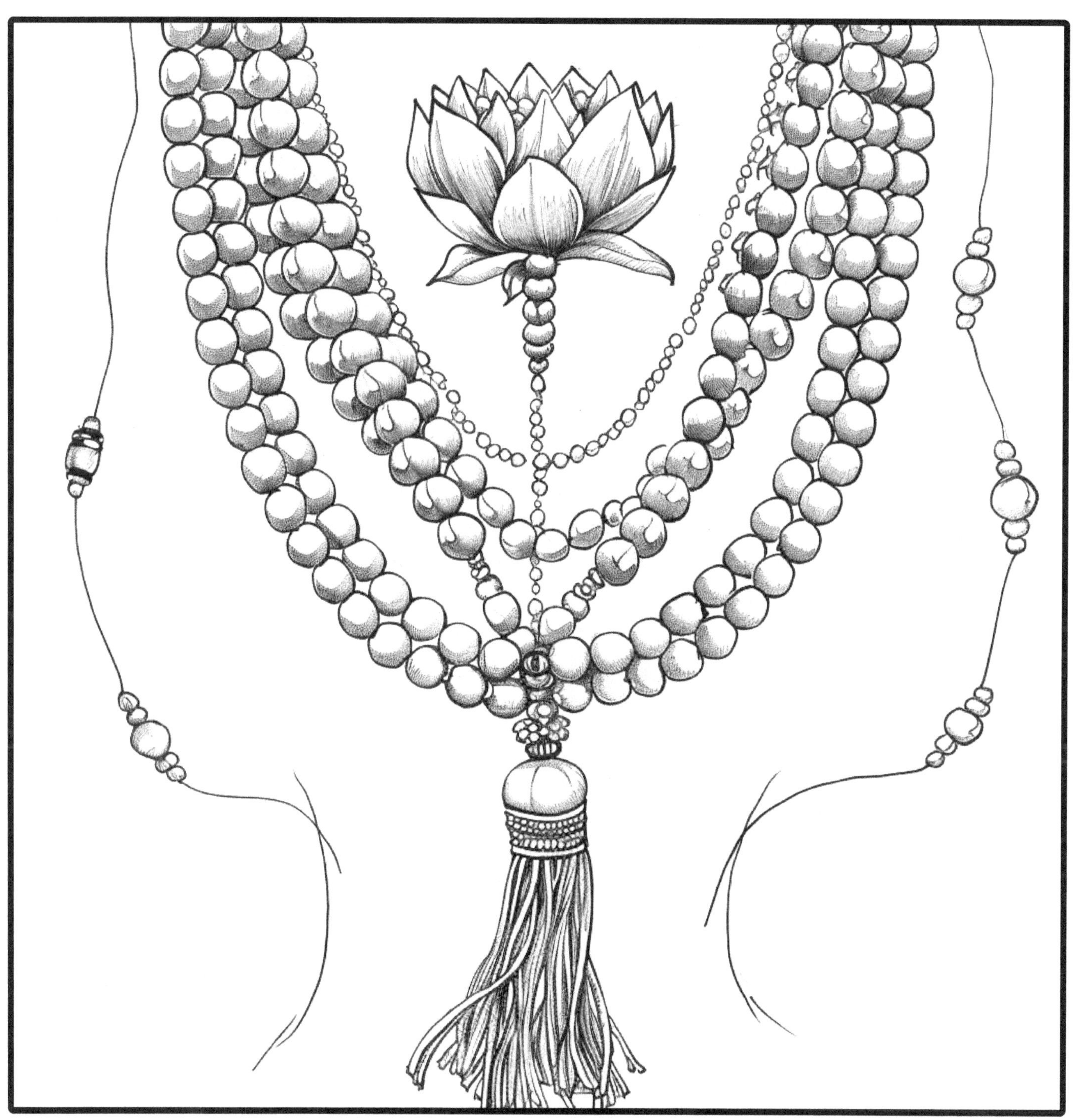

The Deeper the Breath

The Richer the Life

Day 108

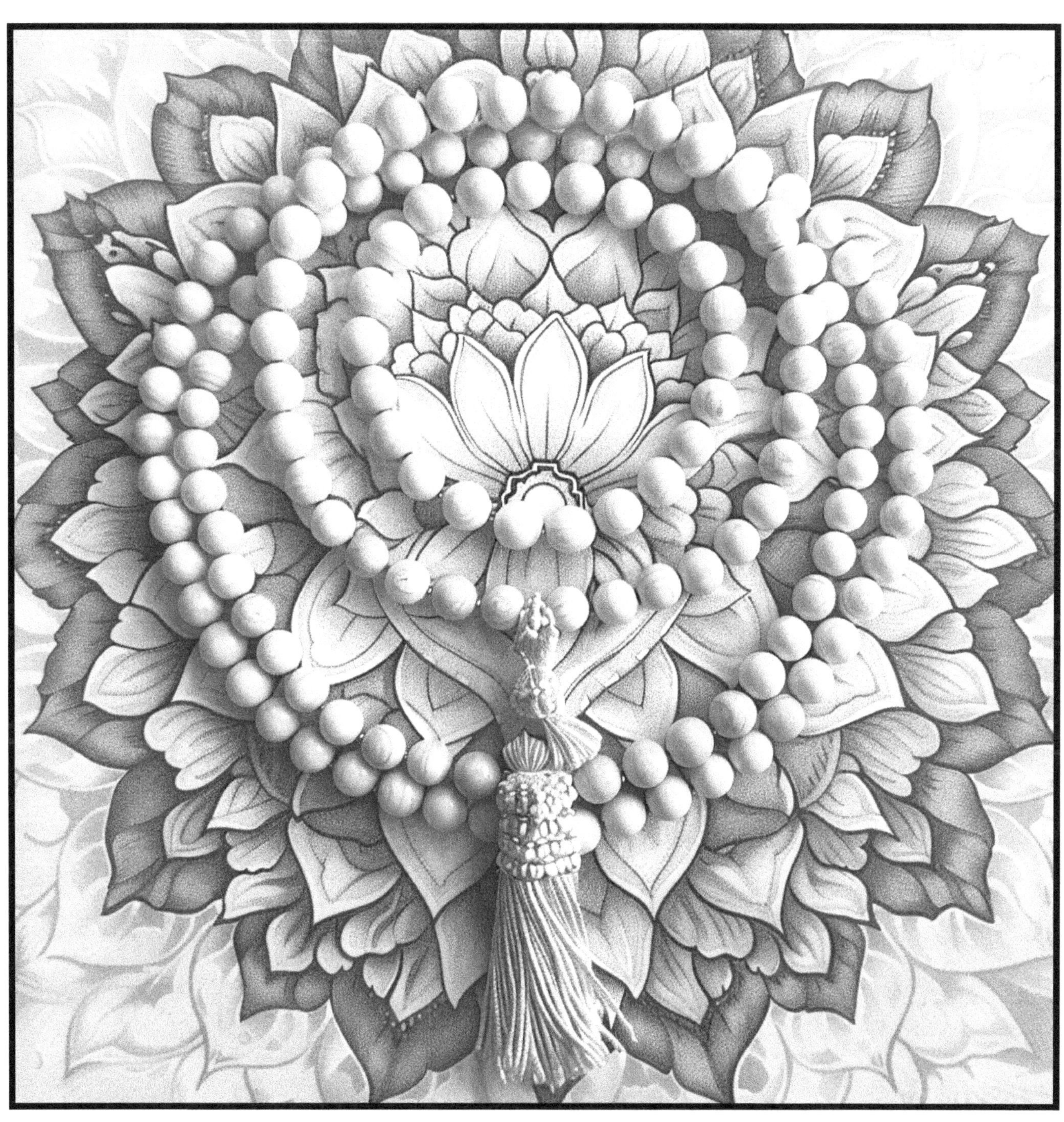

Peace &
BLESSINGS

The Origins and Meaning of Mandala

Mandalas, with their intricate geometric patterns and mesmerizing designs, have captivated the human imagination for centuries. These circular symbols, which originate from various cultures around the world, hold profound meaning and significance. In this brief exploration, we will delve into the origins and delve into the rich meanings associated with mandalas.

Origins: The word "mandala" finds its roots in ancient Indian languages, primarily Sanskrit, where it means "circle." Mandalas have their origins in India, and they can be traced back over 2,000 years. Initially, they were used in Hindu and Buddhist religious practices. Mandalas were crafted as spiritual symbols representing the universe, wholeness, and the cyclical nature of existence.

In Hinduism, mandalas were used as tools for meditation and were often created as intricate designs on temple floors. They served as a visual representation of the cosmos and a way to connect with the divine. Mandalas were also used in Hindu rituals to symbolize the universe's harmony and balance.

Beyond India, mandalas have been found in various forms across cultures and religions, from Native American medicine wheels to Celtic designs. These diverse representations highlight the universal appeal and significance of the mandala.

Meaning: Wholeness and Unity: The most fundamental concept associated with mandalas is wholeness. The circular shape of the mandala symbolizes the universe, the endless cycle of life, and the idea that everything is interconnected. It represents the notion that all parts are integral to the whole, encouraging a sense of unity and balance.

1. **Spiritual Journey:** Mandalas are often used as a form of meditation or spiritual guidance. Focusing on the intricate patterns and following the path from the outer edges to the center can be a transformative journey. It is believed to lead to a deeper understanding of oneself and one's connection to the universe.
2. **Healing and Therapy:** In modern times, mandalas have found their way into art therapy and psychological healing practices. Creating or coloring mandalas can be a therapeutic process, promoting relaxation, reducing stress, and aiding in self-expression.
3. **Expression of Creativity:** Many artists use mandalas as a creative outlet. The symmetry and structure of mandalas provide a framework for artistic exploration and expression.

Mandalas in Native American Culture: While mandalas, as we commonly know them, are most closely associated with Asian cultures like Hinduism and Buddhism, there are analogous geometric designs and symbols found in Native American cultures that share some similarities with mandalas in terms of their spiritual and symbolic significance. These designs are often referred to as "medicine wheels."

1. **Medicine Wheels**: Medicine wheels are circular stone structures or designs made on the ground. They are primarily associated with the Plains Indians, particularly the Lakota Sioux and the Blackfeet, but variations of these structures can also be found among other Native American tribes. Medicine wheels consist of a central hub or cairn of stones surrounded by concentric circles of stones, with lines radiating outward. These structures are considered sacred and hold deep spiritual significance.
2. **Symbolism:** Much like mandalas, medicine wheels symbolize unity, harmony, and the interconnectedness of all life. The central hub often represents the individual or the community, while the circles and lines represent the cycles of life, the seasons, and the ongoing flow of energy and time. The four cardinal directions are typically represented, each associated with specific qualities and elements.
3. **Spiritual and Ceremonial Use:** Medicine wheels are used in various Native American spiritual and ceremonial practices. They serve as a focal point for rituals, meditation, and prayer. Native Americans believe that by aligning themselves with the natural elements and the sacred directions, they can attain balance and spiritual insight.
4. **Healing and Balance:** Medicine wheels are also associated with healing, both physical and spiritual. Native American healers and medicine people may use the symbolism and energy of the medicine wheel to facilitate healing ceremonies. The belief is that when an individual is in harmony with the natural world and the spiritual realm, they are more likely to experience health and well-being.

Teaching Tools: Medicine wheels are educational tools as well, used to pass down traditional knowledge and wisdom. Elders and spiritual leaders use them to teach younger generations about their culture, history, and the relationship between humans and nature.

It's important to note that the specific symbolism and rituals associated with medicine wheels can vary among different tribes and regions. While some elements are common, the details may differ, reflecting the diversity of Native American cultures.

In summary, while not exactly the same as Eastern mandalas, Native American medicine wheels share a similar circular and symbolic nature. They represent the profound connection between people, the natural world, and the spiritual realm, and they are integral to the spiritual and cultural practices of many Native American tribes. These sacred symbols continue to be revered and utilized in Native American communities as a means of preserving tradition, promoting balance, and fostering spiritual growth.

I am in control of my thoughts,
and I choose to focus on the positive.

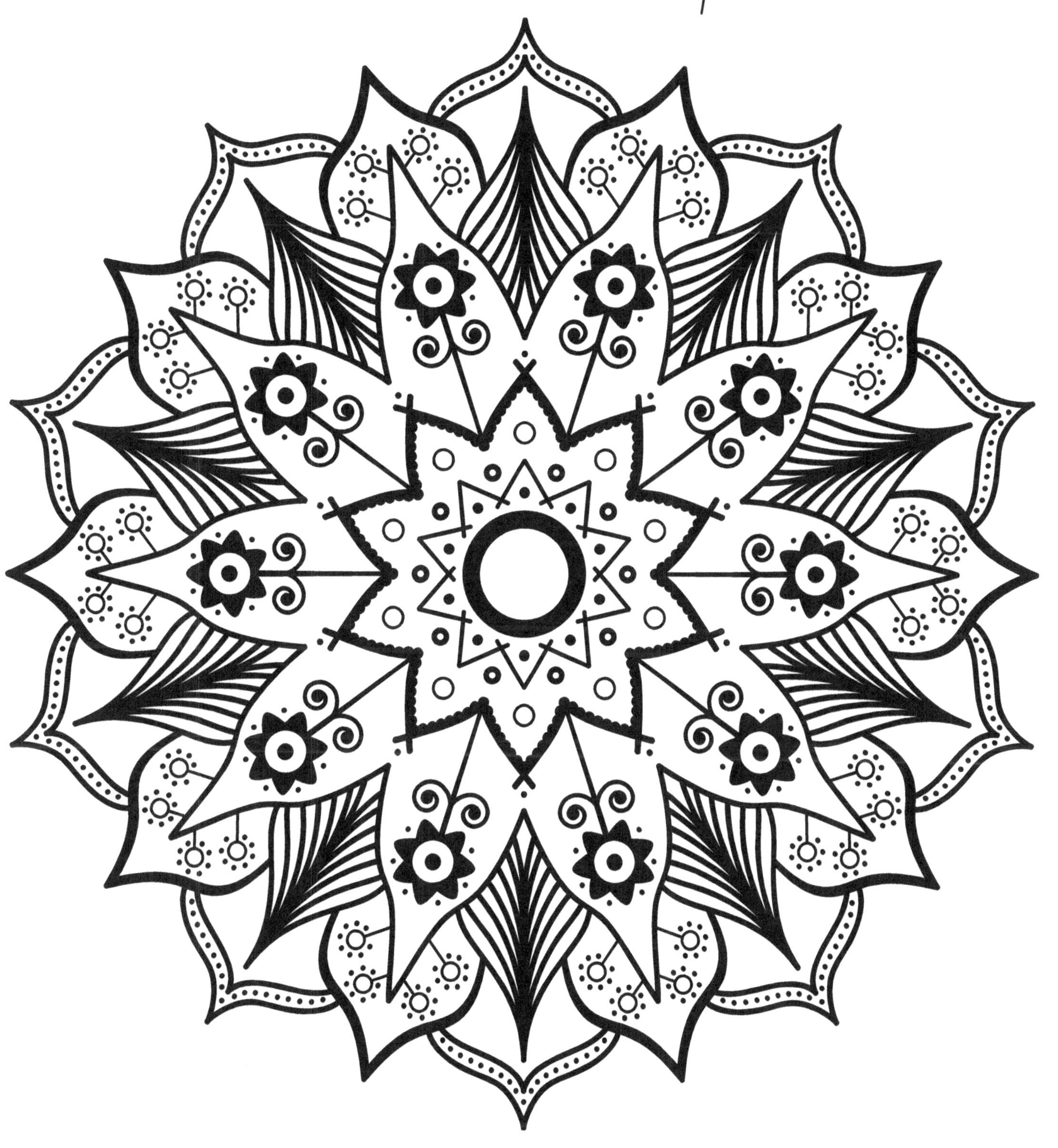

I am capable of overcoming any
challenge that comes my way.

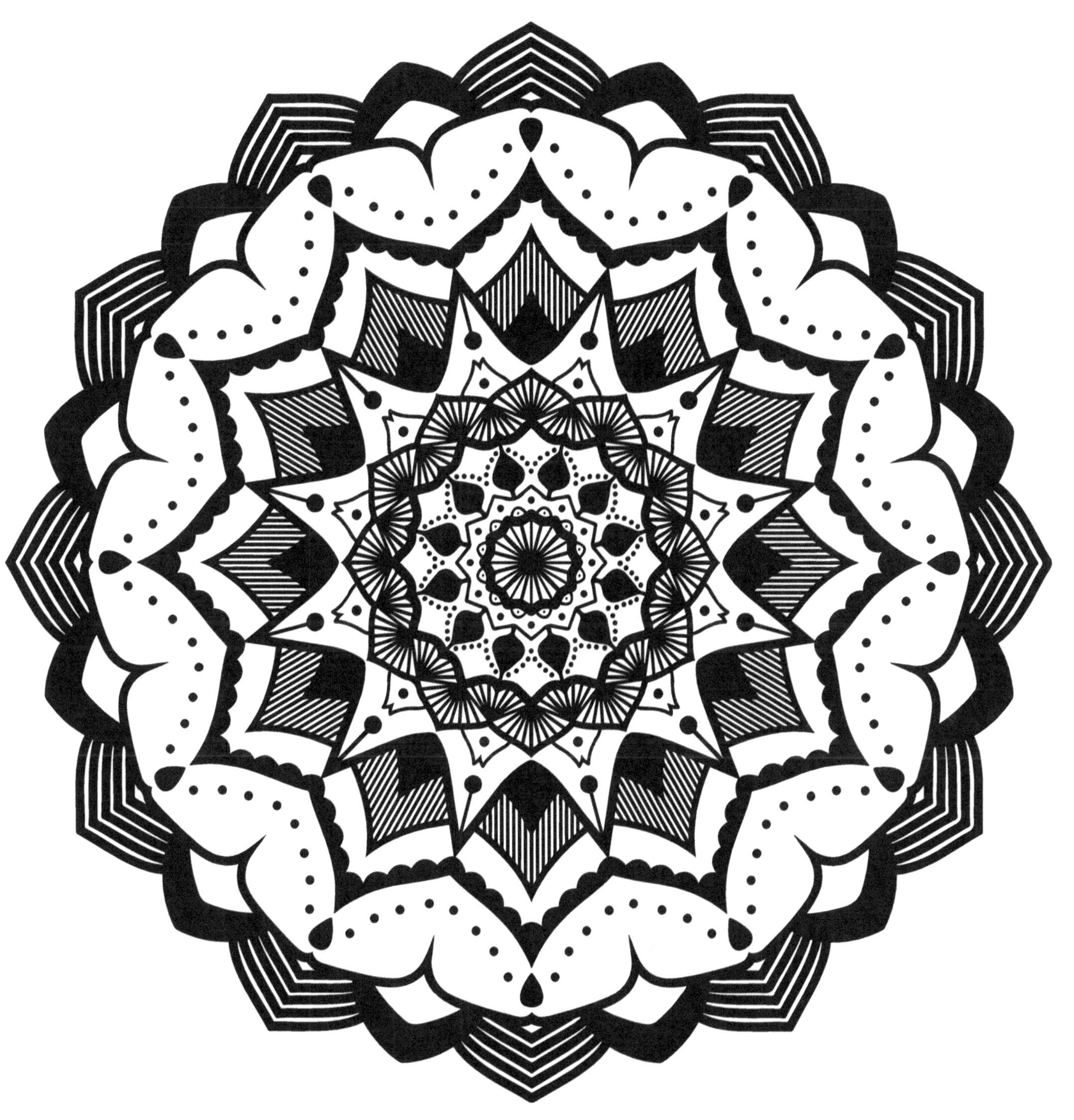

I trust in my ability to create
positive change in my life.

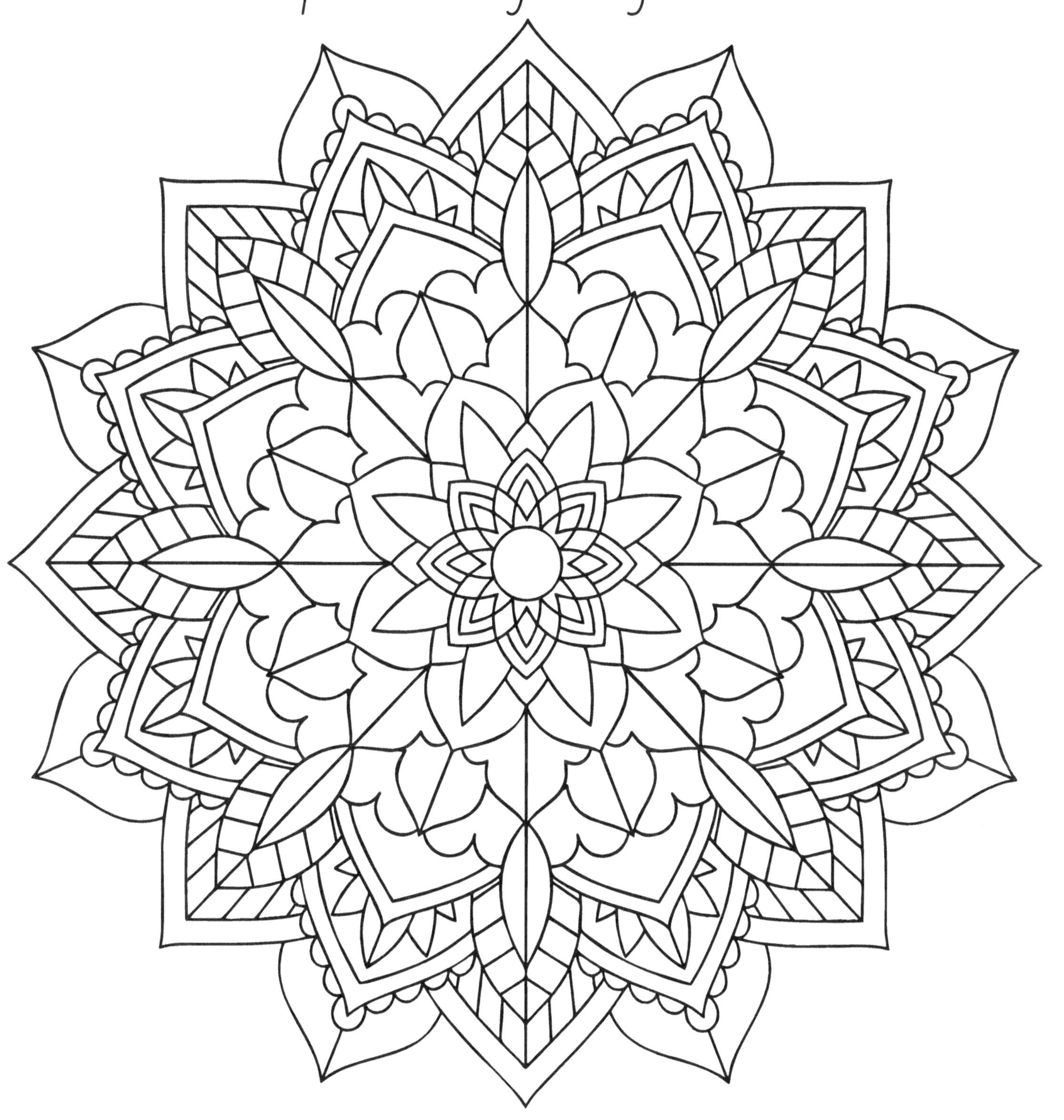

I am resilient, and I bounce
back from setbacks with strength.

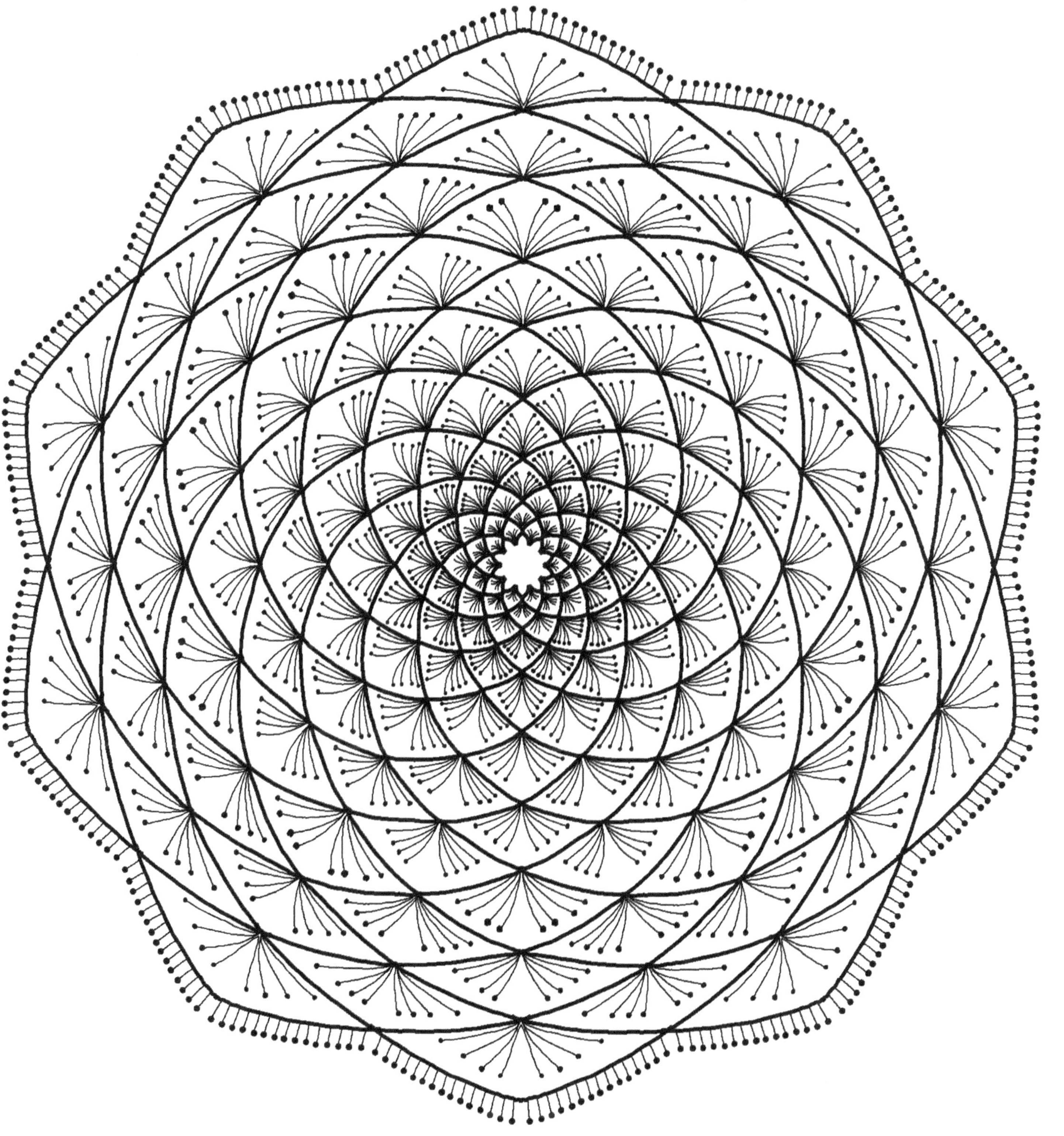

My potential is limitless,
and I am constantly evolving.

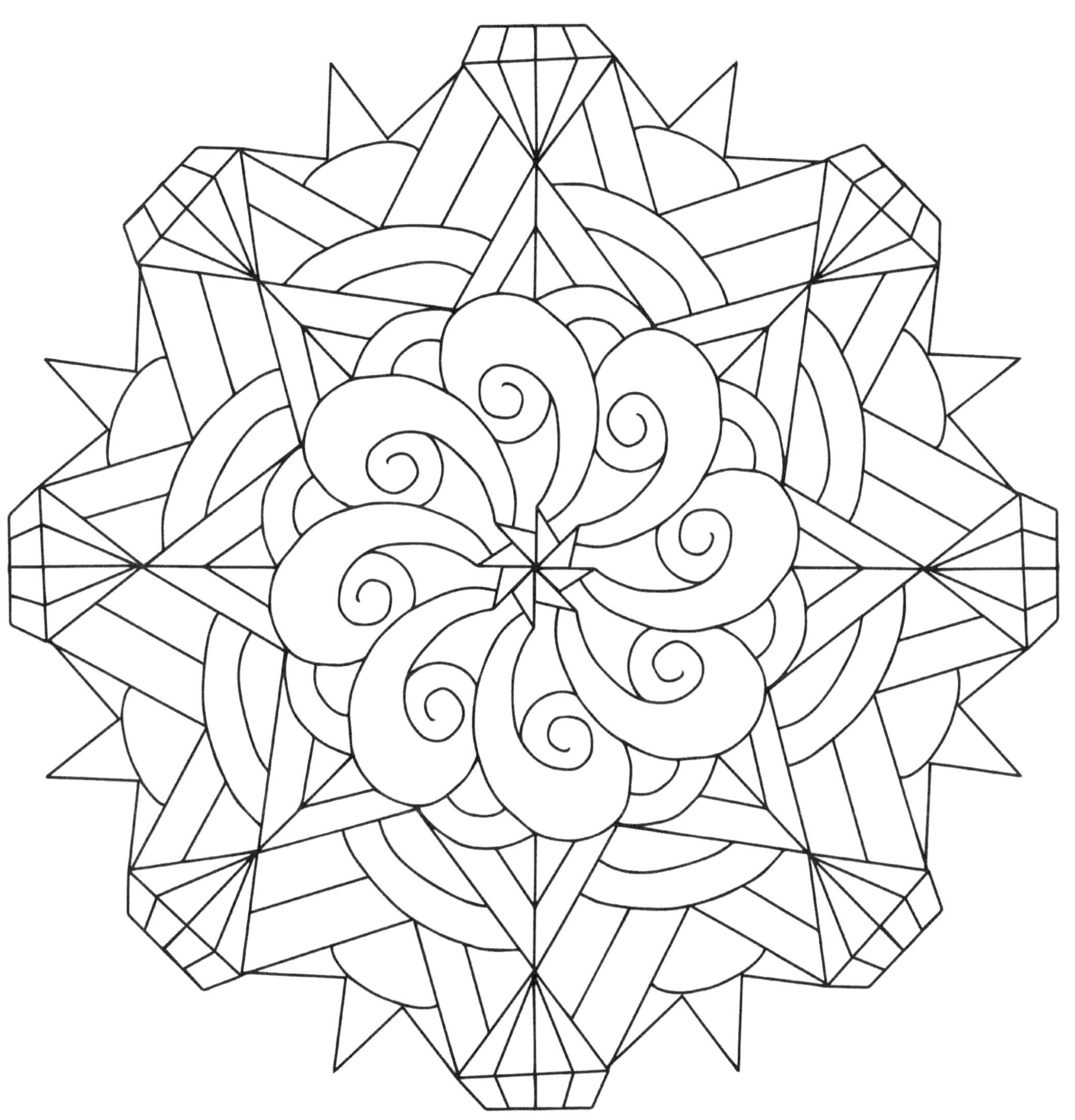

Every day, I am becoming
a better version of myself.

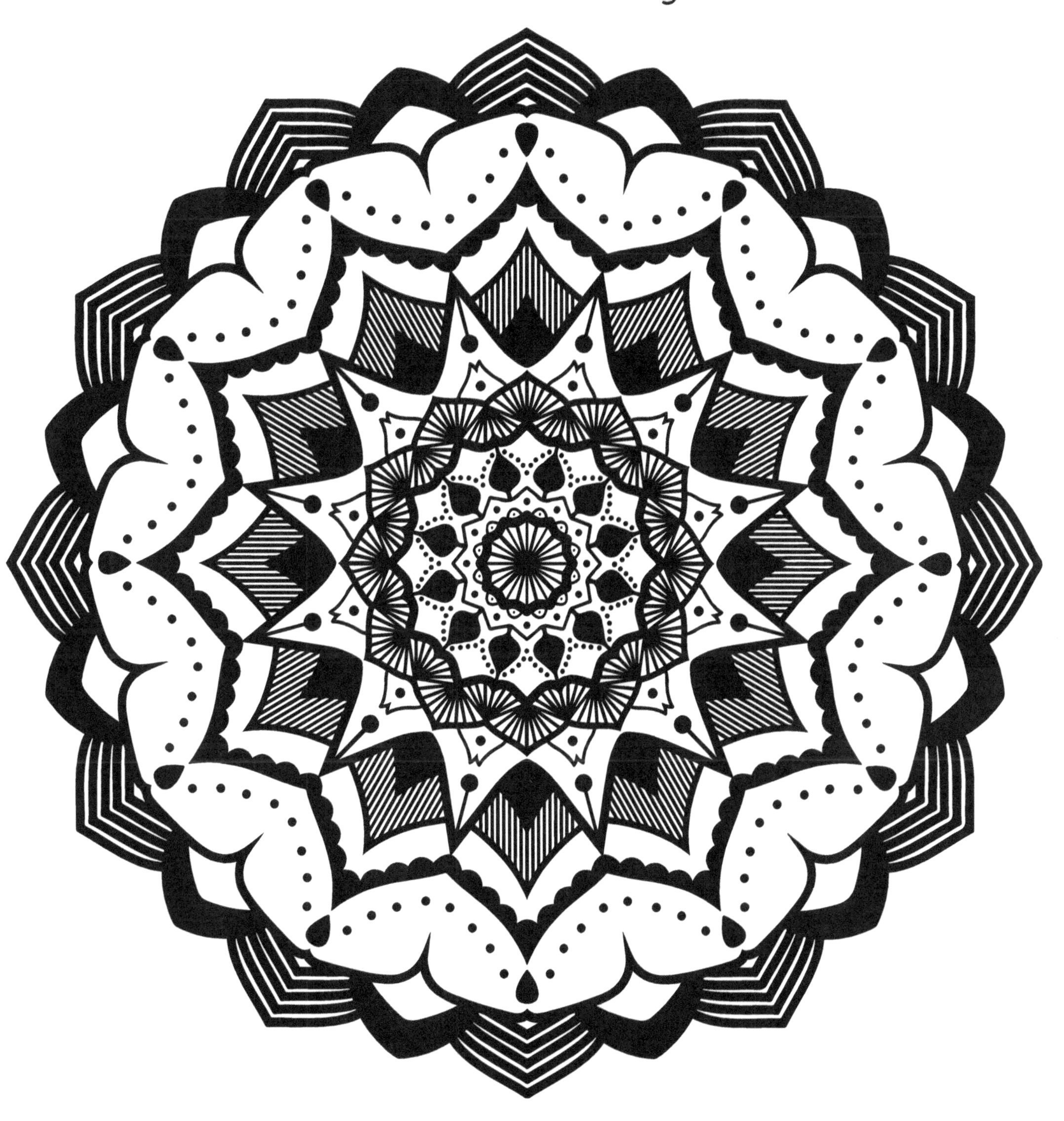

I am worthy of success,
happiness, and fulfillment.

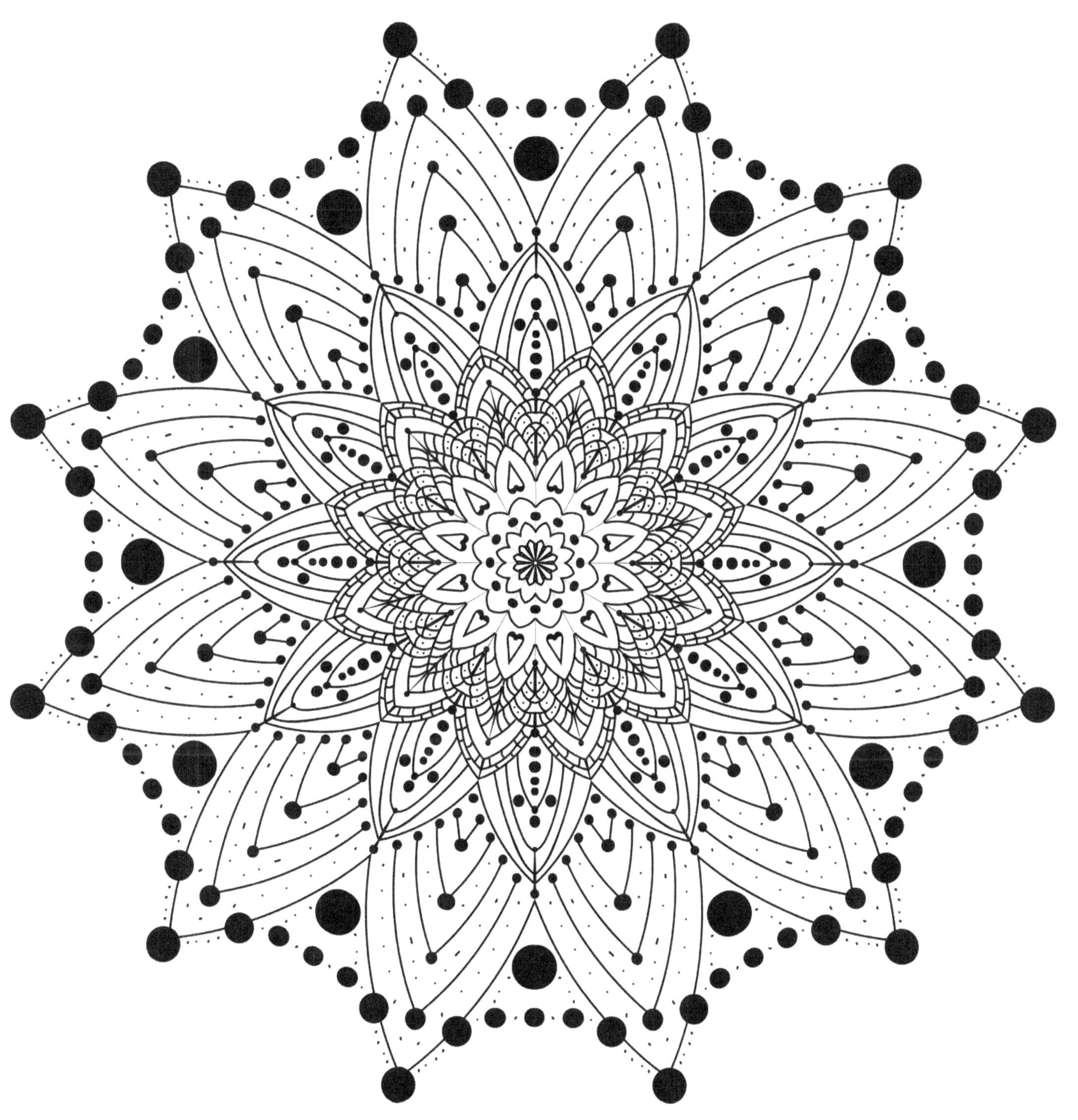

I embrace challenges as opportunities
for growth and learning.

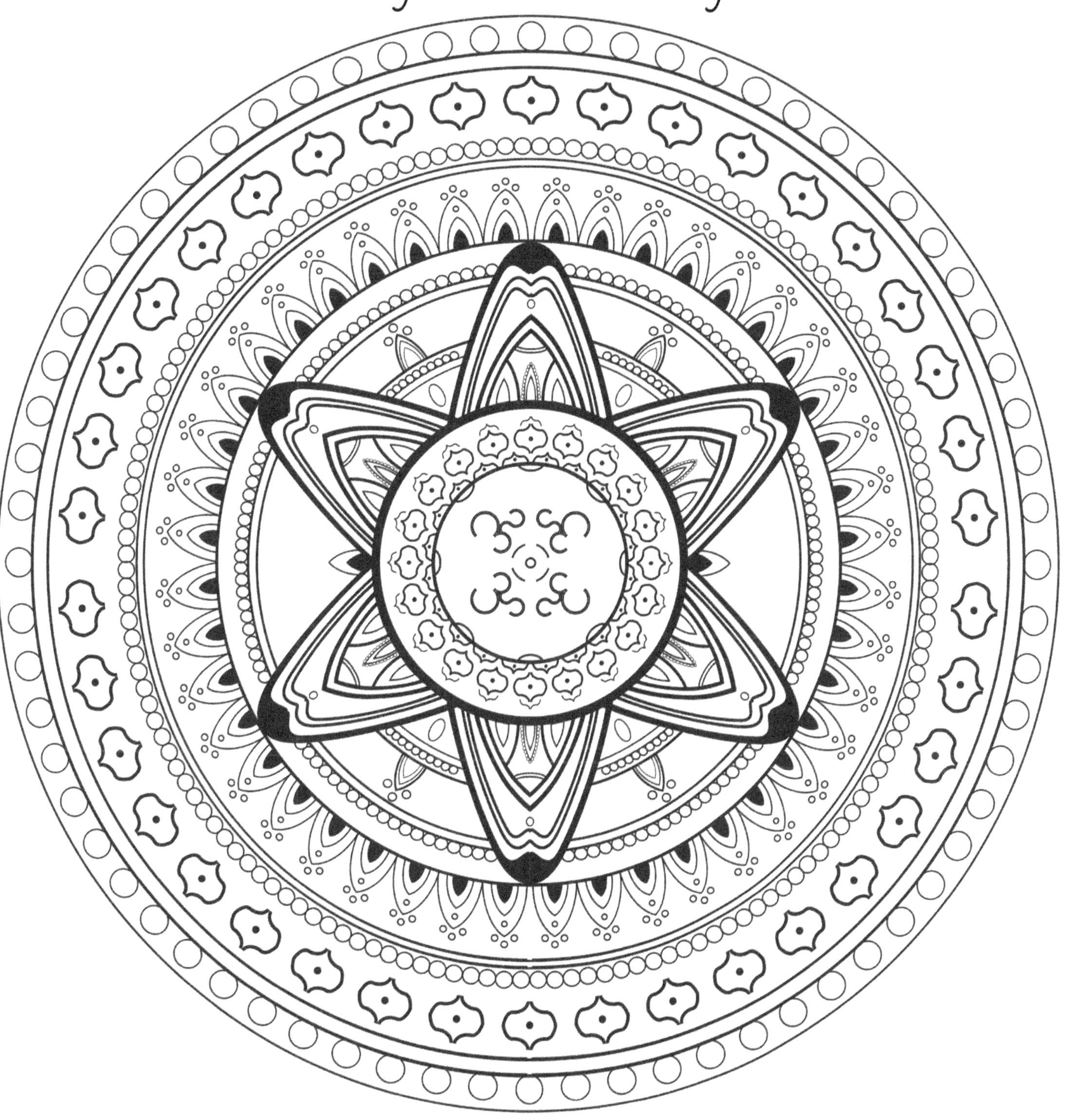

I radiate confidence, self-respect,
and inner harmony.

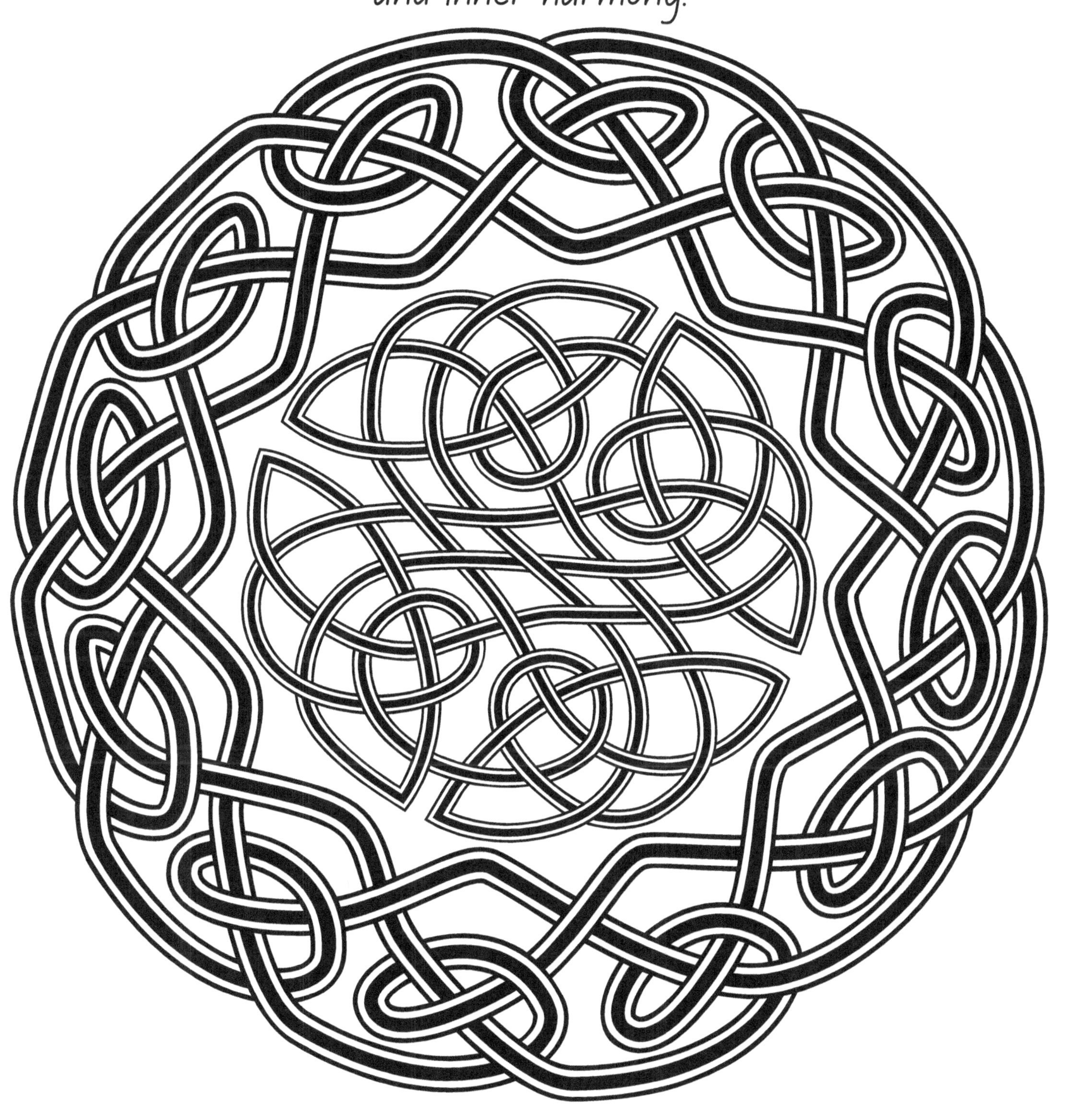

My mind is filled with positive
and empowering thoughts.

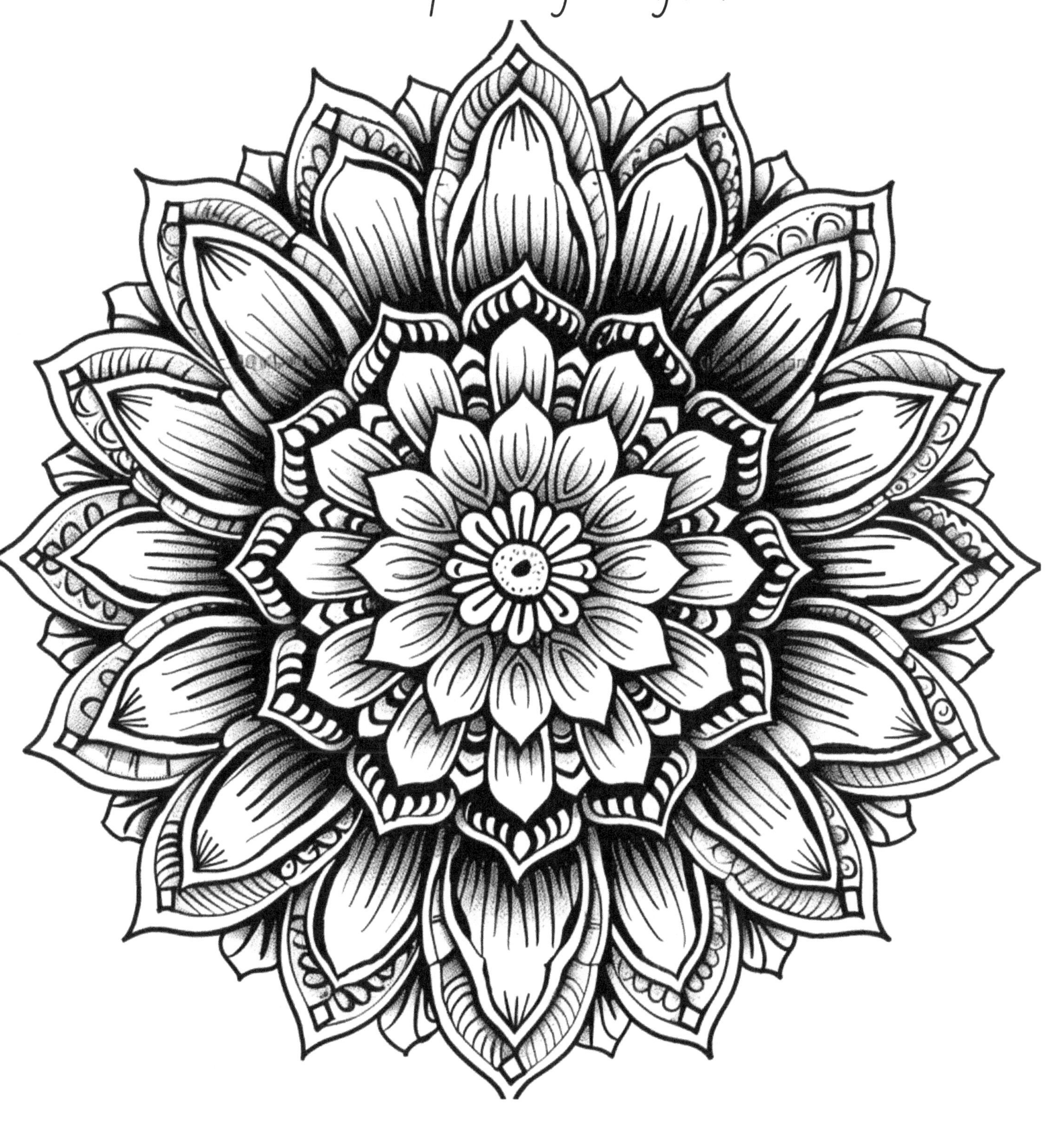

I am the architect of my destiny,
and I am building a life I love.

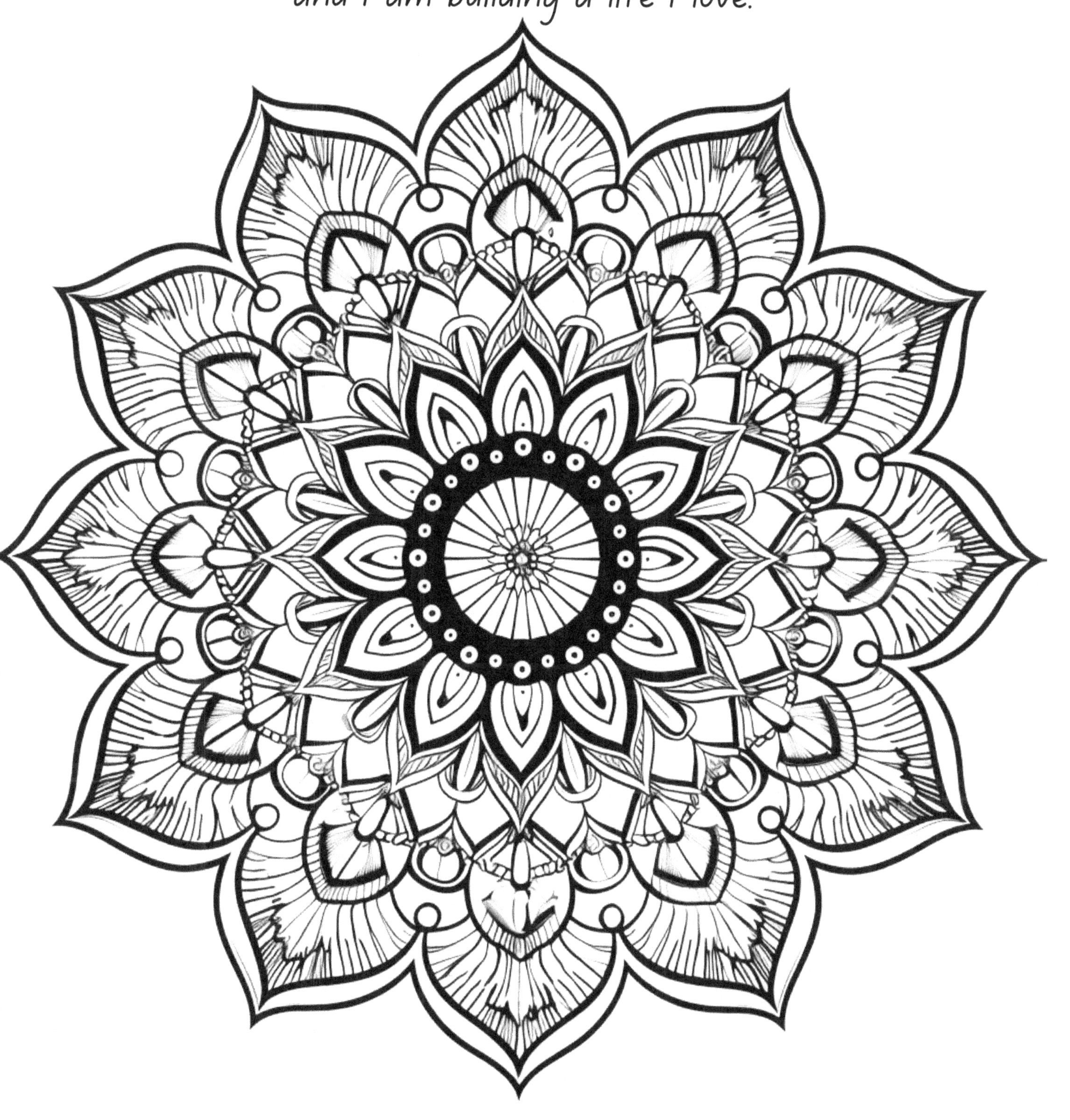

I am a magnet for success, and
I attract abundance effortlessly.

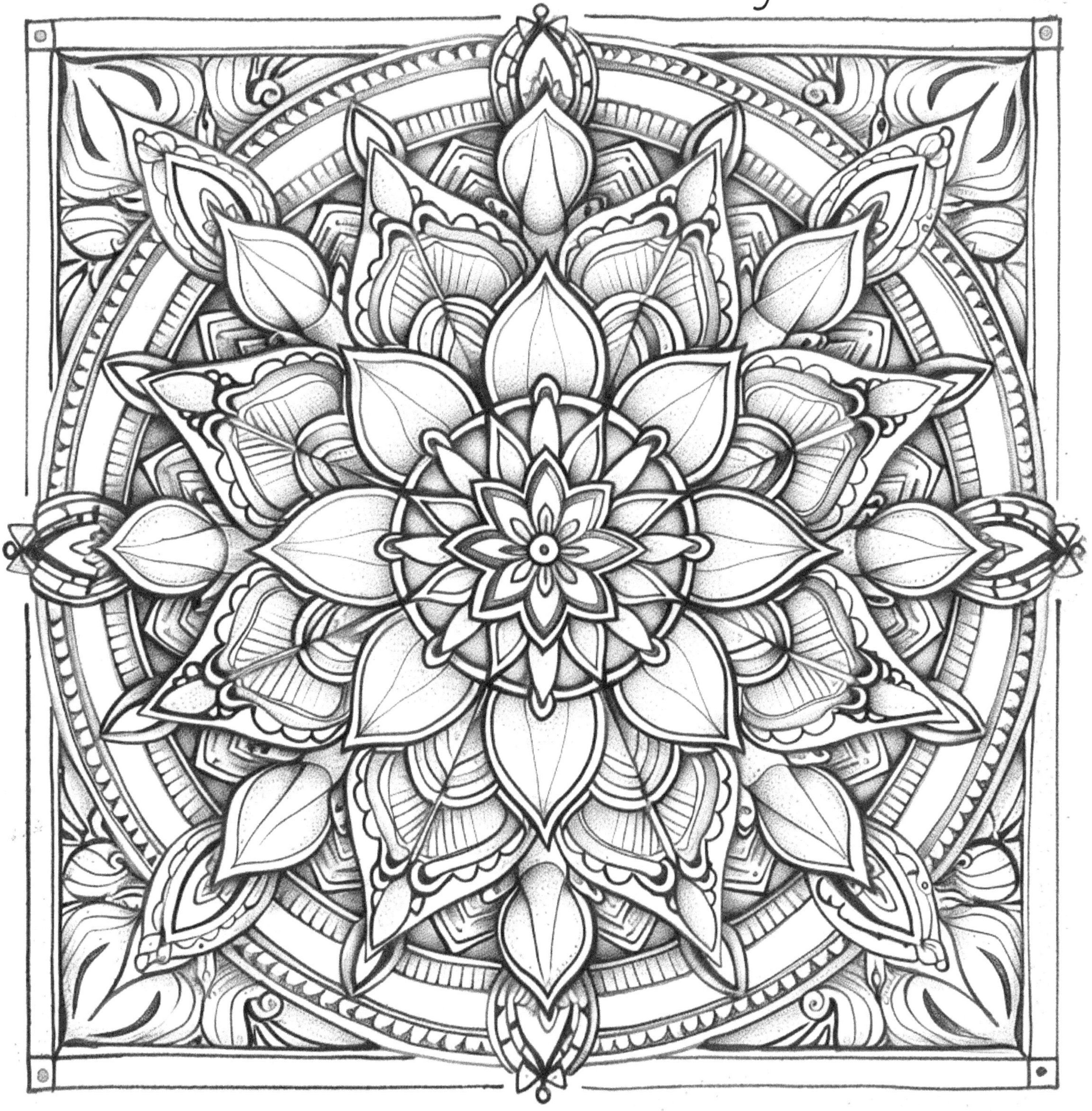

I choose joy, love, and
positivity in every situation.

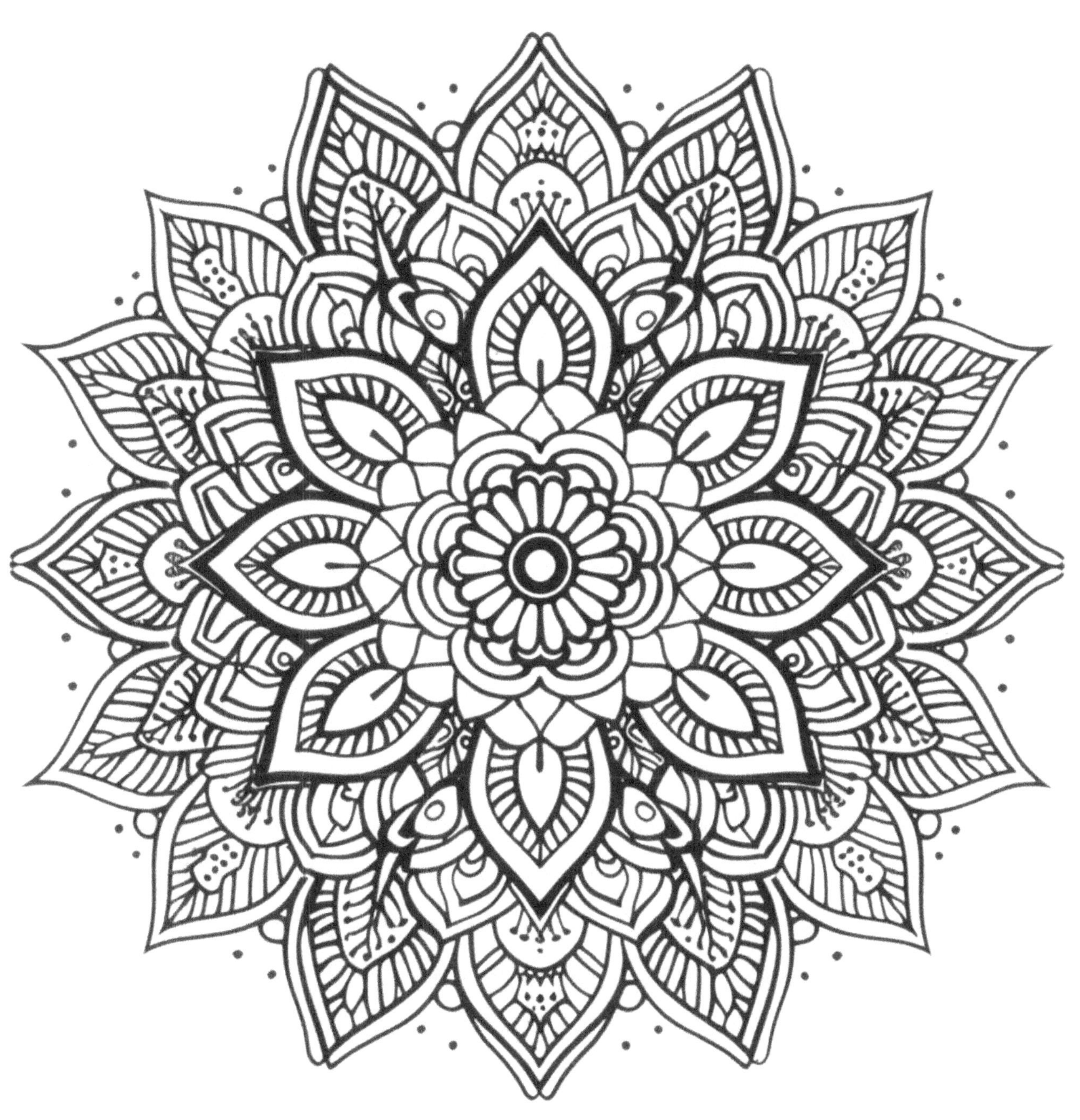

My life is a reflection of the
love and positivity I put into it.

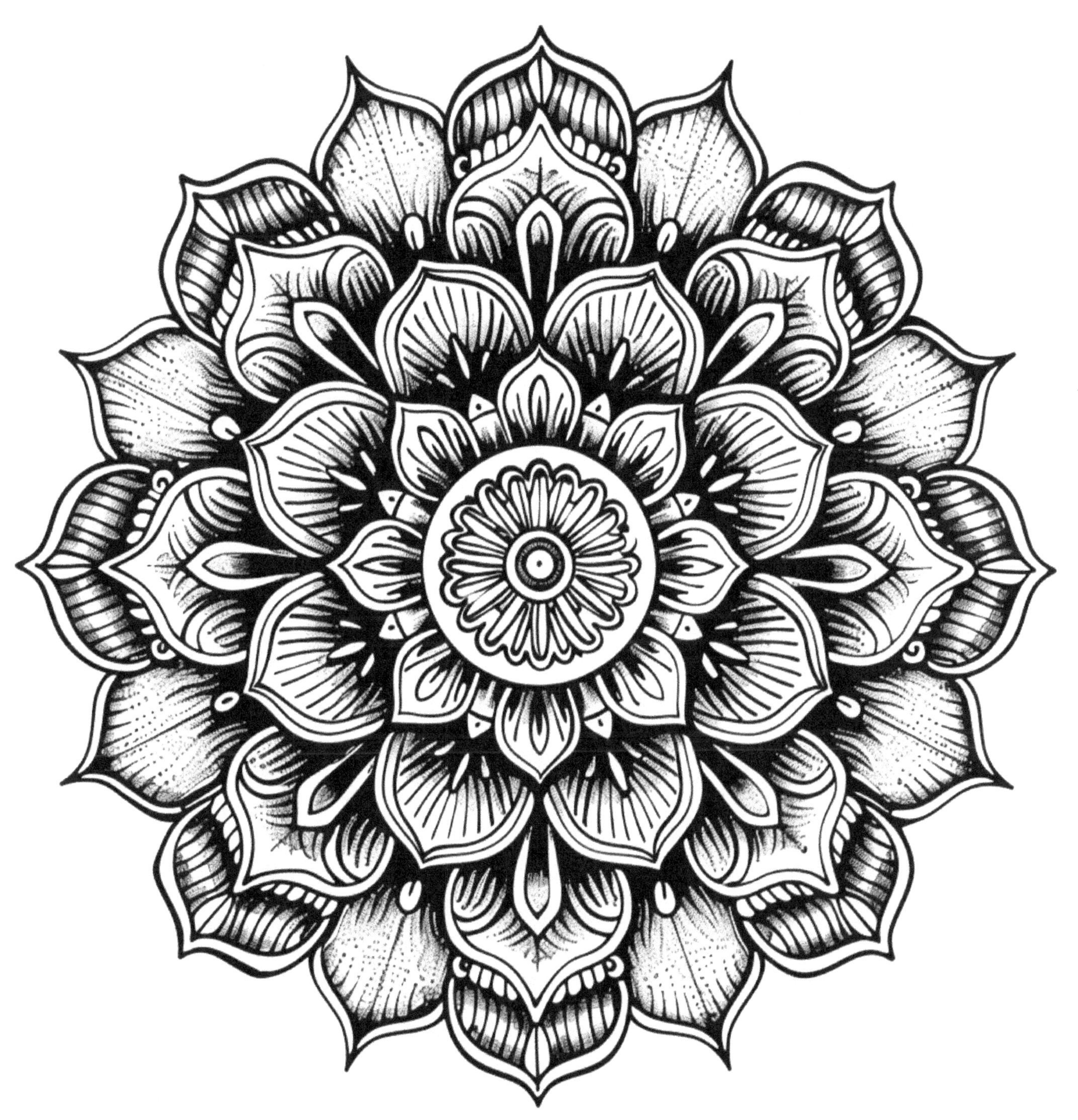

I am surrounded by opportunities,
and I seize them with gratitude.

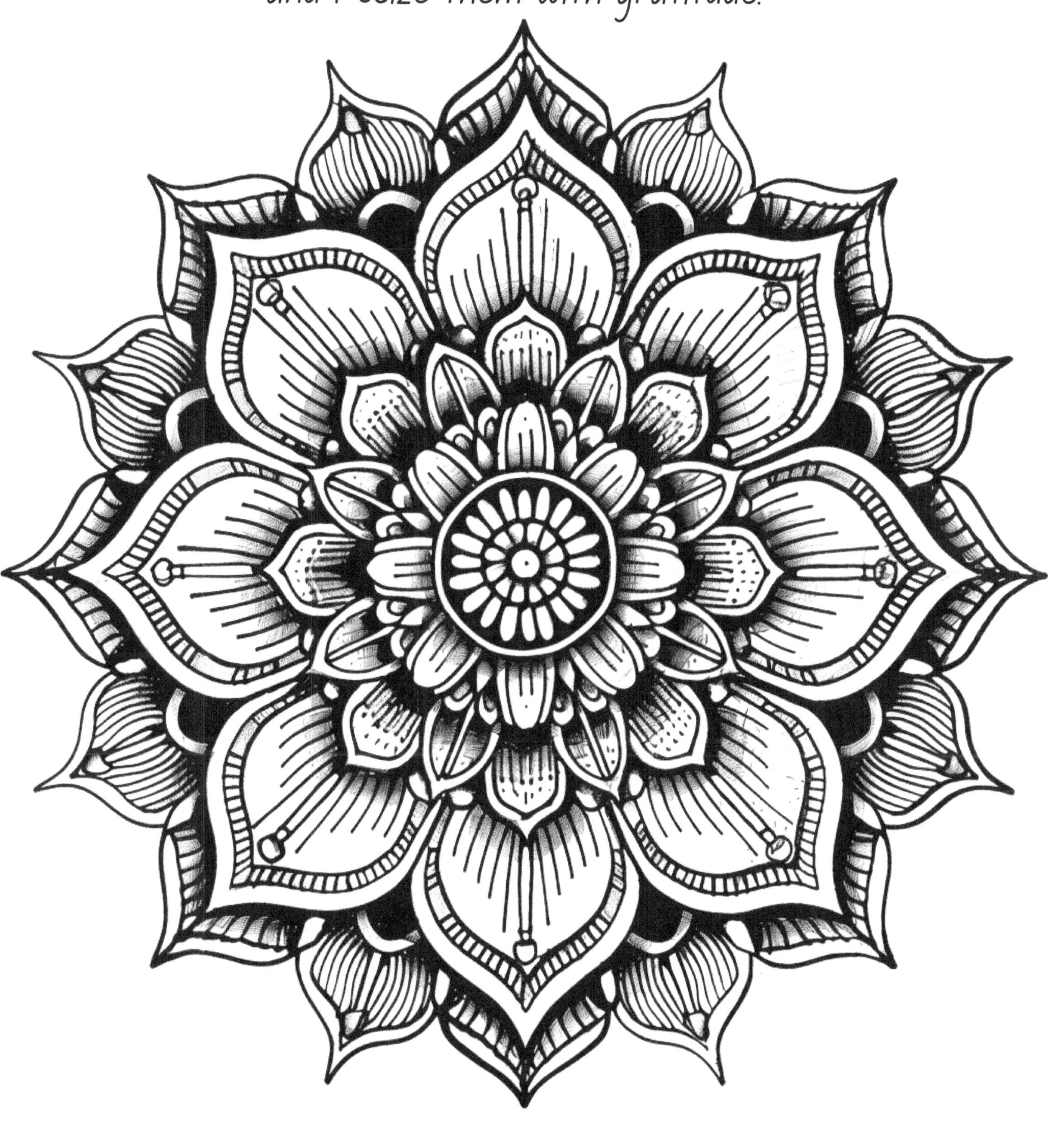

I trust in my ability to make
the right decisions for my life.

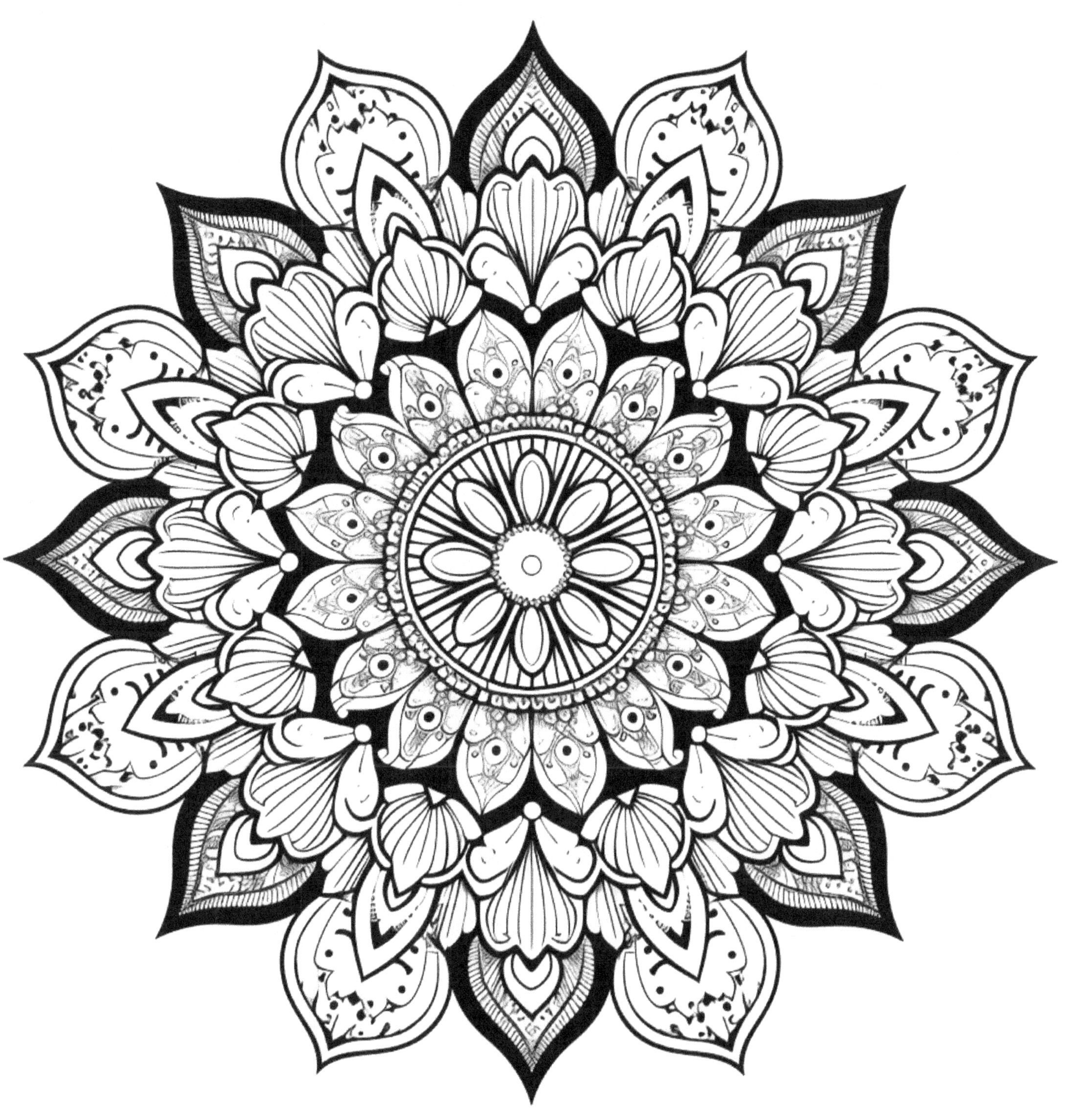

I am a beacon of light, inspiring
others with my positivity.

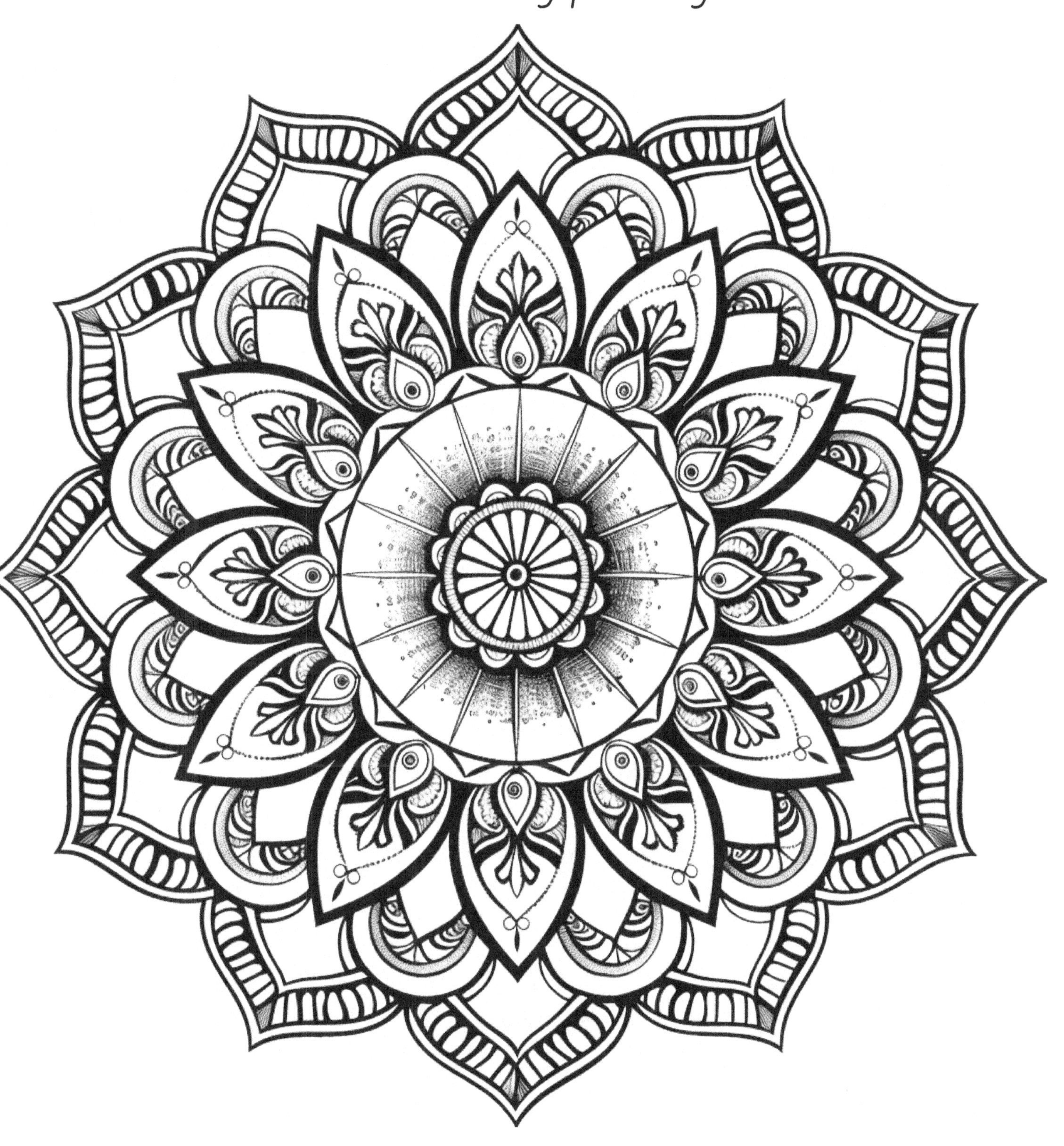

Metamorphosis of the Soul: Unveiling the Spiritual Symbolism of the Butterfly

The spiritual meaning of a butterfly varies across different cultures and belief systems, but it is often associated with transformation, change, and renewal. The life cycle of a butterfly, from egg to caterpillar to chrysalis and finally to a beautiful winged creature, is seen as a metaphor for personal growth and spiritual evolution.

In many spiritual traditions, the butterfly is considered a symbol of the soul and its journey. The process of metamorphosis represents the soul's journey through different stages of life, with the ultimate transformation symbolizing spiritual rebirth and transcendence. The fleeting and delicate nature of a butterfly's existence also underscores the idea of the impermanence of life and the transient nature of material existence.

In some cultures, the butterfly is associated with resurrection and immortality. The ability of a butterfly to emerge from its cocoon and take flight is seen as a symbol of the soul's ability to transcend physical limitations and achieve a higher state of being.

It's important to note that interpretations of spiritual symbols can vary widely, and personal beliefs play a significant role in how individuals perceive and derive meaning from symbols like the butterfly.

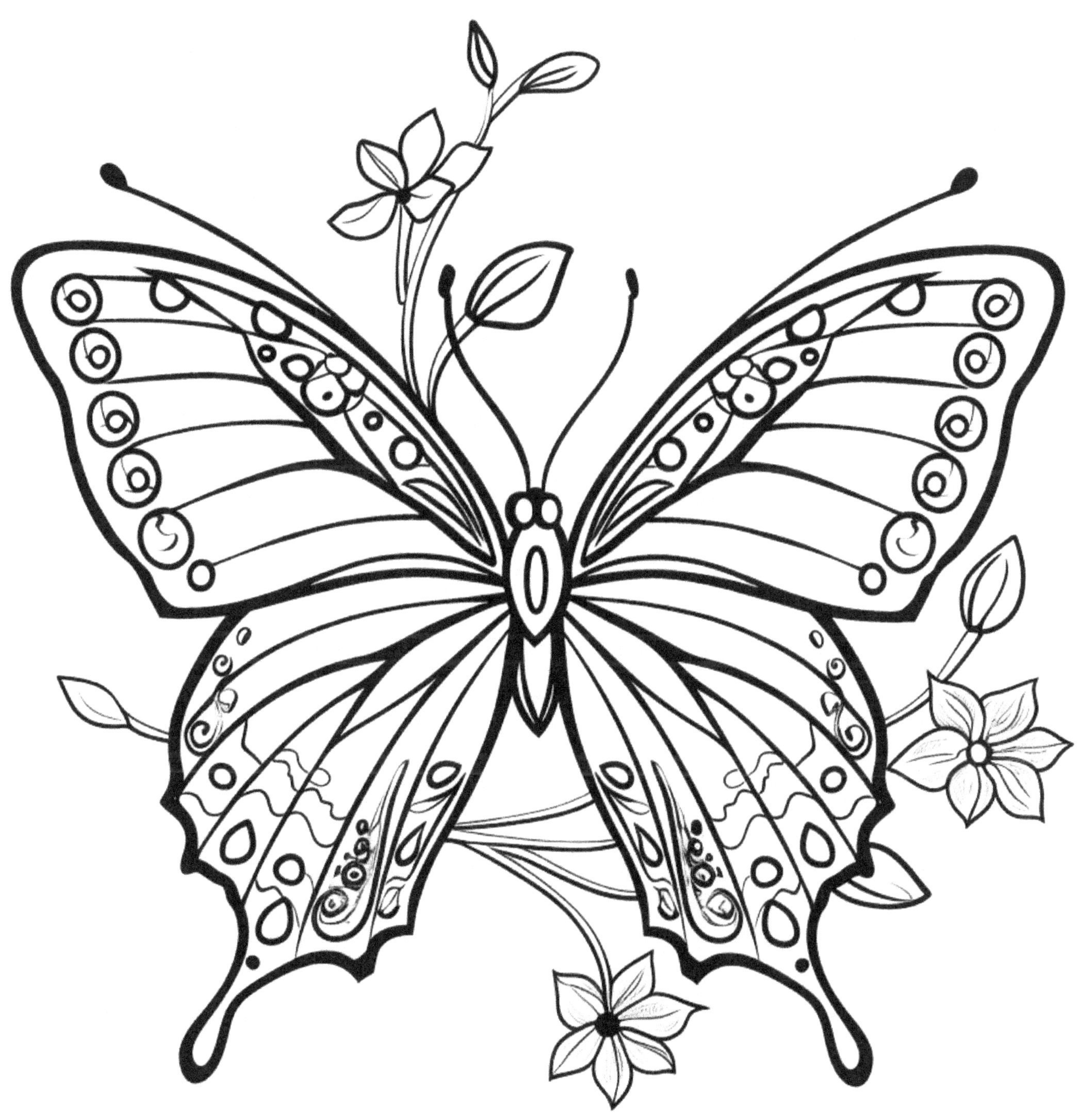

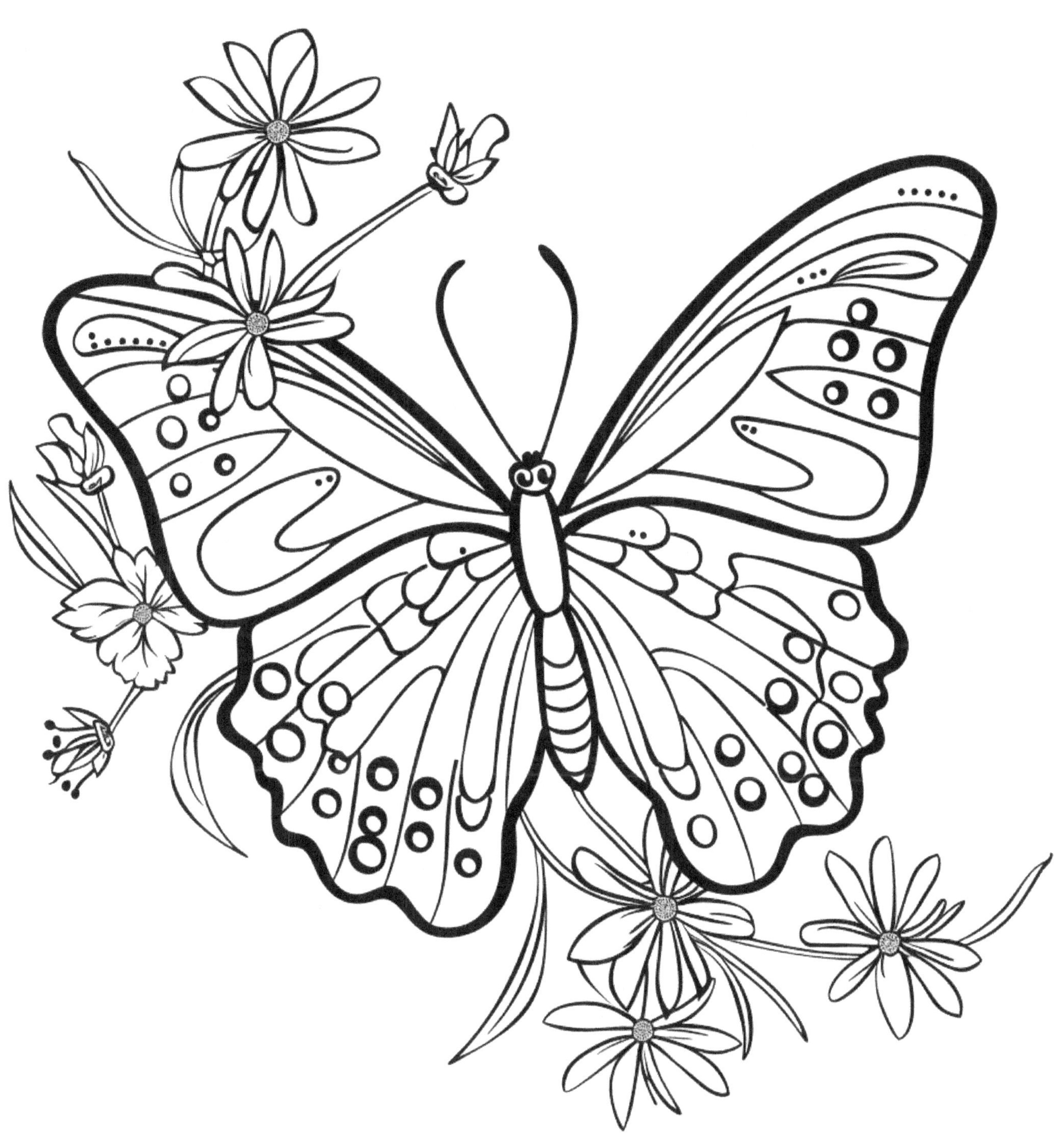

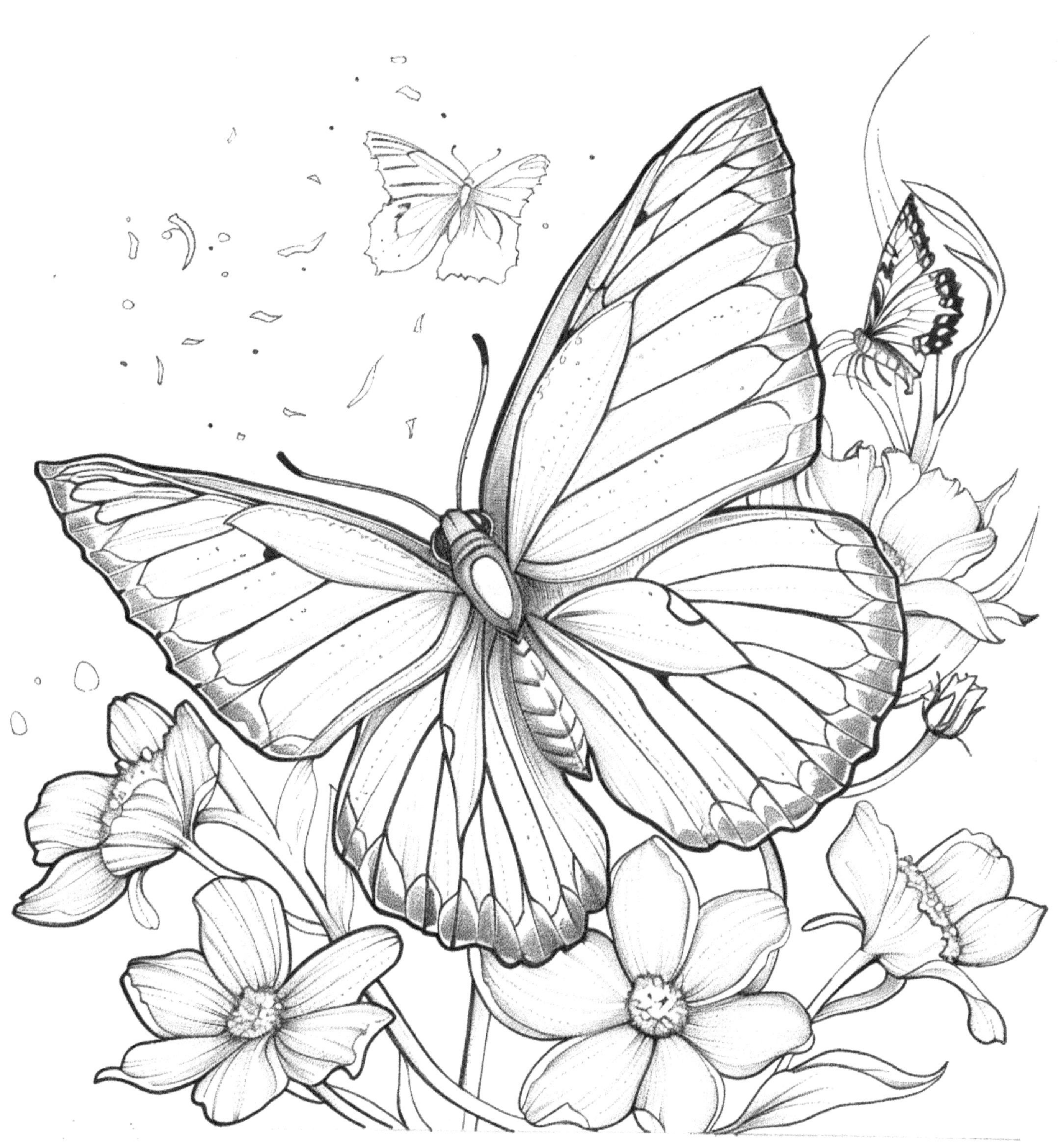

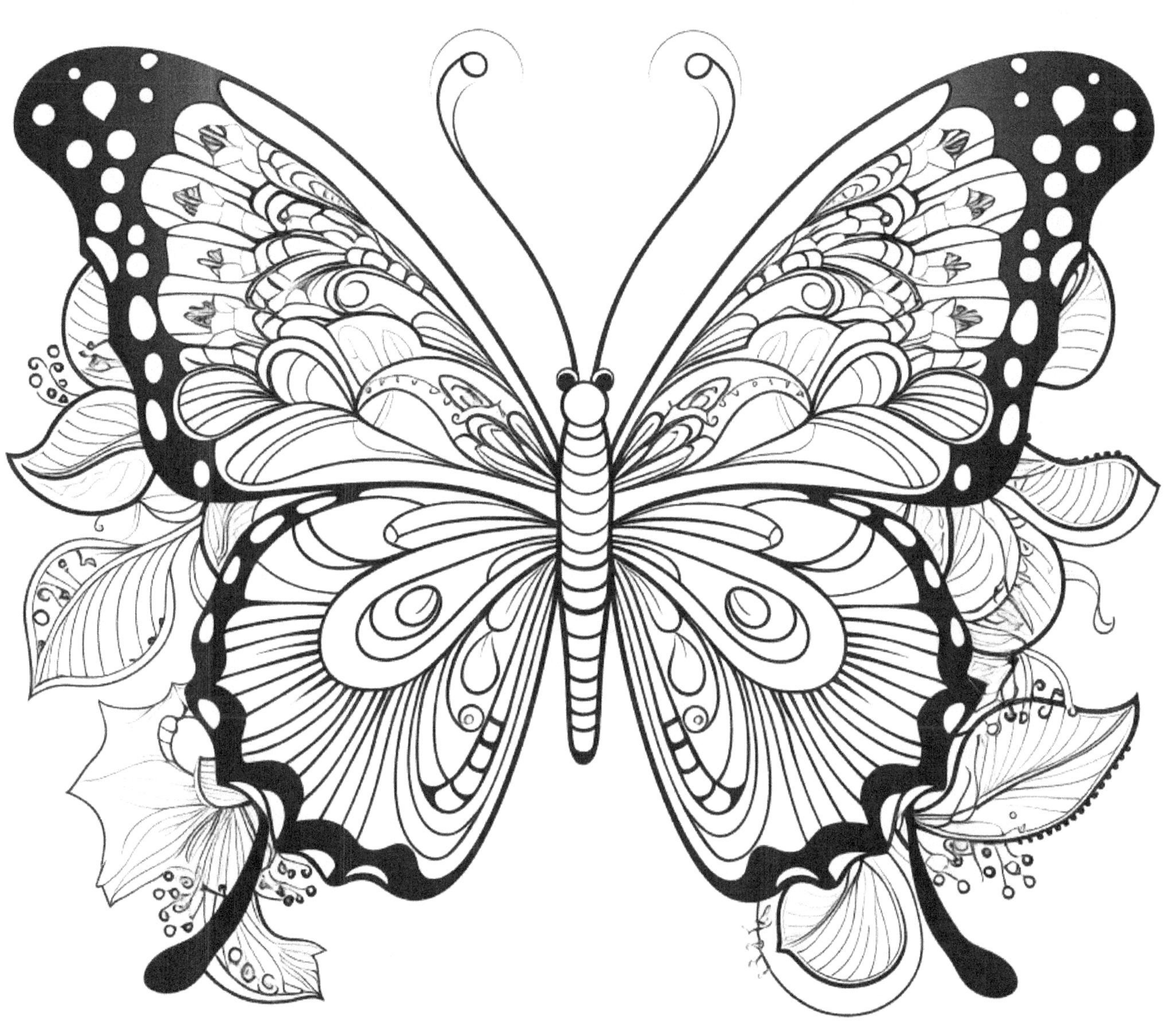

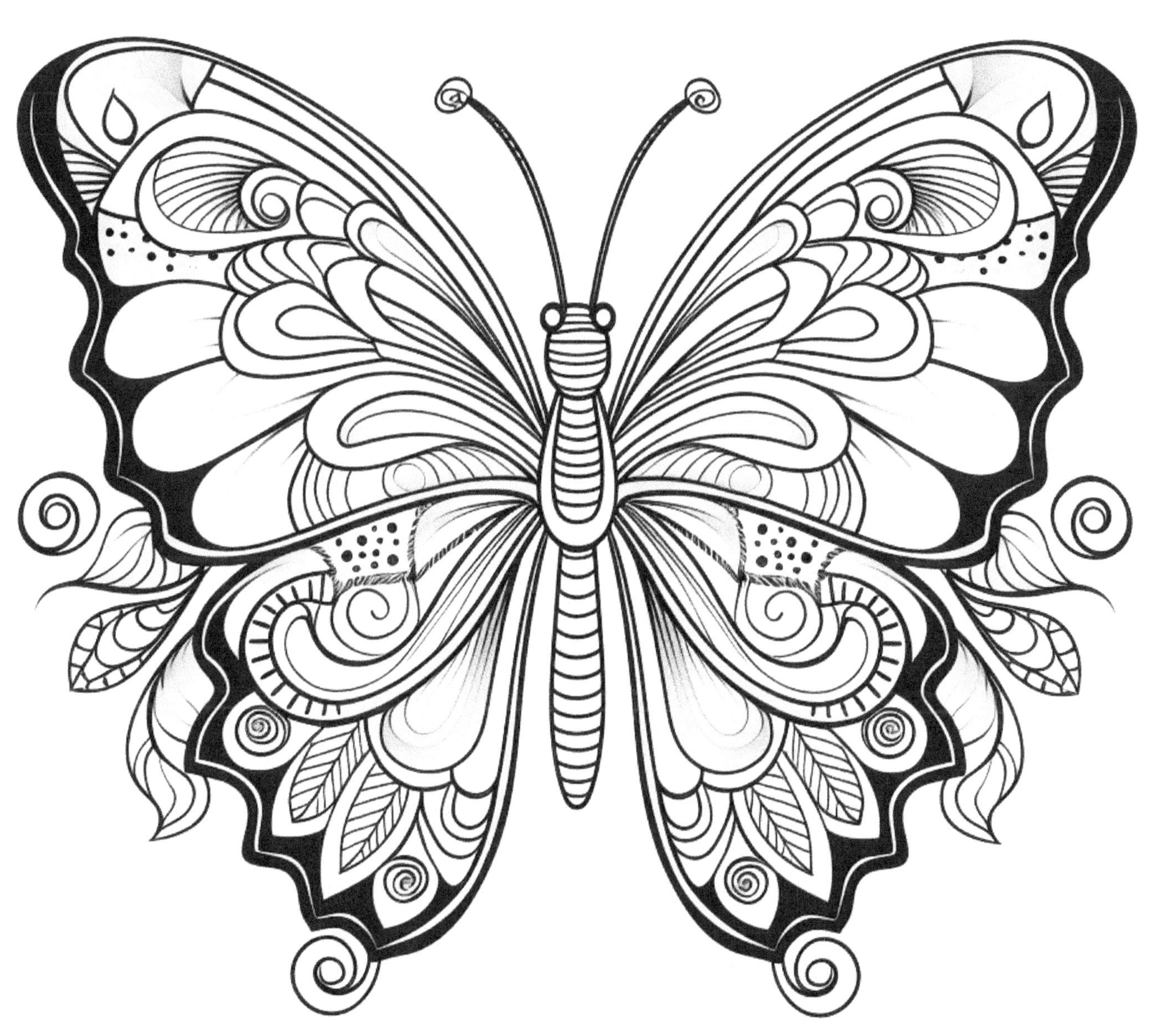

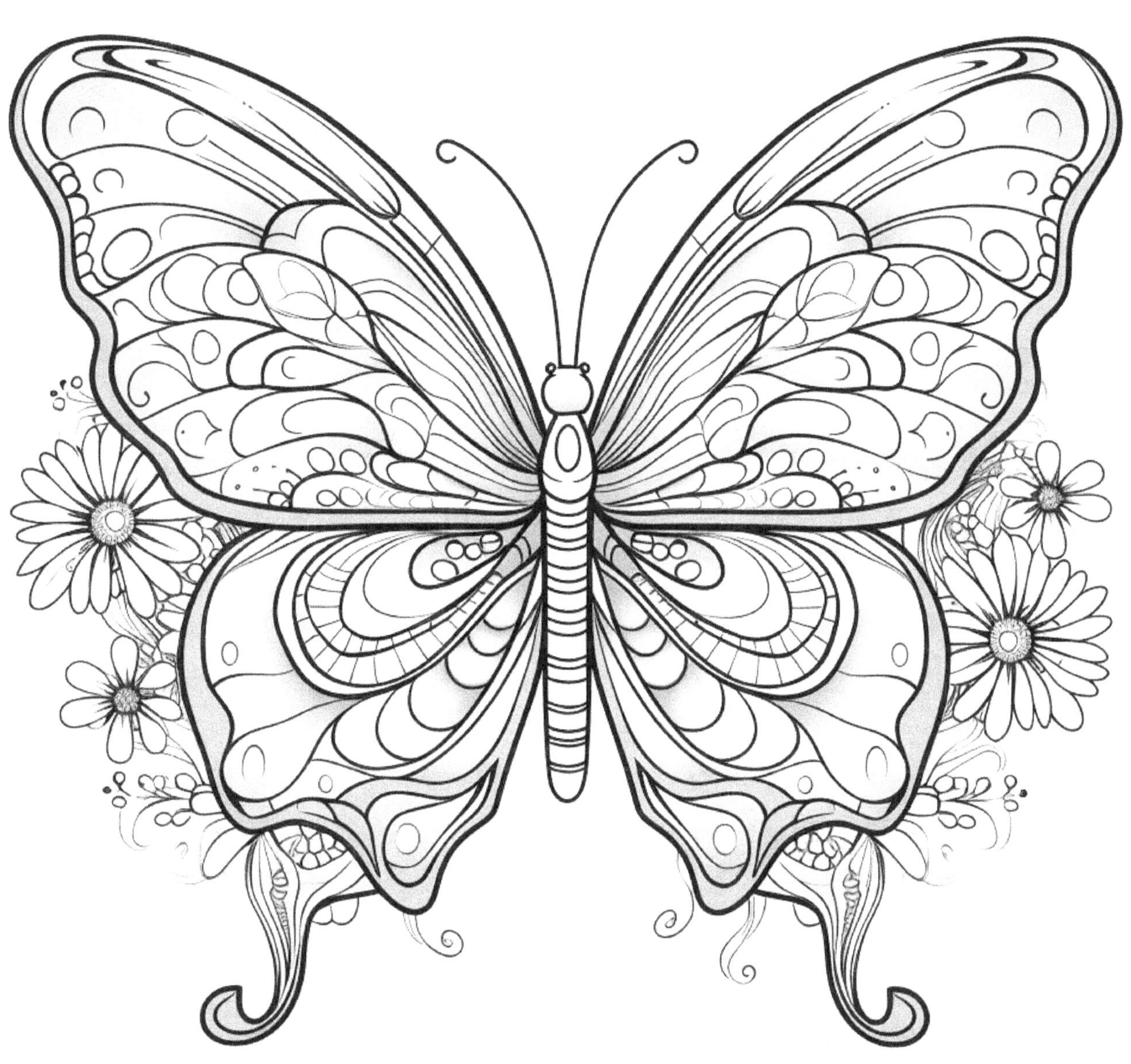

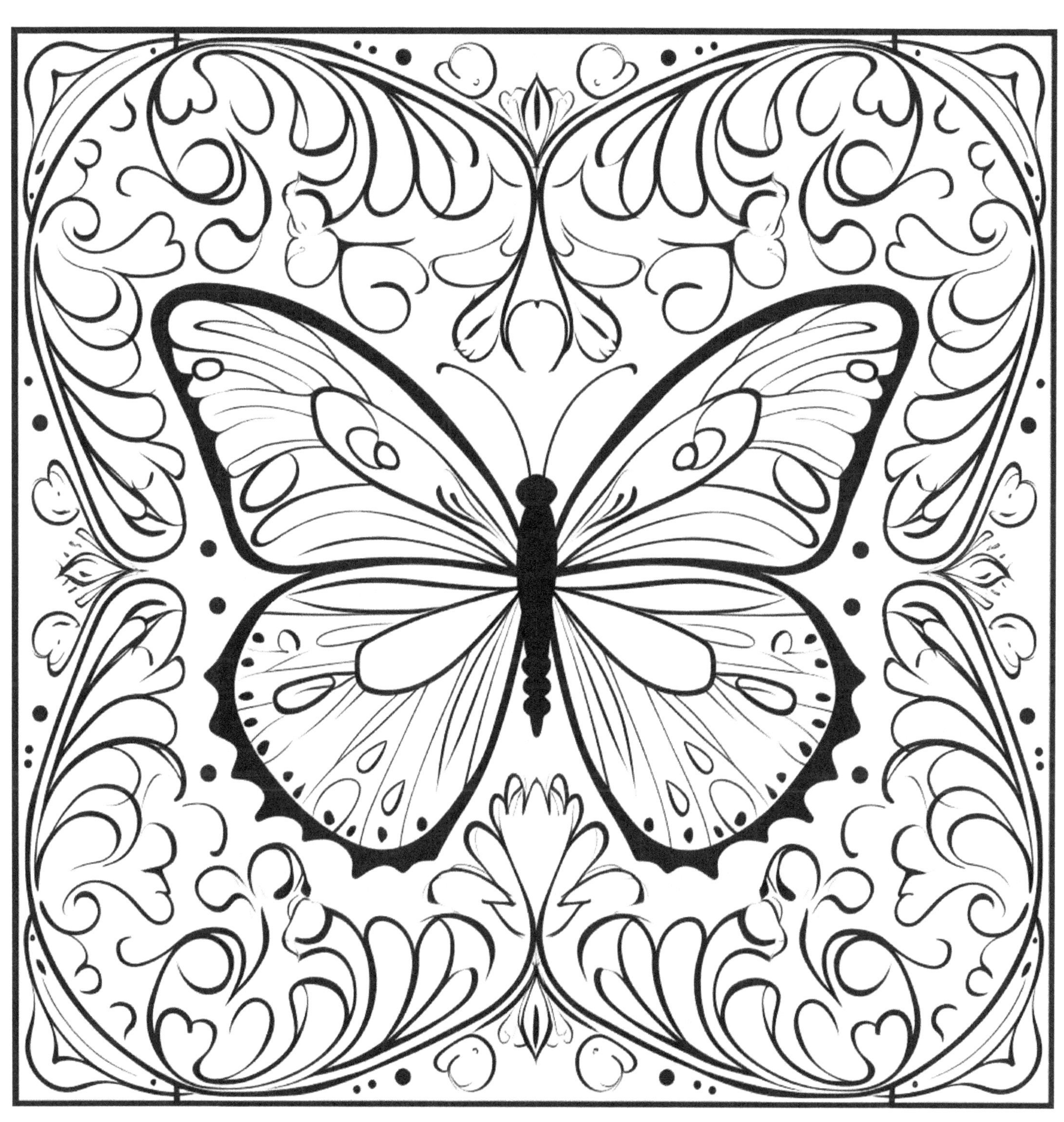

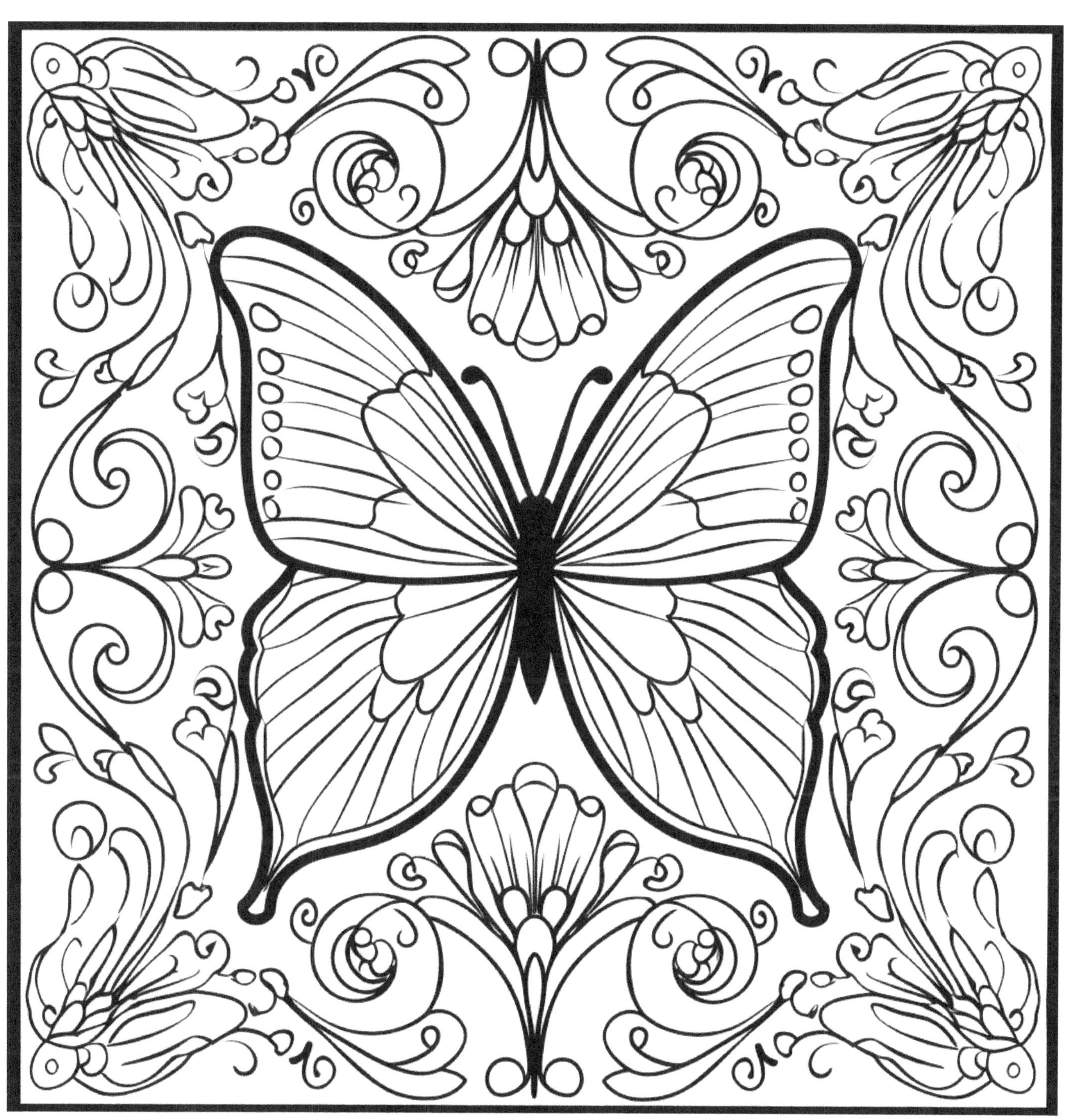

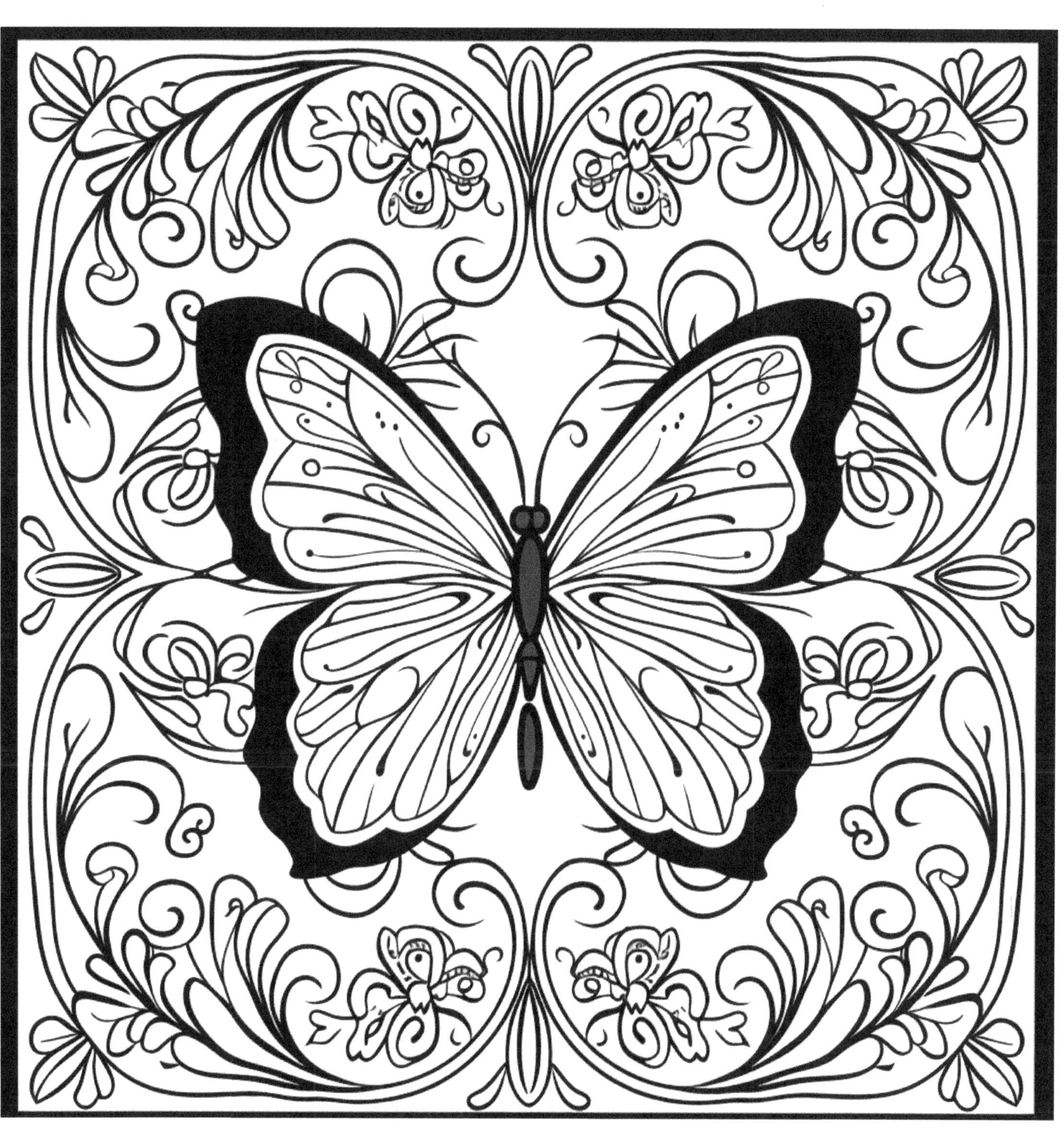

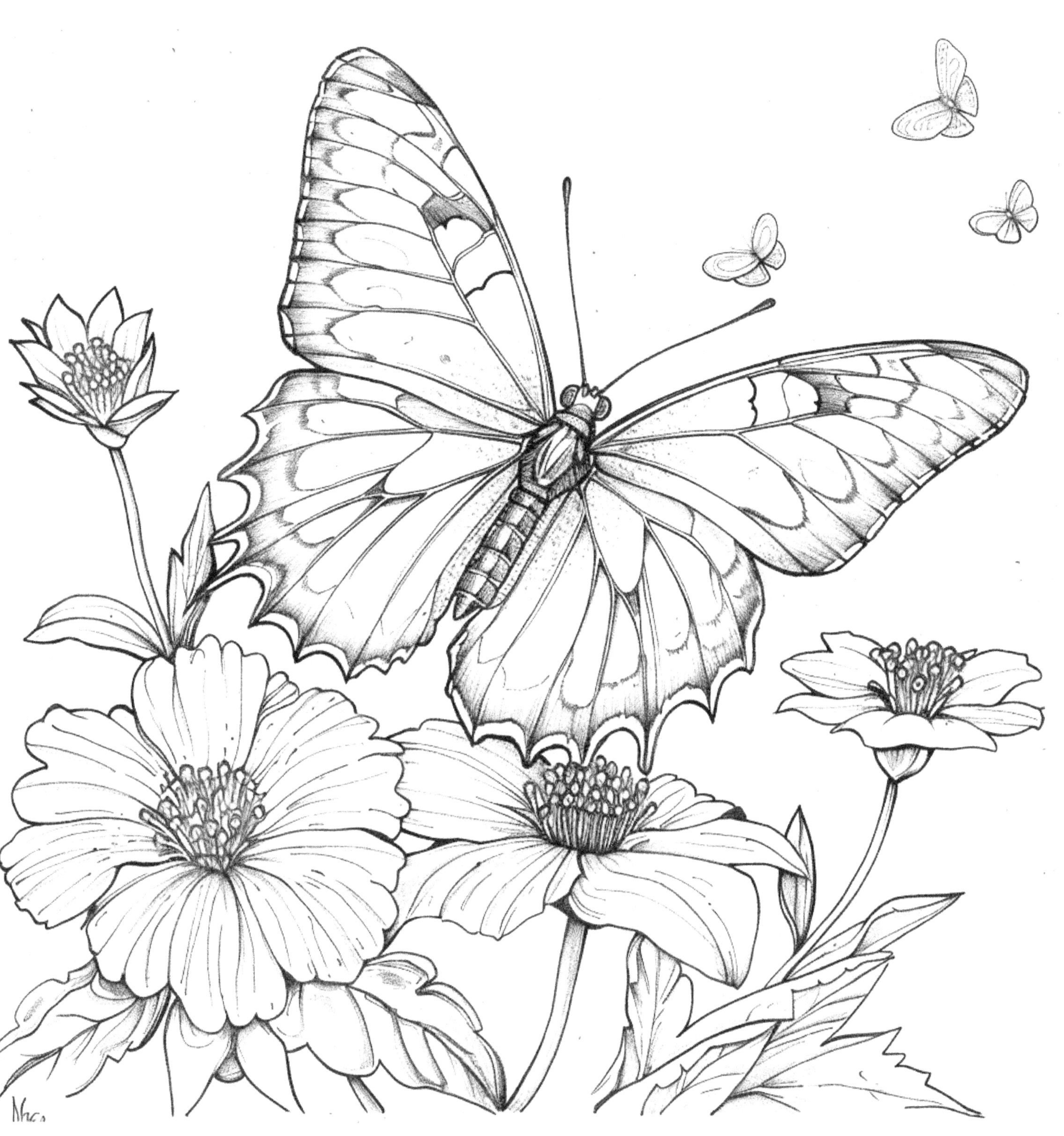

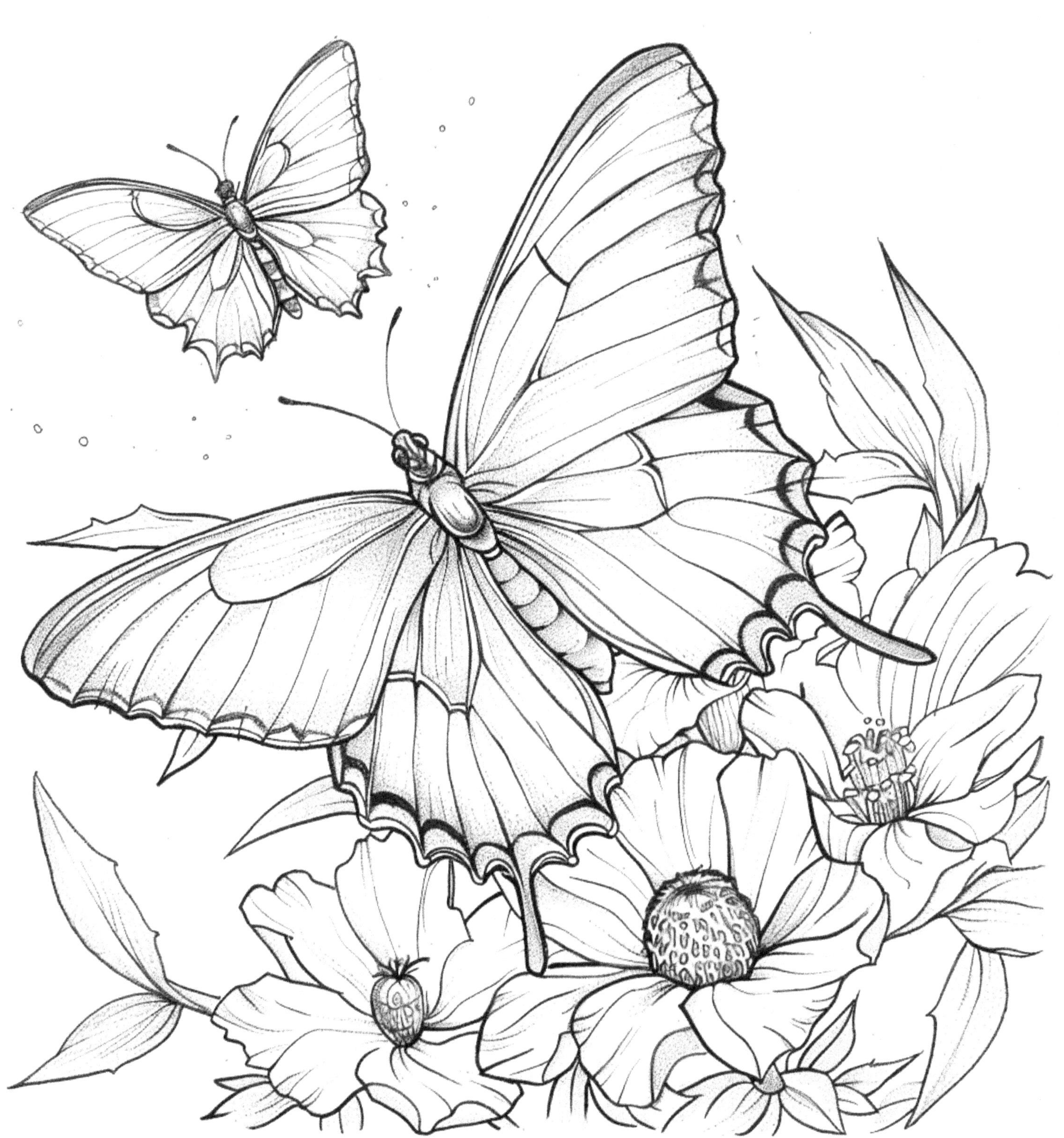

Wisdom, Strength, and Endurance
in Every Elegant Step.

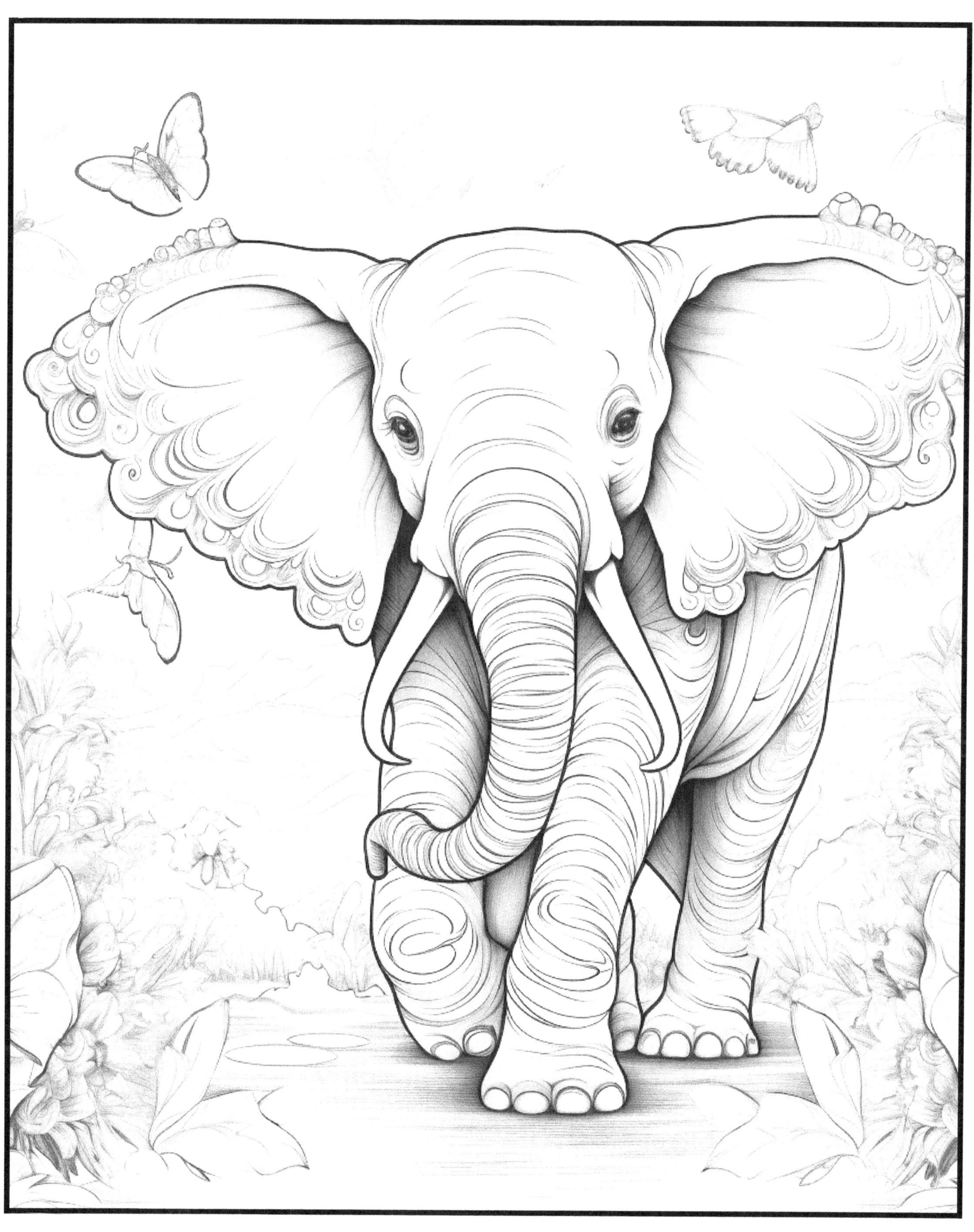

Grace will always grant you peace

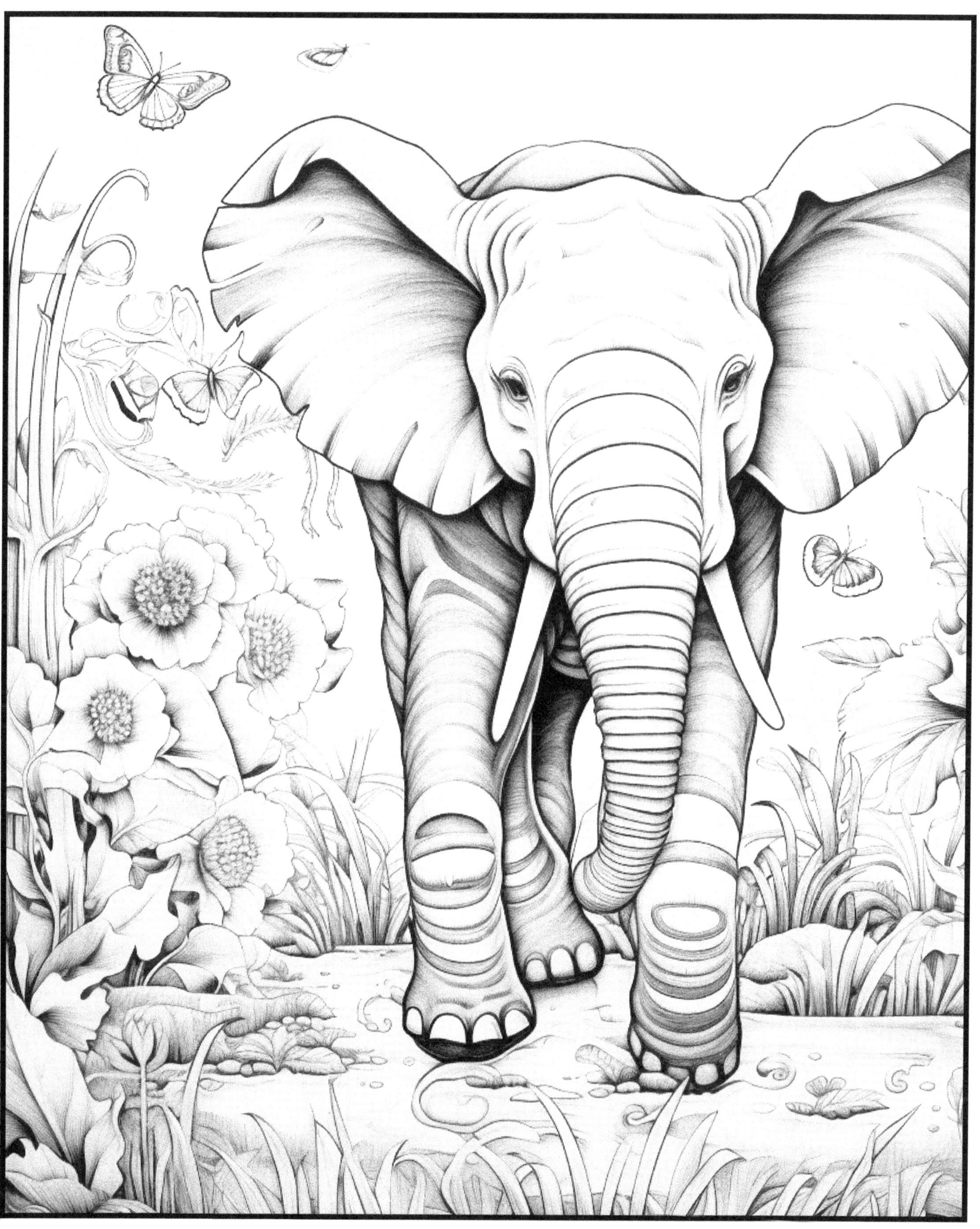

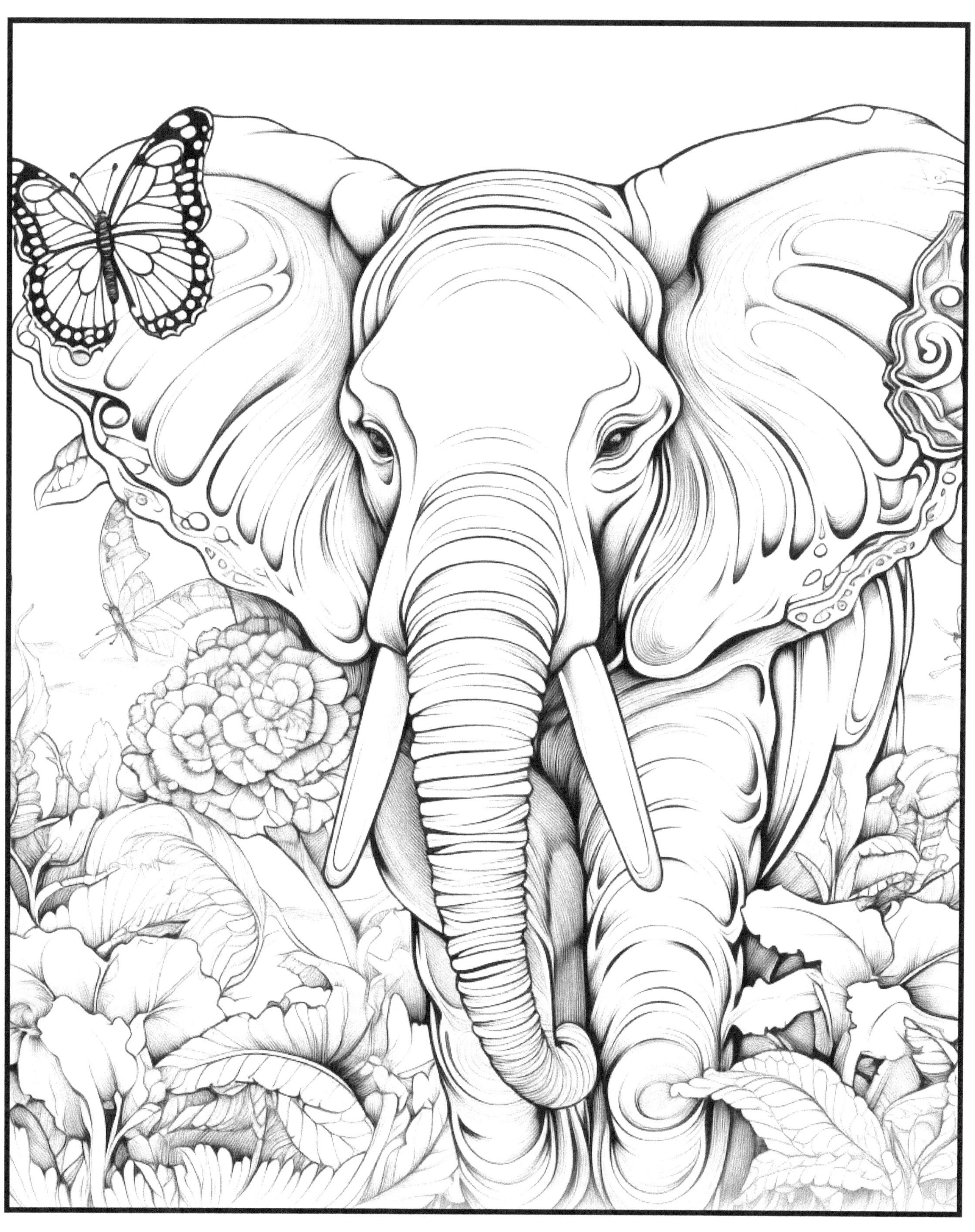

BE Brave
be Kind
BE A Light
Be Wise